State and Local Taxation:

Principles and Planning

SECOND EDITION

Charles W. Swenson, PhD, CPA
Professor
Leventhal School of Accounting
University of Southern California

Sanjay Gupta, PhD, LLB, CPA
Professor
W. P. Carey School of Business
Arizona State University

John E. Karayan, JD, PhD

Joseph W. Neff, JD
PricewaterhouseCoopers

J.ROSS
PUBLISHING

Copyright © 2004 by J. Ross Publishing, Inc.

ISBN 1-932159-17-7

Printed and bound in the U.S.A. Printed on acid-free paper
10   9   8   7   6   5   4   3   2   1

Library of Congress Cataloging-in-Publication Data

State and local taxation: principles and planning / by Charles W. Swenson... [et al.].—
2nd ed.
   p. cm.
   ISBN 1-932159-17-7
1. Tax planning—United States.   2. Taxation—Law and legislation—United States—
States.   3. Local taxation—Law and legislation—United States.   I. Swenson, Charles W.
   KF6297.S73 2003
   658.15′3—dc21

                                 2003010526

Phone: (561) 869-3900
Fax: (561) 892-0700
Web: www.jrosspub.com

TABLE OF CONTENTS

PREFACE

Entrepreneurs, managers, and their tax advisors know what law schools, business schools, and their students are beginning to learn: careers are greatly enhanced by knowing the fundamentals of state and local taxes. This book imparts these fundamentals, which the authors have gleaned from a combined century of experience — as lawyers and accountants, and as professionals and professors — living with (and living off) such knowledge.

The emphasis placed on state and local tax planning by tax advisors can be seen in their staffing. Each of the major accounting firms has a dedicated state and local tax practice, as do most large law firms. Successful practitioners know the importance of state and local tax planning in acquisitions and expansion. They also know that such planning is even more important in cost-effective downsizing. So do companies; between a third and a half of the time typically invested by tax professionals working in business is devoted to state and local taxes, with the percentage increasing the higher up one goes on the corporate ladder.

There are many good reasons for this focus by businesses, and their tax advisors, on state and local tax planning. In recent years, more and more transactions and ventures have become subject to different state and local taxes. This largely is because the Web has greatly reduced the costs of operating across borders, even for small companies. Indeed, advances in electronic commerce have spawned the rise of a new form of business, the micro-multinational. Today even sole proprietors working out of their garage routinely generate transactions spanning the country: a Web-based retailer can close a sale in his/her home office in Florida for a supplier in Montana to ship to a customer in New Hampshire. In this way, a retail sale that used to be local can readily involve a multitude of jurisdictions, each eager to tax both the transaction and the parties involved.

Companies can easily become ensnared in the Byzantine web of different taxes imposed by the many governments touched by (or seeking to touch) cross-border transactions. Not only can many different levels of government be involved, but also many different kinds of taxes; some jurisdictions rely more heavily on income taxes, others on sales or property taxes. Adding complexity, even the same kinds of taxes can differ across borders. For example, the definition of taxable income at the Federal level usually is different from that used by the many states that impose income taxes. Differences among definitions often are subtle, yet important. Indeed, the various tax rules have only one thing in common: they seldom are easy to understand or permanent, because they are created at different times and thus reflect changing government policies.

The stunning advances made in the past decade in telecommunications, capital mobility, and distribution channels not only greatly increased the number of transactions and ventures subject to multiple taxation, but also have made it easier, for those who know what to look for, to plan around such taxes. This is because these environmental changes have reduced the costs of discovering and implementing such plans. The Web has brought greater, quicker, and far less-expensive access to the sources of state and local tax rules. The wall of tax treatises and loose-leaf services that state and local tax planners used to need to maintain is being replaced by on-line portals. Furthermore, these technological advances have made it much easier (and less costly) to negotiate (and relocate people, property, and operations) when shopping among jurisdictions for the most tax-favored locations.

In recent years, state and local taxes also have become increasingly important because they simply are costing more. They are costing more directly: the trend has been for states and local jurisdictions to raise income, sales, and other taxes to avoid budget deficits and expand social programs. State and local taxes also are costing more indirectly. Being for the most part deductible against the regular Federal income tax, state and local tax costs have been Federally subsidized. However, lower Federal income tax rates have likewise reduced this subsidy. The lowered rates also have greatly increased the number of noncorporate taxpayers forced into paying the Federal alternate minimum income tax (AMT), for which state and local taxes are not deductible.

Another reason why state and local taxes play an important role in management decisions is that paying taxes typically claims a high priority on a taxpayer's cash flow and capital. That is, not only are state and local taxes often a big expense, but they also must be paid, and must be paid rather quickly. In addition, companies publicly traded in U.S. capital markets can be especially sensitive to state and local taxes.

This is because financial statement income (which usually has a major impact on stock prices) must be reported on an after-tax basis. Unlike almost all other expenses, state and local tax expense reduces earnings per share dollar for dollar. Furthermore, not only must earnings be reduced by taxes expected to be paid in the current year, but reported earnings also must be reduced by taxes expected to be paid in the *future*. Because senior managers' compensation usually is tied to earnings *via* stock prices (e.g., through stock options), key business and investment decision makers often have a high personal stake in reducing state and local taxes.

In sum, to maintain a competitive edge, entrepreneurs and managers must have a fundamental understanding of the state and local tax implications of key transactions. Those who are able to identify state and local tax issues also can make more effective use of tax consultants because challenges and opportunities can be spotted as they arise, before basic negotiations are concluded and the outline of the deal solidified.

Knowledge of state and local taxation is even more crucial for professionals who advise organizations, particularly accountants and lawyers. By understanding the role of state and local taxes in a strategic setting, consultants — especially "number crunchers" — can greatly increase value for a business.

All in all, there are many factors that combine to motivate efforts to optimize state and local taxes. Those who want to do so, and students who aspire to be someone who does, should buy this book.

ABOUT THE AUTHORS

Charles Swenson, PhD, CPA, is Professor of Taxation — and the Elaine & Kenneth Leventhal Research Fellow — at the Leventhal School of Accounting of the University of Southern California, where he teaches (among other courses) graduate classes on state and local taxation. His professional experience includes service as a tax consultant at PricewaterhouseCoopers. Professor Swenson also has been a Visiting Scholar at the University of California at Los Angeles's Anderson School of Management and a Visiting Professor at the California Institute of Technology. Winner of several American Taxation Association Outstanding Tax Manuscript Awards, Professor Swenson has published extensively in leading journals such as the *Accounting Review, Advances in Taxation, Journal of Accounting and Public Policy, Journal of the American Taxation Association*, and *National Tax Journal*.

Sanjay Gupta, PhD, LLB, CPA, is the Director of the Master's of Taxation Program at the W. P. Carey School of Business at Arizona State University, where (among other things) he teaches State and Local Taxation. A CPA with a law degree, Professor Gupta has served as a consultant to the Big 4 and national CPA firms, as well as multistate giants such as Motorola and Charles River Associates. Dr. Gupta has published in such prestigious venues as the *Journal of Accounting and Economics, National Tax Journal, Accounting Review, Journal of the American Taxation Association, Journal of Accounting and Public Policy*, and *Tax Notes*. His awards include the 1993–94 Price Waterhouse Fellow in Taxation, one of two awarded nationally, as well as receiving a nationally competitive Ernst & Young Tax Research Grant. Sanjay also has been recognized by his peers for his superb teaching. For example, in 2000 he received the Arizona Society of CPAs Accounting Education Innovation Award.

John E. Karayan, JD, PhD, is a tax attorney with a Big 8 CPA firm background who retired from professional practice to become a university professor. Formerly Director of Taxes of one of the world's largest software companies — a NYSE-listed group which operated in all fifty states and over a hundred countries — Professor Karayan has remained active outside of academia as an expert witness on accounting issues in complex business litigation. He also served for over 15 years on the Board of Directors of the world's foremost manufacturer of antiterrorist vehicle access barricades. Dr. Karayan's books include *Strategic Corporate Tax Planning* (2002) with Charles Swenson and Joseph Neff. John also has published articles in journals ranging from *The Tax Advisor* to the *Marquette Sports Law Review*, and has spoken before professional groups such as the World Trade Institute, California Continuing Education of the Bar, the European Accounting Association, and the California Society of CPAs. Recognized by students with several teaching awards, he also was President of the American Accounting Association's 34th Annual Western Regional Conference on Electronic Commerce.

Joe W. Neff, JD, is the National Partner-in-Charge of State Tax Consulting Services for middle-market companies at PricewaterhouseCoopers and serves on large engagements in the Southern California practice. He has held numerous leadership positions, including serving as a member of his firm's three-member executive committee that directed the Multistate Tax Practice nationally. He also had responsibility for developing new services and products in the state tax arena. Before assuming his current position, Joe was the Western Region Director of State and Local Taxation and National Director of State Taxes at another national accounting firm. Prior to that, he served as State Tax Counsel for Texaco, Inc. With over 20 years of experience in the state and local tax area, Joe is a frequent lecturer and has authored numerous articles and publications. He has served as Vice-Chair for the American Bar Association's State and Local Tax Section for environmental taxes, as an editor for the American Bar Association's *State Tax Journal*, and as an adjunct professor in the graduate tax programs at both the University of Southern California and Brigham Young University.

ACKNOWLEDGMENTS

Being able to function in a field of such complexity was not won easily, and likely would not have happened without the help and guidance of people and institutions too numerous to list here. However, some should be named, first and foremost being our families, who inspire us constantly.

Also high on the list are Drew Gierman, Steve Buda, Lynn Cannon, Barbara Caras, and the other fine people of J. Ross Publishing, who inspired us on this venture.

We are always interested in hearing readers' thoughts on how to enhance this book. Feel free to e-mail us care of jekarayan@csupomona.edu with comments, suggestions, advice, and critiques.

Chuck Swenson
Sanjay Gupta
John E. Karayan
Joe Neff

Free value-added materials available from
the Download Resource Center at www.jrosspub.com

At J. Ross Publishing we are committed to providing today's professional with practical, hands-on tools that enhance the learning experience and give readers an opportunity to apply what they have learned. That is why we offer free ancillary materials for download on this book and all participating Web Added Value™ publications. These online resources may include interactive versions of material that appears in the book or supplemental templates, worksheets, models, plans, case studies, proposals, spreadsheets and assessment tools, among other things. Whenever you see the WAV™ symbol in any of our publications, it means bonus materials accompany the book and are available from the Web Added Value Download Resource Center at www.jrosspub.com.

Downloads available for *State and Local Taxation: Principles and Planning* consist of PowerPoint slides, key links and updates, model syllabi, sample exams, an instructor's guide, and a solutions manual.

PART I:
A FRAMEWORK FOR UNDERSTANDING STATE AND LOCAL TAXATION

THE IMPORTANCE OF STATE AND LOCAL TAX PLANNING

INTRODUCTION

State and local tax planning has increased in importance in recent years, as Federal tax planning opportunities have declined and new taxes have been levied at the state and local level. For many companies, state and local tax planning consumes a considerable amount of their in-house tax staff time, and such taxes account for a significant amount of their tax burdens. For example, in a survey by one of the Big 4 accounting firms, state and local tax planning was found to consume 48% of the surveyed companies' overall in-house tax staff time, and accounted for 46% of the companies' overall tax burdens.[1] Each of the Big 4 accounting firms, and most large CPA and law firms, maintain a dedicated state and local tax group, with the sole goal to advise entrepreneurs and managers on how to address state and local tax challenges (as well as taking advantage of opportunities for state and local tax benefits) to enhance the bottom line and cash flow.

The force driving the need to understand (and use) state and local tax knowledge is largely a function of the dynamism — some would say chaos — that is driving state and local public finances in the information age. State and local taxes have become increasingly important over the past few years due to enhanced social needs for education, safety, and health care. Their importance also is the result of massive changes in Federal tax law during the past 2 decades.

More is at stake. Although state and local income tax laws now conform to the Federal more than ever, stubborn nonconformity to some of the recent Federal tax law changes, coupled with deep cuts in statutory Federal tax rates, have greatly increased the relative burden of state and local taxes. Furthermore, until recently, most state legislation conforming to the Federal was enacted after a time lag. However, more and more states have automatically linked their tax law to that of the Federal. The years of Federal tax reform focusing on widening the tax base — e.g., 1981 through 1991 — created a windfall of state and local income taxes. The reverse occurred when the pendulum swung the other way over the next decade of Federal tax law changes. These largely chipped away the income tax base with new (and above the line) deductions (such as that for tuition). For many jurisdictions, this automatically reduced the state and local income tax base. (Masked by enhanced revenues from employee stock options and stock market profit taking in the high-technology boom of the late 1990s, the bust that ensued revealed the shortfalls in state and local taxable income that had been building up.)

Because there have been time lags, as well as specific efforts to reject Federal law changes, there often have been basic differences for assets. That is, the remaining cost for Federal purposes often has been different from that used by other jurisdictions. This is particularly evident for long-lived assets, such as qualified retirement plans and depreciable assets. Another example is investments in flow-through entities, such as Subchapter S corporations.

More importantly, even after years of steady efforts to conform state income tax laws to the Federal, there remains a basic difference — the "unitary tax" concept — complementing the multitude of other Federal-state differences. This concept is employed by unitary states — basically, those west of the Mississippi — for two purposes. The first is to combine commonly controlled but separate legal entities, such as a group of corporations or a corporation and a partnership, where all of the entities are part of one economic unit. This is much like the consolidation rules for financial accounting found in U.S. generally accepted accounting principles. Although consolidated returns can be elected for Federal purposes, most foreign corporations cannot be included in one. To the contrary, unitary states usually require that foreign subsidiaries be included in the combined state income tax. In some cases, states can require that foreign parent corporations be included, as well as their other subsidiaries even if they are not incorporated or do not operate in the U.S.

The second aspect of the unitary approach is to allocate and apportion income earned by a taxpayer operating a multistate business. The purpose is to let states being touched by the firm tax a fair portion of the business's worldwide income. Unlike the Federal "arm's length" rule — the international standard, by the way — the unitary approach does not look at the fairness of transactions between related companies. Instead, it seeks to fairly apportion to a state all of a company's income that was generated by contacts with the state. This is done by applying an averaging formula. However, different formulas are applied by different jurisdictions, leading to the specter of states as a whole taxing more than 100% of a firm's income. Many states have adopted, albeit often only in part, the model proposed by the Multistate Tax Compact. This is an association sponsored by various states. Under the Compact, a model statute was developed: the Uniform Division of Income for Tax Purposes Act. It typically is referred to by the acronym UDITPA.

Another reason that state and local taxes are important is that substantial penalties can apply even to honest mistakes if they are negligent because sufficient research was not done. Taxpayers have an affirmative duty to know the state and local tax law of the jurisdictions in which they generate revenue, and breach of this duty due to ignorance of the law is punishable by monetary penalties.

Finally, intense legislative pressures on the state and local tax authorities to raise revenues have motivated creativity in "enforcing" the law. This particularly is the case because in order to effectively challenge creative tax enforcement, taxpayers almost always must pay the tax assessed and then find recourse only in a lawsuit for a refund in an expensive court action. This is not the case with Federal tax rules, which may be challenged in the U.S. Tax Court before taxes are paid.

VARIOUS TYPES OF TAXES LEVIED ON BUSINESSES

Each of the states, and most of their political subdivisions, impose a variety of taxes. Table 1.1 identifies several common state and local taxes levied on busi-

TABLE 1.1. Taxes Levied on Businesses

Type of Tax	No. of States	% of Total Taxes
Property Tax — Real	49	41.58%
Property Tax — Personal	41	11.07%
Property Tax — Other	41	6.02%
Alcoholic Beverage License	47	0.25%
Amusement License	34	0.19%
Corporation License	48	3.05%
Motor Vehicle License	49	7.44%
Public Utility License	31	0.03%
Corporation Net Income Tax	45	19.71%
Severance Tax	33	4.00%
Document and Stock Transfer	30	1.89%
Taxes on Nonemployee Compensation	15	0.16%
Unemployment Insurance	49	4.33%
Other	50	0.28%
Total		100.00%

nesses, the number of states imposing each tax, and the relative burden of each tax.[2] (To accomplish this, Table 1.1 does not include sales and use taxes. Although these are major sources of revenue, they have been excluded because public records do not distinguish between the amount of sales and use taxes paid by businesses and the amount paid by individuals. Note that because purchases for resale almost always are exempt from such taxes, the vast majority of sales and use taxes are paid by individuals.)

VARIOUS BUSINESS TRANSACTIONS SUBJECT TO TAXATION

Each state, and many of the counties, cities, parishes, school districts, and other governmental subdivisions, impose taxes in a variety of transactions. Illustration 1.1 shows businesses, parties essential to business operations, and (in parentheses) various transactions that are subject to taxation.

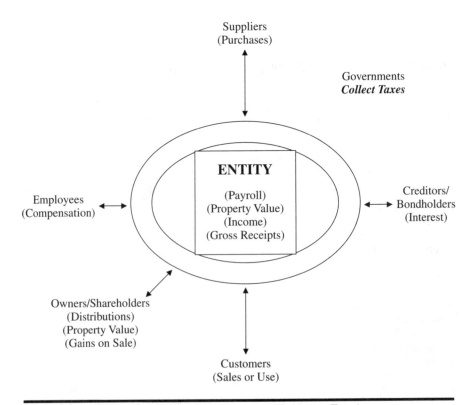

ILLUSTRATION 1.1. Various Business Transactions Subject to Taxation.

TABLE 1.2. Effective Business Income Tax Rates by State

	Effective Tax Rates on Business Income	Ranking		Effective Tax Rates on Business Income	Ranking
Alabama	12.45%	40	Nebraska	6.63%	48
Arizona	25.70%	7	Nevada	10.69%	43
Arkansas	9.96%	45	New Hampshire	25.82%	6
California	15.97%	30	New Jersey	23.24%	8
Colorado	14.47%	34	New Mexico	16.86%	24
Connecticut	21.26%	11	New York	26.84%	5
DC and Maryland	14.44%	36	North Carolina	12.01%	41
Delaware	32.92%	3	North Dakota	11.14%	42
Florida	20.92%	13	Ohio	15.60%	31
Georgia	13.98%	37	Oklahoma	16.62%	26
Hawaii	7.84%	46	Oregon	16.28%	28
Idaho	7.22%	47	Pennsylvania	17.03%	23
Illinois	21.19%	12	Rhode Island	18.47%	19
Indiana	18.76%	18	South Carolina	19.72%	15
Iowa	10.24%	44	South Dakota	4.22%	49
Kansas	14.71%	32	Tennessee	14.62%	33
Kentucky	21.30%	10	Texas	17.65%	21
Louisiana	21.46%	9	Utah	12.63%	39
Maine	19.30%	16	Vermont	16.61%	27
Massachusetts	16.26%	29	Virginia	13.91%	38
Michigan	39.74%	2	Washington	19.83%	14
Minnesota	17.74%	20	West Virginia	26.89%	4
Mississippi	16.82%	25	Wisconsin	17.50%	22
Missouri	14.47%	35	Wyoming	42.63%	1
Montana	19.09%	17			

DISPARITY OF TAX RATES ACROSS JURISDICTIONS

Tax rates vary dramatically across state and local taxing units. Table 1.2 lists the effective income tax rates on business income for each state.[3] Note that two states have effective income tax rates higher than the "highest" Federal corporate income tax rate of 35%.[4]

Tax Liabilities Arising in Multiple Jurisdictions

Each state taxes transactions occurring within its borders. Consequently, two or more states may tax the same cross-border transaction. Even within a state, many political subdivisions — notably counties, cities, and school districts —

may get into the act. As highlighted in the Preface to this book, such cross-border sales have increased due to technological advances, such as the Web, as well as other changes in the economy that have lowered the risk and cost of expanding markets. Mergers and acquisitions involving entities in multiple states have increased as well.

While advances in telecommunications, distribution channels, and management information systems have dramatically reduced internal barriers within the economy, they also have increasingly exposed the parties to these transactions to the multiple tax jurisdictions. More and more, state and local governments have joined the Federal government as, in effect, a third party to these transactions, even if the business being taxed does not operate out of bricks-and-mortar establishments located in these jurisdictions. Today's entrepreneurs and managers thus must be well versed in the basics of state and local tax planning to effectively and efficiently deal with the additional tax-related costs arising from cross-border transactions so that the benefits and burdens arising from such transactions are optimized. More importantly, entrepreneurs and managers are looking to their accountants, attorneys, and other outside consultants for help and insight in this area, and are willing to pay well for good advice.

Considering the variety of taxes, the number of transactions subject to taxation, the disparity of tax rates among jurisdictions, and the possibility of owing taxes in multiple states, deciding where, when, with whom, and how transactions are structured can significantly impact the state and local tax burden of businesses. In other words, state and local tax planning really does merit the consumption of half of in-house tax staff time.

The remainder of the chapter introduces the various types of state and local taxes, the key sources of law controlling state and local taxation, and fundamental planning strategies.

TYPES OF TAXES[5]

Corporate Income and Franchise Taxes

Forty-five states tax corporate net income. (For reasons discussed later in this book, some states refer to this tax as a franchise tax. Most states call it a corporate income tax, however.) In contrast, three states levy a corporate "income" tax only loosely related to net income. Michigan imposes a Single Business Tax based on economic value added. Texas assesses a franchise tax based on net worth. Washington levies a Business and Occupations Tax based on gross receipts.

To calculate net income taxes, most jurisdictions "piggyback" on taxpayers' compliance with the Federal tax law. (Interestingly, the Internal Revenue Code

[IRC] specifically allows any state to let the Internal Revenue Service [IRS] administer and collect the state's income tax. Although this long has been the law, no state has ever accepted the offer.) Piggybacking on Federal income is done in three steps. First, the taxpayer starts with Federal net income. (Many states require that the Federal income tax return, or key portions of it, be attached to the state return.) Second, the taxpayer makes some state-specific adjustments. Finally, the state tax rate, and any state tax credits, are applied. State rates are lower than the Federal, with Federal rates (which range from 10 to 39%, but for large firms are a flat 35%) being about three times that for states (where rates range from about 6 to 12%).

As could be anticipated on reflection, jurisdictions that piggyback on Federal income typically apply Federal statutes, Federal rules and regulations, and Federal case law when dealing with controversies. The usual exception is when the state has its own specific Code Sections (where the language is significantly different from that of the IRC). Another exception is where the state has its own regulations or case law. Similarly, to a great extent, Federal elections also apply to piggybacking states. This usually applies not only to elections of accounting methods and periods but also to extensions of due dates and other procedural matters where there is not specific state rule.

However, strict conformity is not required. A taxpayer often may take some action for Federal purposes and not for state purposes, or *vice versa*, as long as Federal-state conformity is not mandated by state law. In addition, significant differences between Federal and state tax rules exist even for piggybacking states. One major set of differences comes from special economic incentives. These usually are targeted for economically depressed areas, or for industries that a state is trying to subsidize. These types of incentives are specified by state or local statute, and often provide panoply of benefits to investments generating employment in these areas. These range from reduced sales taxes for plant, property, and equipment to investment tax credits and accelerated depreciation on the same. Sometimes there are employment tax credits that greatly reduce the after-tax cost even of new minimum wage employees, or special treatment for start-up costs or losses. More, and more favorable, benefits usually are specified for special enterprise zones. Often modeled after Federal law, these programs usually provide special and higher levels of tax incentives and other benefits (such as sweetheart access to local utilities or other governmental services) for businesses established in designated depressed areas.

Among the key issues for state and local taxes are (1) when is a business subject to a state's taxing jurisdiction and (2) how to split the income of a multistate operation among the various states involved. The latter can be problematic for multistate businesses. For them, many states use an averaging mechanism. Typically, a variant of the three-factor "Massachusetts" formula is used. It averages the ratios of property, payroll, and sales within and without the state, and is used to apportion business income into the state. This roughly divides up income to where it is earned, but because it is only an approximation, it causes a great deal of controversy. The silver lining in this cloud is that the method also allows for tax planning to source more income to lower tax jurisdictions.

State and local tax procedures and appeals are slightly different from the Federal. They vary quite a bit by state. In California, for example, income taxes are enforced by the Franchise Tax Board. Overseen by three *ex officio* officers — the State Controller, the Director of the Department of Finance, and the Chairman of the State Board of Equalization — the Franchise Tax Board is run by an Executive Officer, with duties like the Commissioner of Internal Revenue.

State and local tax audits are run very much like those by the IRS, except that there often is an extended statute of limitation for honest, timely filing taxpayers. Rather than the Federal standard 3-year statute of limitations, 4 years is often used, giving state tax auditors a year to follow up on the reports they receive about IRS action for taxpayers giving permanent addresses in the state. In a similar vein, a state amended return often must be filed within a short time — usually 90 days — of the filing of a Federal amended income tax return and also within a similar period from a final determination of changes, such as from a Federal audit.

Instead of appealing a revenue agent's report to an appellate conferee, appeals of the Franchise Tax Board action go to the State Board of Equalization. This is an elective body that rides circuit throughout the state, hearing appeals. Virtually all are decided in favor of the state, but large, well-represented taxpayers have also won important victories.

State tax appeals processes typically are less taxpayer friendly than the Federal. For example, in California appeals to the State Board of Equalization are similar to those to an IRS conferee. Appeals from the Board of Equalization, however, are not like those from an IRS appellate conferee. There is no state equivalent to the Tax Court. Thus, taxpayers must pay any taxes demanded, and then sue for a refund in the regular state courts. A blue ribbon panel studying California tax reform during the late 1980s recommended that a state tax court be established; none of the bills introduced in the legislature to effect this change has ever passed.

Income Taxes on Employees and Sole Proprietorships

A similar approach, and similar issues, are involved in state and local income taxes on employees and sole proprietorships. Typically, the calculation of the tax base also starts with Federal taxable (or adjusted gross) income. Then Federal-state differences are listed in coming down to state and local taxable income. Last, the state and local tax rates and credits are applied. It is not unusual to find a state alternate minimum tax modeled on the Federal.

As with corporations, key issues include who is subject to a state's power to tax and how the income of a multistate operation is parceled out between the states involved. These are treated much as discussed above. In addition, in most states there are two major divisions of personal income taxes that affect employees and sole proprietorships. The first division is for residents, and the second is for nonresidents and part-year residents. The distinction is made because in many states residents are taxed on their worldwide income, whereas nonresidents are only taxed on their income from sources within the state.

Income generally is sourced where it is earned. For example, it is usual for rents to be sourced (and thus taxed) by the jurisdiction where the property is physically located. Similarly, royalties are sourced where the underlying intangible is being used. Services typically are sourced to where they are rendered. Sourcing may be simple for income from real estate (because it does not move around much), but can become devilish for multistate business operations where the various steps in a firm's value chain are located in different jurisdictions. As noted above, often the resulting income is merely divided among the jurisdictions involved using some averaging convention.

A nonresident usually is defined, if at all, as an individual who is not a resident. A person typically is a resident if physically present in the state for other than a temporary or transitory purpose. (Case law dealing with the question of residency is discussed later in this book. The law is embedded in cases because issues are so fact ridden and many groups of individuals are similarly situated.) As a rule of thumb, a person who moves to a state to take a job, start a business, retire, or who is physically present in the state for a substantial period (e.g., more than 9 months during a tax year) becomes a resident on entering the state.

Income Taxes on Other Entities

Income taxes on other entities tend to follow the Federal lead. For example, mutual funds, publicly traded partnerships, cooperatives, real estate investment trusts, and tax-exempt entities generally are treated the same for Federal income taxes as for state and local income taxes. Nevertheless, there is a wide variety of Federal-state differences. Some of these differences are fairly obscure. Whereas the Federal treatment of homeowners' associations is much like that of any other tax-exempt organizations, some states (such as California) initially classify these as taxable, albeit with special deductions rendering all but the most solvent homeowners' associations tax free. The differences that are not obscure largely are in the area of flow-through entities, such as partnerships, S corporations, and limited liability companies.

Taxation of Flow-Through Entities

Firms often use flow-through entities. Examples include joint ventures with other firms, or a new business in a state where the flow through of tax losses to a financing partner is advantageous. State and local tax treatment of three flow-through entities — partnerships, limited liability companies, and S corporations — is much the same as Federal taxation. However, there are some important differences.

Partnerships

A partnership is an association of two or more persons carrying on for a profit. A partnership can be limited or general.[6] For Federal tax purposes, partnerships have two major advantages: partnerships are not subject to tax, and their losses pass through to their partners.

Most states also do not tax partnerships. Instead, distributive shares of partnership profit or loss are passed through to the partners. Exceptions are the District of Columbia (Unincorporated Business Tax), Illinois (Personal Property Replacement Tax), New Hampshire (Business Profits Tax), New York City (Unincorporated Business Tax), and Michigan (Single Business Tax). Some states (e.g., California) impose a withholding tax on allocations to nonresident taxpayers, and allow the partnership an election to effectively pay state income taxes on behalf of such partners.

Generally, a partner is subject to state and local taxation if the partner is either a resident of the jurisdiction of the partnership or is a nonresident but is doing business there. Individual partners are also subject to taxation by their state of residence on their entire taxable income, including their distributive share of partnership income. However, most jurisdictions provide a resident individual with a credit for taxes paid to nonresident states.[7] Most states do not provide a credit either for a tax paid by the partnership directly or for taxes paid by the partnership on behalf of its nonresident partners.

Sales and Use Taxes

Forty-five states tax consumers on the retail purchase of personal property intended for in-state use. Sales taxes apply to in-state retail purchases; use taxes apply to out-of-state retail purchases. Tax rates are set at the state level, but counties and cities often may add a smaller tax of their own. This can result in a variety of total sales and use tax rates within the same state.

A sales tax normally is imposed directly on the consumer. Sales taxes are complemented by use taxes. To stop consumers from avoiding taxes by simply purchasing in other, lower tax, jurisdictions, vendors there typically are required to collect the taxes from the consumer and remit them to the appropriate government. That is, a use tax is not designed to disadvantage out-of-state vendors, but to level the playing field with in-state vendors. The use tax discourages a state's residents from making purchases in another state in order to avoid the sales tax. (The success of this approach is increasingly challenged by the existence of e-tailers such as Amazon.com or Lands' End.) In addition, both in-state and out-of-state vendors incur similar tax-related collection and remittance costs.

The sales tax is merely a percentage of the purchase price. The use tax is imposed and collected in a similar manner. The notable difference is that in this case the vendor is an out-of-state firm and thus may not have a legally enforceable obligation to collect and remit the use tax. As discussed extensively throughout this book, the existence of a legal obligation depends on the extent of the vendor's contact with the consumer's state.

Many purchases, however, are exempt from sales and use taxes. Purchases of necessities, such as groceries and medicine (as well as snack foods in California), commonly are exempt. So is property used in the production of inventory. Purchases for resale, as well as packaging, ingredients in the final product, and equipment (or parts thereof) used to make products also are not taxed. This prevents double taxation when the product is resold to consumers.

Property Taxes

Taxes are usually assessed on both realty and personalty; however, in some states, only realty is taxed. Taxes are based on the value of the property at a specific assessment date or point in time. Property owners are liable for payment of the tax. States directly assess some realty, but local governments, typically counties, assess most realty taxes. In contrast, states directly assess most personalty. Most states do not tax intangible personalty. Valuation methods, tax rates, and assessment dates vary by state.

In response to a variety of lawsuits regarding large differences in the amount of per pupil funding where property taxes finance schools, there has been a shift to financing schools using state-level funds. This may have broken the traditional link between property taxes and local spending. In any event, several jurisdictions (notably California, Massachusetts, and Michigan) have changed their property tax system. A good example of this dynamic can be found in California's Proposition Thirteen.

This was a constitutional amendment passed in the late 1970s that limits tax increases (property taxes in particular) in general unless supported by a two-thirds supermajority vote. In addition, there is a maximum tax of 1% of assessed value, which in turn is based on historical cost, rather than estimates of fair market value. These changes were important. Like most state and local jurisdictions, intangibles such as stocks and bonds are not subject to property taxes. Nor are personal use assets in general, other than cars, boats, and planes, which are subject to value-based registration fees (typically cost less straight-line depreciation over roughly 7 years). Business inventories are free from property taxes, too.

Proposition Thirteen followed U.S. generally accepted accounting principles in applying the historical cost principle. It mandated that the tax base for real property be limited to its acquisition cost. This can only be changed by three factors. The first is an annual inflation adjustment limited to 2%. Because the California government's spending increased annually by several times this rate for many years, one can see why property taxes have financed a decreasing part of government activities in recent years. Declines in value can reduce the assessed value of a piece of real estate. It also can be increased due to a change of ownership or new construction. Because a majority of common stock for most publicly traded corporations turns over every year, and this has been deemed to amount to a change in ownership, their realty effectively is taxed at market value.

Several challenges to Proposition Thirteen's limits on property taxes have been rejected by the California courts. Among them was Macy's attack on Proposition Thirteen's mandate that property taxes be based on acquisition cost, indexed for inflation, rather than fair market value. Macy's attack in the U.S. Supreme Court also was unsuccessful. (This is interesting in that the company had hired the foremost boutique state and local tax law firm in the country to litigate the issue, but dropped the case after California customers started mailing in cut up credit cards in protest of the action.)

The constitutional argument was simple. Consider someone who bought a home in 1976 for $30,000. The 1991 property tax on it would run about $500. However, if someone were to buy the identical home next door, which now might sell for $300,000, their taxes would be $5,000 per year. In essence, the tax discriminates against new California residents, new California real property owners, and publicly traded companies like Macy's.

In 1989, the U.S. Supreme Court ruled against a Pennsylvania coal mine valuation method that came to the same results. Most commentators believed that the Pennsylvania case could not be distinguished from California. In addition, although historically reluctant to rule Federal tax laws unconstitutional, ever since the *Michelin* decision in the mid 1970s the Court has increasingly examined and struck down state tax schemes. Nevertheless, in *Nordlinger v. Lynch, sub nom Nordlinger v. Hahn*, 505 U.S. 1, 112 S. Ct. 2326 (1992), the Court rejected a challenge to California's system of property tax valuation.

Other Taxes

While the majority of state tax collections are from income, sales and use, and property taxes, other taxes significantly affect businesses and transactions. The vast bulk of the other taxes raised are payroll and excise taxes. These include utility taxes, such as those on cable TV or electricity, as well as "sin" taxes on tobacco products and alcoholic beverages and "bed" taxes on hotel rooms.

State payroll taxes have become increasingly important. Along with withholding where there is a state personal income tax, states impose unemployment insurance taxes. Like Federal Social Security taxes, these may include both an employer tax and an employee tax. The most common example of the latter is taxes for state disability benefits levied on employees that must be withheld from employees' wages. This may be a trend. When California mandated a new "family leave" requirement in 2002, it was financed by a new payroll tax levied only on employees.

Other taxes include insurance company taxes (which typically are on gross receipts, rather than on income), motor vehicle registration taxes (along with those for boats and planes), state business and occupations taxes, realty transfer taxes, and the hazardous waste taxes. There also are local business and occupation fees. Some are inconsequential, some are large; some are flat rate; some are measured by gross receipts or payroll. An excellent example is the Los Angeles City Gross Receipts or Payroll tax, which has been accused by the film industry as a reason for moving its activities outside of the city's jurisdiction. Attempts in 2003 to enforce the tax on home office workers — in particular, journalists — met with many an irate newspaper column by afflicted media scofflaws.

Capital Stock Taxes

Capital stock taxes usually are levied on domestic (in-state) corporations for the right to exist as a corporation. They also apply to foreign (out-of-state) corporations for the right to do business in the state. States often base capital stock taxes on a corporation's net book value, which includes capital, surplus, and retained earnings.

License Taxes

License taxes are imposed for the right to conduct certain businesses or professions. These taxes are intended not only to raise revenue but also to regulate certain businesses and professions. State and local governments both impose these taxes.

Estate, Gift, and Inheritance Taxes

With California and Florida as notable exceptions, most states impose estate and gift taxes modeled after the Federal system. Except for the "pick-up" tax, where the state gets the maximum amount that can be taken as a state death tax credit against the Federal estate tax liability, these taxes usually cost more to collect than they bring in. Instead of estate taxes, which tax the property left by a decedent, some states impose an inheritance tax, which imposes a tax on those who inherit the property. Collection issues aside, it is much the same thing as an estate tax.

Taken together, these basically are a tax on the privilege of giving property away.[8] The gift tax applies to transfers of property interests made during the owner's lifetime, provided the giver (called a donor) does not get something of legal value in exchange. An estate or inheritance fundamentally results from the decedent's last gift. Often, these taxes model the Federal, and have the same rates as well as the same tax base. Some states have a lower rate for gift taxes; rates and exemptions for inheritance taxes usually are based on the level of kinship with the decedent (for example, a surviving sister is charged much less than a first cousin, twice removed).

Unlike income taxes, which are based on annual income, Federal estate and gift taxes are based on the fair market value of property given away over a lifetime. That is, although paid annually, the gift tax base is the total of current year plus all prior gifts, less a credit for previous gift taxes paid. The Federal estate tax base includes both the property passing at death plus the gifts made by the decedent after 1976 (when the system was overhauled). As more taxable gifts are made, higher tax rates apply to subsequent gifts. Similarly, prior taxable gifts increase the estate tax rates applicable to taxable property passed at death. Some states conform to the Federal pattern; those with inheritance taxes, however, rarely include prior gifts in the tax base.

Because transfers to a spouse usually are not taxed, and there are exemptions and credits that reduce taxes for "small" amounts,[9] these taxes are more of an administrative nuisance than a revenue raiser. Indeed, in some states, the estate tax is set at the maximum amount that the estate can claim as a tax credit against the Federal tax.

The same issues noted above under income taxes arise with regards to conformity of rules and elections to the Federal. However, states generally have yet to conform to existing Federal law that eliminates the estate tax in 2010, only to see it reappear in 2011.

Transfer Taxes

States impose transfer taxes on changes of property ownership. The tax usually is imposed on the transferor. For example, some states impose a transfer tax on the transfer or sale of stock or securities, typically exempting initial public offerings from the tax. Other states impose a tax on the transfer or sale of realty at the time of recording or transfer.

Incorporation Taxes

States levy incorporation taxes on the incorporation of domestic corporations, and similar taxes on the qualification to conduct business in the state by foreign corporations. The tax is based on the value of a corporation's stock, or is merely a flat fee.

Excise Taxes

As noted above, a wide variety of jurisdictions impose taxes on the consumption of regulated goods and services. These range from gasoline to air travel, from cigarettes to hotel rooms, from cable TV to parking, from electricity to entertainment.

Severance Taxes

States assess severance taxes on the removal of natural resources, such as timber, minerals, and petroleum. The tax is based on the value of the extracted resources. In some states, these taxes are quite substantial. Texas traditionally has financed its schools on taxes like these, as well as royalties; Alaska effectively has a negative income tax on its residents, which in the past largely has paid out "dividends" from severance taxes and royalties.

Additional Miscellaneous Taxes

States also levy an array of other taxes. Most notable are motor fuel taxes, telecommunications taxes, tourism taxes, value-added taxes, commercial rent taxes, and highway use taxes.

SOURCES OF LAW[10]

This section identifies important sources of law that authorize, set forth, and limit state and local taxes. The sources of state tax laws are similar to the sources of Federal tax laws. States have legislative bodies that enact tax laws, agencies that administer the laws, and courts that hear disputes between taxpayers and tax authorities. States also have quasi-judicial tribunals to hear tax disputes in order to expedite the resolution of disputes and to ease the burden on the courts.

U.S. Constitution

The U.S. Constitution is the highest authority on state tax law. Any state tax law that violates the Constitution is "unconstitutional" and thus invalid.

The Constitution generally performs three functions. First, the Constitution enumerates specific rights of persons in relation to the government. State tax laws infringing on these rights are invalid. For example, states can only levy corporate income/franchise taxes on corporations having *nexus* (a certain level of business contact) to the taxing state. State tax law attempting to impose such taxes on a business without *nexus* is invalid.

Second, the Constitution divides governmental power between the Federal and state governments. This division of power does not necessarily result in two separate arenas or jurisdictions of government action. Sometimes Federal and state governments exercise overlapping jurisdiction regarding public concerns. The Supremacy Clause of the Constitution provides that Federal law controls and state law is invalid when a conflict arises between Federal and state law.

Third, the Constitution divides Federal governmental power among legislative, executive, and judicial branches. These branches are responsible for enacting, enforcing, and interpreting Federal laws.

State Constitutions

State constitutions perform two functions. First, state constitutions establish the supreme law of the state by enumerating specific individual rights. However, state constitutions cannot be in violation of the U.S. Constitution. Second, state constitutions divide power among legislative, executive, and judicial branches. These branches are responsible for enacting, enforcing, and interpreting state tax laws.

Legislative Law Sources

State legislatures enact statutes, the laws of the state. All state legislatures consist of two houses, except Nebraska, which has only one house. The houses perform slightly different but overlapping lawmaking functions. Statutes are enacted after receiving the approval of both legislative houses and the governor. Local laws are enacted according to local government procedure. Subject to constitutional limitations, statutes are the highest authority of state and local tax law.

Administrative Law Sources

State governments create agencies to administer the law. Most agencies are created by statute, but some are created by constitutional provision. Agency heads are either elected or appointed by the governor and approved by the legislature.

In most states, a single revenue agency administers the state tax laws. However, counties and cities typically assess and collect property taxes. In addition, specialized agencies often collect capital stock taxes, employment taxes, and public utility taxes. For example, California divides tax administration between two revenue agencies. The unelected Franchise Tax Board administers income taxes, and the elected State Board of Equalization administers sales and use taxes, as well as hearing appeals from income tax audits.

Revenue agencies issue various authoritative pronouncements. First, agencies regularly issue rules and regulations. They are only the issuing agency's official interpretations of state tax laws. Occasionally, legislatures permit a rule or regulation to operate with the force of law, like a statute.

Second, agencies often follow the IRS model of drafting letter rulings in response to taxpayer requests for guidance. These letters are taxpayer specific and thus do not have broader application. They cannot be relied on as authority by other taxpayers. However, they may be useful in ascertaining an agency's position.

Third, agencies publish hearing decisions that are the results of quasi-judicial and administrative tribunals that hear taxpayer disputes. Like letter rulings, hearing decisions cannot be relied on as law, but they illuminate agency positions on certain issues. Agencies routinely publish departmental announcements, including news releases, newsletters, and tax advisories that identify agency positions. They are not sources of law and are generally not binding on the agency.

Judicial Law Sources

Judges publish legal opinions to resolve litigation and thereby create case law. Case law consists of the interpretation and application of the various sources of law: constitutional, statutory, administrative, and common. Judicial decisions only bind states and localities over which the court has jurisdiction. For example, the Idaho Supreme Court's interpretation of a U.S. constitutional provision is binding within the state of Idaho, but is not binding in the state of Nevada.

All states maintain two or three levels of courts. Each level performs a specific function. The lowest level is the trial court. A trial court determines the facts of a dispute and then applies the relevant law to the facts. The next level is the intermediate appellate court. This appellate court reviews the trial court judge's use and application of the relevant law to the determined facts. These courts rarely re-evaluate or redetermine the facts found at the trial level. Some states do not have intermediate appellate courts. At the highest level, the final appellate court reviews the decisions of the intermediate appellate court. If no intermediate appellate courts exist, the final appellate court directly reviews the decisions of the trial court. The final appellate court exercises jurisdiction over the entire state. Further review on questions of Federal law may be sought in the U.S. Supreme Court, which decides just a handful of such cases annually.

Multistate Law Sources

In 1967, the Multistate Tax Commission was created when a group of states endorsed the drafting, and adoption into law (in whole or in part), of the Multistate Tax Compact. The Multistate Tax Compact is an interstate compact law enacted by Compact Member States. Over half of the states are full or associate members of the Commission.

The Commission encourages states to adopt uniform tax laws and regulations that apply to multistate and multinational enterprises. The goals of uniformity in multistate transactions are

- Reduce compliance burdens for multistate businesses
- Prevent undertaxation or overtaxation of interstate commerce
- Lessen the possibility that Congress will intervene in state taxation

In 1971, the Commission developed general business income tax allocation and apportionment regulations. Called the Uniform Division of Income for Tax Purposes Act (UDITPA), these are embodied in Article IV of the Multistate Tax Compact. UDITPA rules and regulations seek to properly and, more importantly, consistently determine the state and local tax liability of multistate taxpayers. The Commission concluded that universal adoption of UDITPA would not only lead to a more equitable apportionment of the tax base among the states, but would also reduce the likelihood of the taxpayer being subject to duplicative taxation. Most states have agreed, adopting the act in whole or part.

GENERIC STATE AND LOCAL TAX PLANNING STRATEGIES[11]

Planning may occur in isolation or in conjunction with a planned transaction (e.g., an acquisition of another company by the client). The goal of planning is to optimize/minimize a taxpayer's state and local tax liability. Furthering this goal, planning should never interfere with business operations or objectives; the tax tail should not wag the business dog. This is commonly referred to as the tax neutrality doctrine.

Tax savings arise from a permanent reduction in tax liability or a temporary postponement of liability. The savings arising from the former are obvious. The savings arising from the latter are due to the time value of money. The postponement increases the discounted cash flow of the company by permitting the business to hold onto its money longer. This, in turn, enhances financial statement net income. For publicly traded firms, the financial statement effect of tax planning is of utmost importance, because shareholders and financial analysts can only see the results of tax planning in reductions in the firm's tax expense and effective tax rates. In addition, financial statement impact is important to the firm's decision makers. At most large firms, executive compensation includes bonuses and stock options that are maximized by increasing the firm's financial net income.

The basic state and local tax planning strategies can be recalled by use of the acronym for State and Local Tax (SALT): **S**hifting and splitting, **A**dded value, **L**ocation, and **T**iming and transforming (Illustration 1.2). Tax advisors, consultants, and managers add value to the firm by utilizing these techniques.

> **Example 1.1.** A business wants to build a manufacturing plant in a new city, but the local property tax is very high. The business persuades the local officials that the plant will bring many benefits to the city; consequently, the business is able to negotiate a lower property tax rate. The tax cost is **split** between the city and business.
>
> **Example 1.2.** A manufacturing firm needs to replace a substantial portion of its aging equipment. The firm plans to purchase $19 million

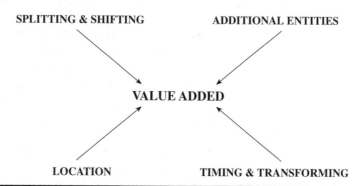

ILLUSTRATION 1.2

worth of equipment; the purchase would be subject to a 7% sales tax in the firm's state. The sales tax can be paid over time as the lease payments are made, if a subsidiary leasing company is set up that purchases the equipment and then leases it to the manufacturer. Tax savings are created by use of **shifting** the tax base to an additional entity and by **timing** that causes a reduction in the present value of taxes. (Appendix B is devoted to the concept of present value.)

Example 1.3. A corporation forms a subsidiary to sell upper management services to other subsidiaries. The management subsidiary is located in a low tax rate state. The other subsidiaries are located in higher tax rate states. **Shifting** to a newly created entity creates tax savings, because the paying subsidiaries deduct their management fee expenses at a higher tax rate than the management fee income recognized by the management company.

Example 1.4. A pharmaceutical company wants to build an assembly plant to service in State C. The company is considering two locations: State A, its current state, and State B. State A has a 9% corporate income tax rate; State B has no corporate income tax. The nontax advantages and disadvantages of States A and B are the same. The company decides to build the plant in the tax-free state. The firm saves significant tax dollars by using **location** as a planning technique.

Example 1.5. A company's marketing department has decided to switch to a more "push" promotion strategy. To do so, it needs a sales force presence in several nearby states. Sales offices are only located in low tax rate states. No business connection or "nexus" is established in high tax rate states. The sales force travels into the high tax rate states from offices in the low tax rate states. Consequently, the company has no tax liability in the high tax rate states, as all sales income generated is allocated to, and subject to the taxation of, the low tax rate states. The firm saves significant tax dollars by using **location** as a planning technique.

Example 1.6. A firm is considering expanding its manufacturing facilities in either its current location or in a nearby city. The nearby city has a number of "enterprise zones." Firms located in such zones not only pay no sales taxes, but they also receive income tax credits for wages paid. If the firm locates in an enterprise zone, it will have **transformed** deductions into credits and taxable into nontaxable sales.

Example 1.7. Near the end of the year, engineers from the production department approach management about acquiring new production machinery. If state tax rates are scheduled to increase next year, any tax deductions for depreciation taken next year have more cash value than if they were taken this year. Management may adjust the **timing** of the transaction by acquiring the machinery early in the next year.

Example 1.8. A state offers a $5,000 tax credit to firms for each employee hired if the employee is in a targeted group (i.e., individuals who normally have difficulty obtaining employment). By hiring such employees, a firm would **transform** a deduction into a credit.

Example 1.9. A manufacturer ships a finished product to a warehouse where the product is then packaged for sale to wholesalers. The packaging is subject to sales tax. Management moves the packaging to the manufacturing plant. This results in the packing materials not being subject to tax, because under most state laws any part of the manufacturing process is exempt from sales tax. This results in a **transforming** of a taxable into a nontaxable transaction.

Example 1.10 — Using Apportionment Techniques to Reduce Tax Liability. Because business income tax rates vary across jurisdictions, it is possible to benefit from tax rate arbitrage. Location strategies focus on this: all other things being equal, it is better to have income from jurisdictions that impose lower taxes. For organizations operating in jurisdictions that apportion cross-border business income — something that most states do — taxes can be reduced through the use of some simple apportionment techniques.

The goal is straightforward: optimize the amount of income apportioned to a lower tax state. As noted above, most states use a variant of the three-factor "Massachusetts" formula to divide the business income of multistate firms among the various states involved. Under this formula, total business income is allocated to a particular state in proportion to the relative amount of property, payroll, and sales the firm had in the state that year. That is, a firm first calculates the ratio of its payroll within the state to its total payroll. This is done again for property, and for sales. Then these three ratios are averaged (some states weight factors differently), and the result is multiplied by total business income. This is the business income taxed by that state.

Because of formula apportionment, it often is possible to reduce the total state and local income tax of a firm by moving the firm's property and payroll to the lower tax state. (It may be possible to "move" sales, too, but it is much more difficult.) High tax states know about this, and have developed a series of rules to hamper taxpayers' efforts to arbitrage away the higher state tax rates. Usually, a minimum amount of payroll is moved to the lower tax state in order to establish a business connection in the lower tax state, or at least to reduce the business connection with the high tax state. (The business connection is referred to as "nexus," and is discussed in detail in the following chapters.)

For example, consider a firm that manufactures in State X and sells its product in States X and Y. State X has a corporate income tax rate of

10%, and State Y, 5%. If the firm sells by mail order into State Y, where it does not currently have nexus, it is not subject to State Y income tax. The firm's income generated from sales into State Y is allocated to (and thus taxed by) State X. But if the firm obtains a business license and has sales personnel make regular incursions into State Y, the firm can establish nexus in State Y. The firm will become liable for State Y income tax based on the sales revenue earned there, and this will reduce overall state taxes.

To illustrate this, suppose the following facts for the firm:

	State X	**State Y**	**Total**
Sales	$100	$100	$200
Payroll	50	0	50
Property	75	0	75

Corporate taxable income is $40.

If the firm does not have nexus in State Y, all $40 of taxable income is taxed by State X. The firm's total tax liability is $40 × 10% = $4. If the firm establishes nexus in State Y, the firm must apportion its taxable income between State X and State Y. Assume both states double-weight sales. Allocation to State X is:

$$\text{Sales} \quad \left(\frac{100}{200}\right) \times 2 = 100\%$$

$$\text{Property} \quad \frac{50}{50} = 100\%$$

$$\text{Payroll} \quad \frac{75}{75} = 100\%$$

Average factors (100% + 100% + 100%)/4 = 75%.
State X tax = $40 × 75% × 10% = $3.00.

Allocation to State Y:

$$\text{Sales} \quad \left(\frac{100}{200}\right) \times 2 = 100\%$$

Payroll = 0%
Property = 0%
Average factors = (100% + 0% + 0%)/4 = 25%.
State Y tax = $40 × 25% × 5% = $0.50.

The firm's total tax liability is $3.50; that is, (0.50/4.00) or a 12.5% reduction in state and local taxes.

Before employing this technique, the firm should consider other aspects of state and local taxation, as well as considering the costs of making such changes. For example, if the firm seeks to reduce its state income tax liability by redistributing workers or facilities between states, it should consider the following:

- What is the cost of the redistribution?
- What is the cost entailed in setting up the workers or facilities?
- What is the **value added** considering marginal productivity?
- What is the overall impact on the "bottom line"? If earnings decrease and management bonuses or debt covenants are tied to earnings, the tax saving may not be worthwhile.

On a more general level, if the firm seeks to acquire an operation or form a subsidiary in a new state, it should consider the following:

- Does this connection with the new state establish nexus?
- Does the change in apportionment reduce the firm's total state income taxes?
- What are the costs of capital and wages (net of any economic incentives offered) in the new state?
- What are the impacts on productivity, value **added**, and the bottom line?
- Can there be **splitting** of incentives with the seller? If the seller is in a lower tax bracket, will it be willing to lease the property instead of selling? (This would not eliminate the property factor in most jurisdictions; for leased property, eight times annual rental values are counted as "property" for apportionment.)
- Is the firm willing to pay moving workers (or hire new ones) higher wages to entice them to relocate (join the firm)?
- With regard to timing, does the firm anticipate the same tax rates and rules to remain in place? Consultation with state political analysts may enable some forecasting for at least a few years in the future. If the tax climate may get less attractive in the near future, the time value of tax savings could actually turn out to be negative.
- What are the transaction costs of acquiring or moving a subsidiary into a new state? Legal and accounting fees, actual transportation costs for personnel and equipment, and other such costs reduce (and could even exceed) the targeted tax benefit.

SCANNING THE CHANGING STATE AND LOCAL TAX ENVIRONMENT

Because the business and tax environment is dynamic, tax planning suggests that it is useful to do — and a tax lawyer, accountant, or other professional consultant's due diligence requires — continuous environmental scanning to anticipate changes that might affect a firm and how it should react. Specifically, there needs to be a continuous review and analysis of (1) nontax changes in the business environment and (2) tax rule changes, particularly for changes in tax rates and tax credits.

Nontax changes should be the primary focus because they are the most dynamic and typically dominate management decisions. Such changes might necessitate a transaction that requires tax management. For example, if a competitor drops its prices, a firm might respond by outsourcing previously manufactured materials so that it can respond with price reductions. Outsourcing has tax implications, such as gains and losses from sales of assets, changes in property and payroll factors used in allocating income among the states, and elimination of nexus.

Although of secondary importance, and much easier to do, scanning for tax rule changes is also important. This is because tax rules constantly change. Sometimes they evolve through deliberate government policy; often the rules change due to administrative and judicial modifications and interpretations. These, too, require tax management.

These scans have become much more effective, and less expensive, in recent years. Indeed, the Web has made it much more practical to continuously monitor changes in the nontax and tax business environment. For example, assume that a county in Texas announces a "no property tax" policy on new investment. If the taxpayer firm's strategic plan is to become a leader in the East Coast market, it makes little business sense to move the firm's plants to Texas. However, it may make sense to move West Coast operations to this Texas county. Prior to the Web, this law change would have been fairly obscure; it would be likely that only Texas tax professionals could be aware of it until the change found its way into tax research services, and even then it may have stayed obscure because even tax professionals might not know enough to consider looking for the change. Now changes can be posted on Web sites and search agents assigned the duty to automatically look for such changes.

One of the advantages of the Web is the vast amount of material on it, particularly primary sources. This especially is the case for state and local taxes. States have found it quite worthwhile — some more than others, some far better than others — to maintain their own Web sites where they post their own pronouncements, rules, regulations, and statutes, as well as the other official documents that make up the basic rules of state and local taxation. Tax Management in Action 1.1 lists those Web sites.

Although these sites are loaded with official documents, which usually are the key sources to be used in courts when litigating tax cases, the sites suffer from the main malady of the Web, i.e., the data provided are unedited, poorly indexed, and too voluminous to be effective. This particularly is the case when one's goal is simply to scan the changing state and local tax environment. In such cases, it makes sense to work through gateway Web sites such as those listed in Tax Management in Action 1.2. These not only strive to contain links to other useful sites, and organize these links so that they are more useful, they also contain secondary material, such as articles and news bulletins. Although not official, these sources help organize the information (albeit at the price of the editor's bias) and thus often are far more useful in an environmental scan than official sources.

Tax Management in Action 1.1

State and Local Tax Web Sites — Scanning the Changing Tax Environment

Alabama	www.state.al.us	Montana	www.state.mt.us
Alaska	www.state.ak.us	Nebraska	www.state.ne.us
Arizona	www.state.az.us	Nevada	www.state.nv.us
Arkansas	www.state.ar.us	New Hampshire	www.state.nh.us
California	www.state.ca.us	New Jersey	www.state.nj.us
Colorado	www.state.co.us	New Mexico	www.state.nm.us
Connecticut	www.state.ct.us	New York	www.state.ny.us
Delaware	www.state.de.us	North Carolina	www.state.nc.us
Florida	www.state.fl.us	North Dakota	www.state.nd.us
Georgia	www.state.ga.us	Ohio	www.state.oh.us
Hawaii	www.state.ha.us	Oklahoma	www.state.ok.us
Idaho	www.state.id.us	Oregon	www.state.or.us
Illinois	www.state.il.us	Pennsylvania	www.state.pa.us
Indiana	www.state.in.us	Rhode Island	www.state.ri.us
Iowa	www.state.ia.us	South Carolina	www.state.sc.us
Kansas	www.state.ks.us	South Dakota	www.state.sd.us
Kentucky	www.state.kt.us	Tennessee	www.state.tn.us
Louisiana	www.state.la.us	Texas	www.state.tx.us
Maine	www.state.me.us	Utah	www.state.ut.us
Maryland	www.state.md.us	Vermont	www.state.vt.us
Massachusetts	www.state.ma.us	Virginia	www.state.va.us
Michigan	www.state.mi.us	Washington	www.state.wa.us
Minnesota	www.state.mn.us	West Virginia	www.state.wv.us
Mississippi	www.state.ms.us	Wisconsin	www.state.wi.us
Missouri	www.state.mo.us	Wyoming	www.state.wy.us

Tax Management in Action 1.2

Gateway Resources on the Web

Prof. Dennis Schmidt's Web Site	http://www.taxsites.com/
Deloitte and Touche	http://www.dttus.com/dtti/home.htm
Ernst & Young	http://www.ey.com/
KPMG International	http://www.kpmg.com/
PricewaterhouseCoopers	http://www.pwc.com/
Accounting Resources	http://www.rutgers.edu/Accounting/raw/
Accounting Research Network	http://www.ssrn.com/ARN/index.html
American Institute of Certified Public Accountants (AICPA)	http://www.aicpa.org/
Corporate Financial Reports	http://www.investorama.com/corp.html
Securities & Exchange Commission, Edgar Data Base	http://www.sec.gov/edgarht.htm

---

STATE AND LOCAL TAX RESEARCH

State and local tax research is done much like that for Federal tax research. The biggest difference is the sheer number of different rules from the multitude of jurisdictions involved and that few states, and no local jurisdictions, are blessed by good, detailed reference works to be consulted.

There are some, however. Among the most highly regarded works are the state tax services that supplement Federal tax services such as the Commerce Clearing House and RIA-Prentice Hall.

Web-based versions of these, and the materials discussed below, are available, too. (These are discussed further in Appendix A.)

More importantly, the leading Federal tax publishers put out a variety of handbooks annually for the dozen states that generate the most state and local tax revenues. A good example is the Commerce Clearing House's *Guidebook to California Taxes*. Also published are multistate handbooks; the Commerce Clearing House equivalent is its All States tax handbook.

These books are an invaluable resource. They typically contain the law up to the early part of November of the prior year. The year of the book is the tax return preparation year. That is, the 2004 edition is what tax practitioners use during the 2004 tax season when preparing 2003 tax returns.

One of their finer features is that they are extensively cross-referenced into the publishers' respective *State Tax Reporters*. These multivolume sets contain extensive detail on almost every aspect of each state's tax law, including the text of the actual laws; headnotes to cases, regulations, and rulings; and the text of current cases.

Another useful feature of a state guidebook is constant cross-referencing both to the state tax law statutes (e.g., California's Revenue and Taxation Code) relevant to the discussion and to the comparable IRC Sections. These tables also indicate if there are no comparable sections. This is important, because most states provide that if there are no specific state rules or regulations relating to a particular topic, taxpayers can rely on Federal law if the underlying statutes are the same.

These cross-references have another useful feature: the Code Sections are in turn cross-referenced into the relevant paragraph of the publishers' *Federal Tax Reporter*. Also included are highlights of new developments and the major tax legislation for the year, tax rates and tables for the major taxes, and cross-reference tables to paragraphs within the guidebooks.

For example, if one knows the section number of the comparable Federal law on a point of interest, a guidebook's "Federal-State Cross Reference Table" can be consulted to find the applicable state tax section, and it provides a reference into the publishers' state guidebook paragraph which deals with the Code Section. Also provided are a topical index, a table of cases, and a table of legal rulings. One important development is that, at least for some publishers, the same topics appear at the same paragraph numbers in each state's guidebook. Thus once a topic is found for one state, it is easily found for all states.

Speaking of rulings by tax agencies, this brings up an important point about finding state tax rules. Most states have relatively little official and unofficial written guidance. Not so for some states, such as New York and California. In these states, there are a mass of official guides, including regulations, rules, and rulings along with extensive publications. In these, significant new rulings, court decisions, and decisions of the state tax agency (e.g., the State Board of Equalization in California) are pointed out in the state guidebook.

There also are many unofficial sources, such as reporters, treatises, and services that package state tax law for practitioners. Just like those for Federal tax rules, some are standard tax reporters, and others are more like tax encyclopedias. There are some multivolume treatises as well as newsletters, published both by the state taxing authority, such as the Franchise Tax Board's *Tax News*, and by private firms, such as Spidell's invaluable *California Tax Newsletter*.

Additional state and local tax research resources are provided in Appendix A.

DISCUSSION QUESTIONS

1. What are the most important state and local taxes in your state?
2. Your sister is thinking about starting a Web-based business selling specialty teas to upper middle class American women who are working out-

side the home for compensation. If the business is to start up in 3 months, what key decisions will your sister face during that period, and how might state and local taxes impact them?

3. You work for a family-owned business located in Coos Bay, Oregon, which manufactures prefabricated metal structures. The owner's granddaughter has just started college at McGill University in Quebec, and he has promised to pay half of her costs provided she majors in engineering and works for the business after she graduates. Over lunch, he asks you to find out whether he should pay his half from his personal accounts or put her on the payroll. What state and local tax issues should be considered in making this decision?

PROBLEMS

Problem 1

How would your answer to Question #2 change if your sister is willing to move anywhere in the U.S.?

Problem 2

Galadriel Elvin, a wealthy entrepreneur, was returning home after taking the eldest of her three children to start college on the other side of the country when she noticed that the person sitting next to her in the first-class cabin was absent-mindedly fiddling with a pink substance. When she asked about it, Bill Halfacre explained that he had developed it because he was spending a small fortune on batteries for his young children's toys. Simply dipping regular alkaline batteries in the substance for an hour had proven to more than double the effective life of the batteries.

When Galadriel mentioned that this was a great idea, Bill replied that he was a bit depressed because he had been trying to connect with someone who could help him develop and market the product, but had been unsuccessful. Galadriel encouraged him, and discovered that he had lived a varied and interesting life. He had earned several degrees in chemistry, but had spent all his time since graduating surfing throughout the world and tinkering with various inventions. (He had inherited enough money that he had not had to work since he finished school 5 years ago, but the money was running out.)

By the time the plane landed, Galadriel and Bill had set a time to meet with Galadriel's lawyer, Elsa Treebeard, to discuss a venture to market Bill's products. They had also invited one of Galadriel's colleagues, Jim Pippin, to attend the meeting. Jim had worked with Galadriel on several occasions; he makes a lot, but keeps very little, money. He is a marketing whiz who has strong connections to several distributors to large office supply outlets. Galadriel's concern with Jim has always been that he plays things a bit fast and loose.

At the meeting with Elsa, the group developed projections of profits and losses for the first 5 years of the business. The expectation is that annual losses will range from $100,000 to $200,000 over these 5 years, with break-even in about Year 5. The business will be capitalized with about $200,000 in cash, along with computers, equipment, furniture, and fixtures (fair market value of $100,000 and basis of $25,000) contributed by Galadriel. Bill will contribute the patent at an agreed value of $150,000. Jim has nothing to contribute but time. He will receive a 25% interest for contributing all of his time for a year to get the business going. Thereafter, he will be compensated based on sales and profits. Elsa believes they will be able to borrow $200,000 initially and perhaps an additional $100,000 per year during the development period. The money will be used for working capital and manufacturing equipment. They feel that they may be able to attract new investors once some of the initial work has been completed.

Galadriel thinks Jim brings some needed talents to the venture, but she is very uneasy about being exposed to liabilities that he might create. Bill says he has nothing to lose so the association with Jim does not concern him. Galadriel has about $500,000 in income each year. Bill's income is about $25,000 a year, and Jim has earned anywhere from $0 to $200,000 annually over the last few years.

How should state and local taxes impact the results of the major strategic decisions faced by the three venturers as they start up the business?

ENDNOTES

1. *State and Local Taxes: The Burden Grows.*
2. Source: Authors' calculations.
3. An effective tax rate is computed by dividing the total taxes paid by businesses in a state by income for businesses operating in the state. Source: Authors' calculations.
4. Wyoming's high effective rate is driven by large severance tax collections.
5. For a more detailed review of the various types of taxes, see Karayan, Swenson, and Neff, *Strategic Corporate Tax Planning* (Wiley: 2002).
6. A special type of partnership, allowed in most states, is a limited liability partnership (LLP). With an LLP, if an action of one or more partners causes liability, personal liability (i.e., extending to the partner's individual assets) is limited to the partner(s) causing the action.
7. The credit is usually limited to the lesser of the amount of tax computed by multiplying the taxpayer's total tax by a fraction or the amount of tax actually paid. The fraction is the amount of taxable income subject to tax in the nonresident jurisdiction under the resident's state tax laws over the resident's entire taxable income.

8. For a detailed description of Federal estate, gift, and generations skipping taxes, see Chapter 7 of Khoury, Karayan, et al. *Wealth Forever: The Story of Stock Markets* (World Scientific Publishers: 2003).

9. The Federal unified credit renders the first block (e.g., $1 million) of funds given away — during lifetime or at death — tax free. Furthermore, Federal law exempts small gifts (e.g., up to $11,000 annually) from taxation. In addition, transfers to qualified charities are tax deductible, as are payments for anyone's qualified tuition or medical expenses.

10. An expansive discussion of the sources of Federal tax law can be found in Karayan, Swenson, and Neff, *Strategic Corporate Tax Planning* (Wiley: 2002).

11. An excellent guide to business tax planning in general is *Strategic Corporate Tax Planning* (Wiley: 2002) by Karayan, Swenson, and Neff.

Free value-added materials available from the Download Resource Center at www.jrosspub.com.

2

CONSTITUTIONAL LAW LIMITATIONS

INTRODUCTION

Constitutional provisions are very important in state and local tax planning, much more so in determining the legality of state and local taxes than for Federal taxes. Consider the constitutional history of the Federal income tax. In 1895, the U.S. Supreme Court ruled that the Federal personal income tax violated the Constitution and therefore was unenforceable. The Court reasoned that the tax was a direct tax not apportioned among the states in proportion to their populations.[12] In response, Congress drafted the Sixteenth Amendment to the U.S. Constitution, ratified in 1913, which specifically sanctioned Federal individual and corporate income taxes. Since the amendment, constitutional challenges to Federal income taxes have essentially ceased.

In contrast, constitutional challenges to state and local taxes are often starting points for much consulting work. Challenges are brought under provisions contained in the U.S. Constitution and in state constitutions. U.S. constitutional provisions frequently used for such challenges are the Due Process and the Commerce Clauses. Less used provisions are the Equal Protection and the Privileges and Immunities Clauses. While the U.S. Constitution limits a state's authority to impose taxes, a state's own constitution is the first level of limitations on the state's authority to impose taxes.

STATE-LEVEL CONSTITUTIONAL ISSUES

Most state constitutions contain a uniformity or equality clause that limits the state's authority to impose taxes. For example, Article 9 of the Arizona Constitution provides:

All taxes shall be uniform upon the same class of property within the territorial limits of the authority levying the tax, and shall be levied and collected for public purposes only.[13]

However, uniformity and equality clauses vary considerably among the states. Some require only that the taxes be uniform (e.g., Arizona's constitutional provision above). Others require taxes to be either equal and uniform or proportional and uniform. For example, the New Hampshire constitution provides that the state may "impose and levy proportional and reasonable assessments, rates, and taxes."[14]

Most uniformity or equality clauses pertaining to a property tax provide that "[t]he assessment of all property shall be equal and uniform"[15] and that "[p]roperty tax levies shall be uniform."[16] On the other hand, some extend the uniformity or equality provision to all taxes, such as Wisconsin which requires that "[t]he rule of taxation shall be uniform."[17]

For tax planning purposes, the basic issue is this: how does a constitutional provision regarding uniformity or equality impact a state's ability to impose taxes? However, before determining the impact, two questions must first be answered:

1. Is the levy being imposed a tax or a fee?
2. If the levy is a tax, is it a property tax or an excise tax?

Question 1: Tax or Fee?

Equality and uniformity clauses typically apply only to taxes and not to fees. Therefore, fees may be imposed by state or local governments without having to satisfy the state's equality and uniformity clauses. Questions naturally arise:

- What makes a levy a tax rather than a fee?
- What criteria are useful in distinguishing between a tax and a fee?
- Does it matter whether the levy is labeled a tax or a fee?
- Does the substance or form of the levy determine whether it is a tax or a fee?

Examples of court cases from the different states provide some guidance.

Example 2.1. In two West Virginia cases, the courts reached different conclusions for two levies. Neither levy was labeled a tax. A solid waste assessment charge was determined to be a "regulatory fee" rather than a tax.[18] A fire service fee was held to be an *ad valorem* property tax.[19] Consequently, the latter levy was subject to the state constitution's uniformity and equality clause but the former was not.

Example 2.2. In a Wisconsin case, the state's Supreme Court held that a property tax credit violated the state's uniformity requirement.[20] The credit was payable from the state general revenue fund, and made available to a group of property owners to offset increased property tax assessments. The Court stated that "[i]t is the effect of the statute, not the form, which determines whether it is a tax statute subject to the uniformity clause,"[21] and that the credit was "in substance a tax statute because it has the effect of changing the individual tax burden by granting a partial exemption."[22]

Criteria for Distinguishing Between Taxes and Fees

Fees characteristically involve: (1) a voluntary payment, (2) made to a segregated fund, (3) for a specific governmental benefit, (4) where payment is imposed by a regulatory agency on those subject to regulation.

In contrast, taxes characteristically involve: (1) an involuntary payment, (2) made to the general treasury, (3) for general governmental purpose, (4) where payment is used to defray general governmental expenditures. Because the same issue arises in determining Federal itemized deductions for taxes, Federal law is relevant by analogy when analyzing this and the following question.

Question 2: Property or Excise Tax?

If a levy is a tax, the next question is whether the tax is a property tax or excise tax. In most states, constitutional requirements of equality and uniformity apply only to property taxes and not to excise taxes. The fundamental distinction between property and excise lies in whether the tax is imposed on all of the privileges of owning a property or only on some of the privileges.

A tax is a property tax if it is imposed because people own property and not because they exercise some privilege entitled them due to this ownership of the property. Property taxes do not impose any condition or place any restriction on the use of the property. Property taxes tend to be recurring in nature and assessed as of a fixed date each period, usually annually, although they may be payable quarterly or semi-annually. In contrast, excise taxes tend to be one-time charges imposed on the privilege of exercising some right.

STATE INCOME TAX — PROPERTY TAX OR EXCISE TAX?

An interesting question that has historical significance is whether an income tax is a property tax or an excise tax. This question was raised at the state level following the 1895 *Pollock* decision that struck down the Federal personal income tax as unconstitutional. Some state courts interpreted the decision as holding that an income tax is a property tax, and thereby made the tax subject to that state constitution's uniformity and equality clause. Depending on each state's constitution, the classification as a property tax had different implications. For example, a graduated income tax was determined to be unconstitutional in many states.

Now, however, an income tax is generally not classified as a property tax, and thus it is not subject to the constitutional limitations that apply to property taxes. An early case establishing this view is *Featherstone v. Norman,*[23] which concluded that Georgia's income tax was not a property tax. Some states' constitutions specifically address the matter of income taxes.

> **Example 2.3.** The Kentucky constitution provides "[n]othing in this Constitution shall be construed to prevent the General Assembly from providing for taxation based on income, licenses or franchises."[24]
>
> **Example 2.4.** The Wisconsin constitution not only expressly empowers the state to impose income taxes but also allows graduated income taxes to be imposed. Article VIII of the constitution reads: "[t]he rule of taxation shall be uniform....Taxes may also be imposed on incomes, privileges and occupations, which taxes may be graduated and progressive, and reasonable exemptions may be provided."[25]

FEDERAL-LEVEL CONSTITUTIONAL ISSUES

Several provisions of the U.S. Constitution affect state and local taxes, including the Equal Protection, Privileges and Immunities, Due Process, and Commerce Clauses. The most frequently raised challenges to state and local tax levies are based on the Due Process and the Commerce Clauses. With much less frequency, state and local taxes have also been challenged under the Equal Protection and the Privileges and Immunities Clauses.

The Equal Protection Clause

The Fourteenth Amendment to the U.S. Constitution provides:

> [N]or shall any State...deny to any person within its jurisdiction the equal protection of the laws[26]

Although the Equal Protection Clause makes no mention of taxation, it has been invoked in a manner similar to the state-level equality and uniformity provisions. Specifically, the clause has been invoked to determine whether the tax treats different "persons" equally.[27] The U.S. Supreme Court's position has been that state legislatures are allowed a high degree of flexibility in classifying taxpayers, if there is a reasonable basis for the legislature's distinctions. Their position is illustrated by the following statements from *Lehnhausen v. Lakeshore Auto Parts Co.*[28]

> The Equal Protection Clause does not mean that a State may not draw lines that treat one class of individuals or entities differently from the others. The test is whether the difference in treatment is an invidious discrimination. Where taxation is concerned and no specific federal right, apart from equal protection, is imperiled, the States have large leeway in making classifications and drawing lines which in their judgment produce reasonable systems of taxation.[29]

In addition, the Court has granted "a presumption of constitutionality" of the state's classification scheme. The Court concluded that the state legislature is uniquely positioned to have intimate knowledge of local conditions and is presumed to have used that knowledge to devise its taxing scheme. As long as there is any conceivable basis for treating classes of taxpayers or members of a class differently, the taxing scheme withstands Equal Protection challenge.

Example 2.5. In *Exxon Corp. v. Eagerton*,[30] the Court found that an Alabama statute exempting royalty owners from an increase in the state's severance tax and prohibiting producers from passing the tax increase to their purchasers did not violate the Equal Protection Clause.

Example 2.6. California's Proposition Thirteen, dealing with the state's real property tax system, is one of the most widely known and controversial state tax initiatives that imposed differential tax burdens. It amended the state constitution to limit property taxes to 1% of 1975–76 valuations and to cap annual increases in valuations at 2%, unless the property underwent a change in ownership (e.g., sale) or was a new construction. Property values were assessed based on the date of acquisition rather than current value. That is, the historical cost principle, indexed for inflation, is used in calculating the property tax base, rather than estimated fair market value.

Consequently, a taxpayer continuing to live in the same property might have a substantially different property tax burden from a taxpayer who newly buys a virtually identical property in the same neighborhood. Proposition Thirteen was challenged under the Equal Protection Clause, but the Supreme Court upheld the California scheme. The Court held that the difference in tax treatment of newer and older owners rationally furthered a legitimate state interest of preserving and stabilizing local neighborhoods.[31]

State Uniformity and Equality Provisions and the Federal Equal Protection Clause

Federal law generally dominates or "trumps" state law, so state equality and uniformity provisions cannot conflict with the Equal Protection Clause. Such state provisions specifically target the state's taxing powers, but the Federal Equal Protection provision is general and extends to all laws. In addition, such state provisions tend to provide stricter tests that state tax statutes must pass with regard to equality then the Federal provision. Finally, as demonstrated above in *Lehnhausen*, the Supreme Court has granted state legislatures tremendous flexibility in devising tax statutes capable of passing muster under the Federal Equal Protection Clause.

> **Example 2.7.** In a recent case, the Ohio Supreme Court held that the state could not treat a long-distance "interexchange" carrier differently from a reseller of telecommunications services for *ad valorem* tax purposes, because both owned essentially the same type of equipment.[32] Under Ohio's law, the long-distance carrier was considered a utility, whereas the reseller was not. Thus, the Court invalidated the state's distinction between the two taxpayers.

The Ohio decision demonstrates the greater willingness of state courts to invalidate state tax statutes by use of state uniformity and equality provisions on behalf of taxpayers. In contrast, the U.S. Supreme Court has been reluctant to allow successful challenges to state legislatures' taxing schemes on Equal Protection grounds.

Distinctions Between Taxpayers, Property, and Activities for State Tax Purposes

A fundamental question is to what extent may the state legislature distinguish between taxpayers, property, and activities without violating the Federal Equal Protection Clause and its equality and uniformity provisions. It is difficult to provide a general answer to this question. A distinction must be tested under both the Federal-state provisions. However, as the state provisions tend to be stricter, the answer is likely to depend on the specific language used in the state constitution. Consequently, one could arrive at different answers to questions such as the following:

- Can taxes be imposed at different rates on different taxpayers, property, or activities?
- Does providing an exemption to a taxpayer, property, or activity amount to differential taxation within the purview of the uniformity and equality clauses?
- Does providing a tax credit to a taxpayer, property, or activity amount to differential taxation within the purview of the uniformity and equality clauses?

The Privileges and Immunities Clauses

The U.S. Constitution has two clauses concerning privileges and immunities that have played a role, although a rare one, in state and local tax matters. The first concerns "interstate" privileges and immunities and states:

The Citizens of each State shall be entitled to all Privileges and Immunities of Citizens in the several States.[33]

The second Privileges and Immunities Clause states:

No State shall make or enforce any law which shall abridge the privileges or immunities of citizens of the United States.[34]

The first has been used occasionally as a basis for claiming unconstitutional discrimination in the tax treatment accorded to state residents and nonresidents. The Supreme Court has stated that:

[T]he primary purpose of this clause...was to help fuse into one Nation a collection of independent, sovereign States. It was designed to insure to citizen of State A who ventures into State B the same privileges which the citizens of State B enjoy.[35]

This clause differs from the Equal Protection Clause in scope: the former applies only to "citizens"; the latter applies to "persons." Because corporate taxpayers are persons but not citizens, corporations are entitled to Equal Protection but not to Privileges and Immunities. The second clause merely bars a state from interfering with a U.S. citizen's rights and has had little impact on tax matters.

The Due Process and the Commerce Clauses

A state's taxing scheme must first survive scrutiny under the Equal Protection and the state constitution's uniformity and equality requirements. Next, the state must have jurisdiction to impose the tax on the taxpayer, property, or activity. If an individual taxpayer is a state resident, the property is located in the state, or the business activity is conducted entirely within the state's boundaries, the state clearly has jurisdiction over the individual taxpayer, property, or activity. The answer is not straightforward when the activities cross state boundaries.

Today, business activities are commonly carried on simultaneously in multiple states. Cross-border activities make the issue of tax jurisdiction much more complicated.

To illustrate, consider the following questions:

■ Can all of the states in which activities are conducted impose a tax?
■ If so, is it possible for the same activity to be taxed more than once?
■ If that occurs, what would it do to the overall tax burden of the tax-payer?
■ More importantly, would such multiple taxation be fair to the taxpayer?
■ Does the threat of multiple taxation imply that an interstate business should not be subject to tax by any state?

In sum, what are the rights of taxpayers engaged in interstate business, and what are the powers of the states to impose taxation on such activities?

Any questions involving fundamental rights and powers require a look to the Constitution for guidance. The Due Process and the Commerce Clauses of the U.S. Constitution limit a state's authority to impose a tax on a foreign corporation, and thereby delineate the rights of these taxpayers. The nexus requirements of both clauses must be satisfied before an out-of-state business may be subject to the taxing jurisdiction of a state. Nexus, as explained, is the extent of contact that the taxpayer must have with the state in order for the state to impose a tax within its constitutional limits. The Due Process Clause of the U.S. Constitution states:

[N]or shall any State deprive any person of life, liberty, or property, without due process of law....[36]

The Commerce Clause of the U.S. Constitution states:

The Congress shall have Power...to regulate Commerce with foreign Nations, and among the several States, and with the Indian Tribes[37]

The Supreme Court has issued numerous decisions based on these clauses. The Court's decisions have evolved over time. To understand the Court's current position, one must understand the historical development of its decisions. Historically, the Court has relied on both clauses to provide answers to controversies arising over taxation of interstate commerce.

Relationship Between the Due Process Clause and the Commerce Clause

In *Quill Corporation v. North Dakota*, the Supreme Court examined the relationship between the Due Process Clause and the Commerce Clause. The Court concluded that the clauses address different constitutional concerns, and that "although the 'two claims are closely related,' the Clauses pose distinct limits on the taxing powers of the States."[38] Thus, a state may be "consistent with the Due Process Clause, have the authority to tax a particular taxpayer, imposition of the tax may nonetheless violate the Commerce Clause."

Regarding their decisions leading up to *Quill*, the Court acknowledged that it had not precisely distinguished between the two clauses. Hence, the relationship between the two clauses and their application to state and local tax jurisdiction has been somewhat confused.

In *Miller Bros. Co. v. Maryland*, an earlier case, the Court held that the Due Process Clause "requires some definite link, some minimum connection, between a state and the person, property or transaction it seeks to tax."[39] In several cases regarding use taxes, the Court held that the minimum connection requirement was satisfied if the seller's local activities were "plainly accorded the protection and services of the taxing state."[40] The minimum connection requirement would therefore be satisfied if the seller had any sort of physical presence. For example, the presence of sales personnel in the state or the maintenance of local retail stores in the state would satisfy the requirement.

In *National Bellas Hess*, the Court suggested that physical presence in the state was not only sufficient but also necessary for jurisdiction under the Due Process Clause.[41] However, in *Burger King Corp. v. Rudzewicz*, the Court eschewed a formalistic physical presence test for a more flexible approach. The Court relied on prior decisions that did not equate the minimum contact requirement with physical presence. Instead, the relevant enquiry was whether the defendant's presence in the state justified requiring it to defend a suit in that state.[42] For that purpose, the Court stated that physical presence was not necessary, as economic presence could suffice. Economic presence is satisfied when a business purposefully avails itself of the benefits of a state's economic market.

The Commerce Clause grants Congress the power to "regulate Commerce... among the several States."[43] The Court has held that the Commerce Clause "is more than an affirmative grant of power" to Congress and that "it has a negative sweep as well." This "negative sweep" aspect is referred to as the "negative" or "dormant" Commerce Clause.

In the seminal case on this issue — *Complete Auto Transit, Inc. v. Brady* — the Court held that a state tax satisfies the requirements of the Commerce Clause if it meets four requirements:

1. The tax is applied to an activity with substantial nexus with the taxing state.
2. The activity, both in and out of the state, is fairly apportioned.
3. The tax does not discriminate against interstate commerce.
4. The tax is fairly related to services provided by the state.[44]

The Court defined Due Process Clause nexus as a minimum connection with the state and Commerce Clause nexus as a "substantial" connection with the state. The Court bifurcated the nexus requirement under the two clauses because they have different principal concerns. The principal concern of Due Process is fairness for the individual defendant; the principal concern of the Commerce Clause is the effect of state regulation on the national economy and the potential for unduly burdening interstate commerce.

Using this rationale, in *Quill* the Court concluded that the Commerce Clause substantial nexus requirement necessitated that an out-of-state mail-order seller have a physical presence in the state in order for the state to require it to collect use taxes on sales made to in-state purchasers. The Court articulated a bright-line physical presence test. However, its decision raised the question of whether physical presence is always required for Commerce Clause nexus.

The Court added to the confusion by stating in *Quill* that "we have not, in our review of other types of taxes, articulated the same physical-presence requirement...established for sales and use taxes." This suggested that the standards of nexus might differ based on the type of tax involved. In addition, the Court's decision seemed to weigh heavily on the fact that the case involved the mail-order industry.

The Court left unresolved its ruling in *National Bellas Hess*, 25 years before *Quill*, that a similar use tax collection requirement created an unconstitutional burden on interstate commerce. However, the Court reaffirmed its holding in this earlier case that those persons whose contacts with a state do not exceed U.S. mail or common carrier do not have substantial nexus and cannot be required to collect use taxes. In *Quill*, the Court apparently sought to preserve the tax status quo of the mail-order industry, because it believed that the industry's tremendous growth was in part due to the Court's *National Bellas Hess* decision.

Historical Development of Commerce Clause

As discussed above, both the Due Process Clause and the Commerce Clause place limits on a state's power to tax interstate commerce. Of the two, the Commerce Clause is more important. Originally, the Court held that interstate commerce should be free from all state taxes as a tax would amount to state regulation of interstate commerce, and only Congress has the power to regulate such commerce via the Commerce Clause. This "free trade" view was well summarized in *Freeman v. Hewit*:

> The Commerce Clause was not merely an authorization to Congress to enact laws for the protection and encouragement of commerce among the states, but by its own force created an area of trade free from interference by the States. In short, the Commerce Clause even without implementing legislation from Congress is a limitation upon the power of the states....This limitation on State power...does not merely forbid a State to single out interstate commerce for hostile action. A State is also precluded from taking any action which may fairly be deemed to have the effect of impeding the free flow of trade between States. It is immaterial that local commerce is subjected to similar encumbrances.[45]

After the Great Depression, this free trade view gradually was replaced with a multiple taxation doctrine. Under the new doctrine, the Court ruled that state taxes could be imposed on interstate commerce, unless there was a risk of multiple taxation and such risk was not borne by local commerce. After a temporary reversal of the multiple taxation doctrine, in *Northwestern States Portland Cement Co. Minnesota* the Court stated for the first time that the Commerce Clause does not prevent a state from levying a nondiscriminatory direct net income tax on a foreign corporation.[46] Since then, the Court has granted increased power to the states to impose taxes on interstate commerce. In 1977, the Court generalized this recognition of state power to tax interstate commerce in the *Complete Auto* case, discussed above.

In *Tyler Pipe Industries, Inc. v. Washington Dept. of Revenue*, the Court held that the activities of local sales representatives of an out-of-state corporation amounted to substantial nexus with the state of Washington, and thus the state could impose and collect a tax on the corporation's local sales.[47] It was irrelevant

---

Tax Management in Action 2.1

Checklist of Relevant Questions

1. Is the levy a tax or a fee?
2. Is the levy a property tax or an excise tax?
3. Does the tax satisfy the state's constitutional provisions regarding uniformity and equality?
4. If the tax is imposed on interstate transactions, does the tax also satisfy the Federal constitutional provisions of the Due Process Clause and the Commerce Clause?
5. What is the tax base?
6. What is the amount of the tax?
7. When is the tax due?

that the local representatives were independent contractors and not employees of the corporation.

DISCUSSION QUESTIONS

1. What factors are used to distinguish between a "tax" and a "fee"? Why do we care whether a levy is a tax or a fee?
2. Explain the importance of distinguishing between a property tax, an excise tax and an income tax?
3. Are tax incentives ethical?
4. Are taxes a quid pro quo?
5. Define the term "nexus." Does nexus require a physical presence? Does nexus mean the same thing for different types of taxes?
6. What is meant by "substantial" nexus? How is it achieved?
7. Does substantial nexus require a physical presence? Does substantial nexus imply or require a substantial physical presence?

PROBLEMS

Problem 1

For your home state, do the following:
- Identify and list the different taxes imposed.
- Obtain the text of the uniformity and equality constitutional provision.
- Compare the provision to the Federal Equal Protection Clause. Evaluate whether it is more, less, or equally demanding as the Federal standard.
- Research the latest case in which the courts (Federal or state) have analyzed and interpreted your state's uniformity and equality constitutional provision.

Problem 2

Prepare brief written summaries of the following cases:
- *Lehnhausen*
- *Complete Auto Transit Corp. v. Brady*
- *Quill Corp.*

Organize your brief using the following sections:
a. Facts
b. Issues presented
c. Analysis of issues
d. Conclusions of the court

ENDNOTES

12. *Pollock v. Farmers' Loan and Trust Co.*, 158 U.S. 601 (1895).
13. Ariz. Const. art. IX, §1.
14. N.H. Const. part 2, art. 5.
15. S.C. Const. art. X, §1.
16. S.C. Const. art. X, §6.
17. Wis. Const. art. VIII, §1.
18. *Wetzel County Solid Waste Auth. v. West Virginia Div. of Natural Resources*, 462 S.E.2d 349 (W.Va. 1995).
19. *City of Fairmont v. Pitrolo Pontiac-Cadillac Co.*, 308 S.E.2d 527 (W.Va. 1983).
20. *State ex rel. La Folette v. Torphy*, 270 N.W.2d 187 (Wis. 1978).
21. Id. at 192.
22. Id.
23. 153 S.E. 58 (Ga. 1930).
24. Ky. Const. §174
25. Wis. Const. art. VIII, §1.
26. U.S. Const. amend. XIV, §1.
27. A person has been held to include corporations.
28. 410 U.S. 356 (1973).
29. Id. at 359 (citations and footnote omitted).
30. 462 U.S. 176 (1983).
31. *Nordlinger v. Lynch, sub nom Nordlinger v. Hahn*, 505 U.S. 1, 112 S. Ct. 2326 (1992).
32. *MCI Telecommunications Corp. v. Limbach*, 625 N.E.2d 597 (Ohio 1994).
33. U.S. Const. art. IV, §2.
34. U.S. Const. amend. XIV.
35. Toomer v. Witsell, 334 U.S. 385 (1948).
36. U.S. Const. amend. XIV, §1.
37. U.S. Const. art. I, §8, cl. 3.
38. 504 U.S. 298, 305 (1992) [quoting *National Bellas Hess, Inc. v. Dept. of Revenue of the State of Illinois*, 386 U.S. 753, 756 (1967)].
39. 347 U.S. 340 (1954).
40. *National Bellas Hess, Inc. v. Dept. of Revenue of the State of Illinois*, 386 U.S. 753, 757 (1967).
41. 386 U.S. 753 (1967).
42. 471 U.S. 462 (1985).
43. U.S. Const. art. I, §8.
44. 430 U.S. 274 (1977).
45. 329 U.S. 249, (1946).
46. 358 U.S. 450 (1959).
47. *Freeman v. Hewitt*, 483 U.S. 232, 107 SCt 2810, 97 LEd 2d 199 (1987).

Free value-added materials available from the
Download Resource Center at www.jrosspub.com.

PART II: PRINCIPLES OF STATE AND LOCAL TAXATION

3

CORPORATE INCOME/ FRANCHISE TAXES

INTRODUCTION

Forty-four states and the District of Columbia have a corporate-level tax based on corporate net income. Michigan, Nevada, South Dakota, Texas, Washington, and Wyoming do not have such a tax. In lieu of a corporate income tax, Washington has a tax based on corporate gross receipts, Michigan has a Single Business Tax that is like a Value-Added Tax (VAT), and Texas has a tax based on the higher of 0.25% of allocated capital or 4.5% of allocated earned surplus.

Those jurisdictions having a corporate net income tax have incorporated many of the guidelines recommended by the Multistate Tax Commission. As noted earlier, the Commission drafted model income tax rules and regulations embodying its guidelines: the Multistate Tax Compact and the Uniform Division for Income Tax Purposes Act (UDITPA). Unless specified otherwise, in this book these rules and regulations are referred to as the general rule because as they have been widely adopted, though in modified form. Common modifications include differences in statutory rates, exemptions, deductions, credits, methods of apportioning income, and reporting requirements (e.g., whether consolidated or separate accounting).

Differences arising from modifications are suggested by the effective corporate income tax rates by state shown in Table 3.1.[48] Effective tax rates are computed by dividing the total corporate income taxes collected for the year by the total corporate net income for the year. For comparison purposes, Table 3.1 also reports statutory rates.

As the table indicates, effective corporate income tax rates vary widely by state. Most states' effective rates are also lower than their statutory rates.

TABLE 3.1. Effective Income Tax Rates by State

State	Effective Tax Rate	Statutory Tax Rate	State	Effective Tax Rate	Statutory Tax Rate
Alabama	3.04	5.0	Nebraska	2.34	7.8
Arizona	5.98	7.9	Nevada	0.00	0.0
Arkansas	2.68	6.5	New Hampshire	6.38	8.0
California	4.49	8.8	New Jersey	4.84	9.0
Colorado	3.96	4.7	New Mexico	3.31	7.6
Connecticut	5.02	7.5	New York	6.35	8.5
DC and Maryland	3.74	0.1/0.07	North Carolina	2.45	6.9
Delaware	4.34	8.7	North Dakota	4.32	0.105
Florida	4.81	5.5	Ohio	3.34	8.5
Georgia	3.06	6.0	Oklahoma	4.39	6.0
Hawaii	2.22	6.4	Oregon	4.84	6.6
Idaho	2.84	8.0	Pennsylvania	4.29	9.9
Illinois	4.76	4.8	Rhode Island	4.02	9.0
Indiana	3.70	3.4	South Carolina	3.94	5.0
Iowa	3.05	12.0	South Dakota	1.79	0.0
Kansas	3.89	4.0	Tennessee	3.45	6.0
Kentucky	4.73	8.2	Texas	4.54	0.0
Louisiana	3.66	8.0	Utah	2.72	5.0
Maine	5.48	8.9	Vermont	4.92	9.75
Massachusetts	3.88	9.5	Virginia	2.80	6.0
Michigan	8.25	2.3	Washington	5.30	0.0
Minnesota	4.42	9.8	West Virginia	5.79	9.0
Mississippi	3.65	5.0	Wisconsin	3.80	7.9
Missouri	3.70	6.2	Wyoming	0.00	0.0
Montana	6.70	6.75			

(Because South Dakota, Texas, and Washington do not have corporate income taxes, they do not have statutory rates. To calculate effective rates, their taxes on financial institutions, franchise taxes on capital, and gross receipts taxes that were equivalent to income taxes — i.e., not sales and use taxes — were used.)

Nexus

A corporation is subject to tax if the firm has nexus with the state. As noted previously, nexus is the minimum contact that an entity must have with a state for the entity to be subject to the state's tax jurisdiction. The nexus requirement is rooted in the Due Process and Commerce Clauses of the U.S. Constitution. Nexus, however, is not a single concept. Instead, it varies with the type of tax imposed.

CORPORATE FRANCHISE TAXES

Each state generally has the right to tax corporations that use their "corporate franchise" inside the state's borders. Some states, most notably California and New York, impose what they refer to as a "franchise tax," but it is computed like a corporate income tax. For franchise tax purposes, nexus exists if a corporation meets any of the following four tests: (1) does business in the state, (2) has commercial domicile in the state, (3) is incorporated in the state, or (4) is qualified or registered to do business in the state.

"Doing business" deals with the performance of certain business activities within the state; this definition varies with the state. "Commercial domicile" exists if the corporation's principal place of business or headquarters is located in the state. "Incorporation" means that a corporation was organized under the laws of the state. "Qualification to do business" means that a corporation that is not incorporated within the state registers to obtain permission to conduct business, which is sometimes required depending on the nature of activities performed.

> **Example 3.1.** Smithco is incorporated in Minnesota. However, its Minnesota operations consist of a small office. Smithco's principal operations (i.e., commercial domicile) are in Illinois. Smithco has nexus in both Minnesota and Illinois.

CORPORATE NET INCOME TAXES

Generally, a corporation incorporated in a state (and thus organized under its laws) is required to file an income tax return. A corporation incorporated in a state is a "domestic corporation." A corporation incorporated outside the state is a "foreign corporation." A foreign corporation is only required to file an income tax return if it has the requisite nexus in the state for income tax purposes.

As indicated previously, a state's ability to assert that nexus exists for income tax or franchise tax purposes is limited by the Federal statute P.L. 86-272. ("P.L." stands for "Public Law"). Normally, Federal statutes that are enacted into law are codified. That is, they are inserted into one of Titles of the Federal Code. Tax laws, for example, are located in Title 26; Federal criminal laws are located in Title 18. Codes are organized bodies of law, divided into pieces — e.g., Title, Subtitles, Parts, Subparts, Sections, Subsections, Paragraphs, Subparagraphs, Clauses, and Subclauses — so that rules governing similar situations can be placed close together, and in an organized fashion.

One great advantage of codification is that to change a rule one often needs only to change some of the language of an existing section, so that the rule for a particular issue — such as the corporate tax rate — always is located in the same section number. P.L. 86-272 was not codified because it is so unique to Federal tax law that there was neither a Code Section nor even a Subtitle in the Internal Revenue Code (IRC) under which it logically could be put. (Being *sui generis*, it has yet to be codified.)

This law limits franchise taxes based on net income. In particular, P.L. 86-272 prohibits the imposition of a net income tax on a seller of tangible personal property if three requirements are met: (1) the seller's activities within the state are "mere solicitation" of sales orders, (2) the orders are sent outside the state for approval, and (3) the orders are filled from a stock of goods located outside the state.

Twelve states have adopted P.L. 86-272 without modification; others, including California, have adopted it with some modification.

In *Wisconsin Department of Revenue v. William Wrigley, Jr., Co.*, the U.S. Supreme Court defined "solicitation."[49] The Court stated that a foreign seller seeking protection under P.L. 86-272 needs to establish that its in-state activities are "entirely ancillary to requests for purchases [from customers]." The Court also stated that tax immunity would not be lost if the foreign seller's activities are not entirely ancillary so long as these nonimmune activities are "trivial."

> **Example 3.2.** Smithco has its commercial domicile in Illinois. It also manufactures consumer electronic products in the state. It sells the products to wholesalers in other states. Sometimes title to inventory passes in Illinois, and sometimes in other states. The company's salesmen never travel to meet the out-of-state customers. Instead, they contact them by telephone and e-mail. Consequently, as Smithco salesmen are engaged only in "mere solicitation" outside of Illinois, Smithco only has nexus in Illinois.

STATE INCOME TAX FORMULA

Multistate Tax Commission

As noted earlier, the Multistate Tax Commission was formed to solve problems through interstate cooperation, avoid double taxation by the use of fair apportionment, increase compliance in tax return filing, and achieve uniformity in tax administration. The Commission drafted UDITPA, which provides a model three-factor formula usable by states to apportion a corporation's net taxable income among the states with which it has nexus.

UDITPA Three-Factor Formula

The UDITPA formula for determining the state income tax in a particular state is:

$$
\begin{array}{ll}
& \text{Federal Taxable Income} \\
\pm & \text{State Adjustments} \\
- & \text{Nonbusiness Income} \\
= & \textbf{Apportionable State Income} \\
\times & \text{Apportionment Percent} \\
= & \textbf{Apportioned Business Income} \\
+ & \text{Nonbusiness Income Allocated to State} \\
= & \textbf{State Taxable Income} \\
\times & \text{Statutory Tax Rate} \\
= & \textbf{Gross State Tax} \\
- & \text{State Tax Credits} \\
= & \textbf{Net State Tax}
\end{array}
$$

Basically, taxpayers start with Federal taxable income and make a number of adjustments to arrive at net state tax. The following thus focuses on the adjustment components of the formula. Note that the formula, depending on a state's requirements, is based on either a single legal entity, such as a corporation (in "separate accounting" states) or on a combined group of entities (in "unitary accounting states"). Separate versus unitary accounting is discussed later in the chapter.

State Adjustments

The state adjustments vary by state but usually involve the following items:

- Interest income on Federal obligations
- State and local interest income (same state)
- Federal income tax (Alabama, Iowa, Louisiana, Missouri, North Dakota)
- State income taxes (most states require add-back of deduction)
- Foreign income taxes (half of states)
- Varying policies regarding use of NOLs (net operating losses), as well as depreciation, depletion, and amortization, along with foreign dividends and Subpart F income
- Deductions forgone because of a Federal credit (e.g., the research and development credit)

Net Operating Losses (NOLs)

A number of states limit the use of NOLs. For example, over the past decade California has limited the carryforward of NOLs to 50, 65, and 0%, with special exceptions. Some states disallow the carryback of NOLs. These include Alabama, Arizona, Arkansas, California, Colorado, Connecticut, Florida, Kansas, Massachusetts, Minnesota, Nebraska, New Hampshire, New Jersey, New Mexico, North Carolina, Ohio, Oregon, Pennsylvania, South Carolina, Tennessee, and Wisconsin. Delaware limits carrybacks to a $30,000 NOL deduction for the loss year. Idaho limits carrybacks to an aggregate amount of $100,000.

Tax Management in Action 3.1 reports NOL carryback and carryforward provisions by state. Most states require the apportionment of postacquisition NOLs. Delaware, Maine, Maryland, Massachusetts, New Jersey, New Mexico, New York, Rhode Island, and Virginia do not require such apportionment.

Tax Management in Action 3.1

Net Operating Loss (NOL) Provisions by State

State	NOL Carryback and Carryforward Years	State	NOL Carryback and Carryforward Years
Alabama	0, 15	Montana	3, 7
Arizona	0, 5	Nebraska	0, 5
Arkansas	0, 5	Nevada	n/a
California*	0, 5	New Hampshire	0, 5
Colorado	0, 20	New Jersey	0, 7
Connecticut	0, 5	New Mexico	0, 5
Delaware	2, 20	New York	2, 20
Florida	0, 20	North Carolina	0, 5
Georgia	2, 20	North Dakota	2, 20
Hawaii	2, 20	Ohio	0, 15
Idaho	3, 15	Oklahoma	0, 15
Illinois	2, 20	Oregon	0, 15
Indiana	2, 20	Pennsylvania	0, 10
Iowa	2, 20	Rhode Island	0, 5
Kansas	0, 10	South Carolina	0, 20
Kentucky	2, 20	South Dakota	n/a
Louisiana	3, 15	Tennessee	0, 15
Maine	2, 20	Texas	n/a
Maryland	2, 20	Utah	3, 15
Massachusetts	0, 5	Vermont	2, 20
Michigan	0, 10	Virginia	2, 20
Minnesota	0, 15	Washington	n/a
Mississippi	2, 20	West Virginia	2, 20
Missouri	2, 20	Wisconsin	0, 15
*Sometimes suspended.		Wyoming	n/a

Dividends Received

States vary in their treatment of the deductibility of dividends received. Treatments generally fall into three categories: (1) a percentage of dividends received is deductible, (2) full exclusion for dividends received, or (3) deduction only for dividends received from subsidiaries or corporations doing business in the state.

Kraft General Foods, Inc. v. Iowa Dept. of Revenue and Finance is the leading case on the differential treatment of dividends received from foreign versus domestic corporations.[50] In *Kraft*, the Supreme Court ruled that a state violates the Foreign Commerce Clause if it taxes foreign source dividends more heavily than domestic source dividends.

Depreciation and Depletion

Most states have adopted the Federal depreciation provisions enacted over the past 25 years (e.g., *The Taxpayer Relief Act of 1986*). Consequently, there now are few differences among the states. However, due to such differences, and time lags in various states' conformance to Federal changes, there often are Federal-state differences in basis. This typically involves long-lived assets, such as realty and intangibles. Because of these differences, there can be differences in gains and losses on dispositions, recapture, and Federal-state alternate minimum tax calculations.

Tax Management in Action 3.2 details state depreciation rules. As usual, there are exceptions. For example, Michigan allows the taxpayer to deduct the entire cost of an asset. On the other hand, California did not adopt the depreciation provisions enacted by various Federal tax statutes immediately, particularly those of the *Taxpayer Relief Act of 1986*. Similarly, California's general conformity in other areas has tended to lag (e.g., for tax years beginning before 2002, the cross-references to the IRC in California's Revenue and Taxation Code were to the IRC as amended on January 1, 2001).

Interest Income

As one might expect in a system based on federalism, all states exclude interest income generated by investments in most Federal obligations from their own state income taxes. (In most jurisdictions, this includes income from flow-through entities, like mutual funds, provided that these entities can show how much of the income flowing through can be sourced to qualifying Federal debt obligations.) On the other hand, most states require Federal taxable income to be increased by the amount of interest received from state and municipal bonds.

However, some states do not tax such interest, if the bonds are issued by that state or its subdivisions. (Similar to the treatment of Federal source interest

Tax Management in Action 3.2

Conformity of Depreciation to Federal Rules, by State

State	Conformity to Fed? If Not, What Rules?
Alabama	Yes, for years after 1990. Al. Admin. Code Secs. 810-3-15
Arizona	Yes. Ariz. Rev. Stat. Ann. Sec. 43-1121(6)
Arkansas	Yes. Ark. Code Ann. Sec. 26-51-404(b)(6)
California	Yes. Cal. Rev. and Taxation Code Sec. 24349(a) and (b)
Colorado	Yes
Connecticut	Yes. Conn. Gen. Statute Sec. 12-217(b)(1)
Delaware	Yes
Florida	Yes, after 1986. Fla. Statute Ann. Sec. 220.03(5)(a)
Georgia	Yes, after 3/11/87. Ga. Code Ann. 48-7-39(a)
Hawaii	Yes. Haw. Rev. Stat. Sec. 235-1
Idaho	Yes. Idaho Code Sec. 63-3004
Illinois	Yes.
Indiana	Yes. Ind. Code Sec. 6-3-1-3.5(b)
Iowa	Yes. Iowa Code Ann. Sec. 422.35
Kansas	Yes. Kan. Stat. Ann. Sec. 79-32, and 109(a)
Kentucky	Yes, after 1989. Ky. Rev. Stat. Ann. Sec.141.01(1)
Louisiana	Yes. La. Rev. Stat. Ann. Sec. 287.65
Maine	Yes, after 1987. Me. Rev. Stat. Sec. 5200-A.2.E.
Maryland	Yes. Md. Code Ann. Tax-Gen. Sec. 10-304(1)
Massachusetts	Yes. Mass. Gen. L. ch.63
Michigan	N.A. Mich. has value-added tax
Minnesota	Yes. Minn. Stat. Sec. 290.01.19
Mississippi	Yes. Miss. Code Ann. Sec. 27-7
Missouri	Yes. Mo. Ann. Stat. Sec. 143.091
Montana	Yes. Mont. Code Ann. Sec. 15-31-113(3)
Nebraska	Yes. Neb. Rev. Stat. Sec. 77-2734.04(11)
Nevada	N.A. Nev. has no income tax
New Hampshire	Yes. NH Rev. Stat. Ann. Sec. 77-A:1, III(a)
New Jersey	Yes, after 7/3/93. NJ Stat. Ann. Sec. 54:10A
New Mexico	Yes. NM Stat. Ann. Sec. 7-2-2(J)
New York	Yes, after 1993. NY Tax Law Sec. 208
North Carolina	Yes. NC Gen. Stat. 105-130.2(5d)
North Dakota	Yes, after 1982. ND Cent. Code Sec. 57-38-01(3)
Ohio	Yes, after 1993. Ohio Rev. Code Ann. Sec. 5733
Oklahoma	Yes. Okla. Stat. Sec. 2353(2)
Oregon	Yes, after 1984. Ore. Rev. Stat. Sec. 317.368
Pennsylvania	Yes, after 1984. Penn. Stat. Sec. 7401(3)1(h)
Rhode Island	Yes. RI Gen. Laws Sec. 44-11-11(a)
South Carolina	Yes. SC Code Sec. 12-6-40(A)
South Dakota	N.A. No income tax
Tennessee	Yes. Tenn. Code Ann. Sec. 67-4-805(a)(1)

Conformity of Depreciation to Federal Rules, by State

State	Conformity to Fed? If Not, What Rules?
Texas	Yes. Tex. Tax Code Ann. Sec. 171.110(a)(1)
Utah	Yes. Utah Admin. R. 865-6-14F
Vermont	Yes. Vt. Stat Ann. Tit. 32 Sec. 5811(7)
Virginia	Yes, after 1987. VA Regs Sec. 630-3-402
Washington	N.A. No income tax
West Virginia	Yes. W. Va. Code Sec. 11-24.3(a)
Wisconsin	Yes, after 1986. Wis. Stat. Ann. Sec. 71.22(4)(j)
Wyoming	N.A. No income tax

Note: Where possible, the specific depreciation conformity rule is cited. Otherwise, the overall taxable income conformity rule is cited.

income, most jurisdictions allow tax-exempt character to survive when interest is allocated from flow-through entities, like mutual funds, as long as these entities can show how much of the income flowing through can be sourced to qualifying debt obligations of the taxing state or its political subdivisions.) If such interest income is taxable for state purposes, related expenses are added to deductible items for state purposes.

State and Local Taxes on Income

Many states disallow a deduction for state and local income taxes and also for other taxes based on net income. Most states disallow a deduction for their own income tax. Some, like California, allow a "foreign tax credit" much like the Federal. That is, if a taxpayer pays another state's income tax on revenue generated in that state, then a tax credit is given if that same revenue also is included in the crediting state's tax base. This happens, for example, when "worldwide" income is included by the state of the taxpayer's "domicile," even if the income is not generated by sources within that state.

Charitable Contributions

Many states impose their own percentage limitations on the deductible amount of a charitable contribution, as opposed to following Federal guidelines. Also, some states have their own special rules relating to deductions for donations of food, impacts on alternate minimum tax, and documentation requirements.

Federal Income Taxes

Only five states allow a deduction for Federal income tax: Alabama, Louisiana, Iowa, Missouri, and North Dakota. Iowa and Missouri limit the deduction to 50% of the Federal tax.

Other Adjustments

Examples of other adjustments allowed are

- Inclusion of foreign source income excluded from Federal Form 1120F
- Special deductions for R&D and pollution control facilities
- Disallowance of deductions for interest paid to some stockholders
- Partial capital gain deductions
- Adjustment of capital gains to reflect an asset's fair market value at the time of tax law changes

Example 3.3. From Example 3.1, assume that Smithco has the following Federal income tax return (in thousands):

Sales	$50,000
Cost of goods sold	30,000
Gross margin	20,000
S,G,&A expense	<5,000>
California taxes	<1,500>
Taxable income	$13,500
Federal taxes @ 35%	$4,825

Smithco's working capital investments are State of California and State of Arizona bonds that provided interest income of $1,000 and $2,000, respectively. Cost of goods sold includes $10,000 of MACRS depreciation. California depreciation rules, however, permit only $8,000 depreciation.

California taxable income is computed as follows:

Federal taxable income	*$13,500*
Add: State of Arizona Bond interest	2,000
Excess of MACRS over California depreciation	2,000
California income taxes	1,500
California taxable income	$19,000

BUSINESS VERSUS NONBUSINESS INCOME

Distinguishing business from nonbusiness income is important because each receives different state income tax treatment. Business income is "apportioned," and nonbusiness income is "allocated." Definitions are provided by UDITPA.

Income Classification

Section 1(a) of UDITPA defines business income as:

> [I]ncome arising from transactions and activity in the regular course of the taxpayer's trade or business and includes income from tangible and intangible property if the acquisition, management, and disposition of the property constitute integral parts of the taxpayer's regular trade or business operations.

Most states that have adopted UDITPA use two alternative tests to determine whether income is business income: the transactional test or the functional test. Income that meets either of these tests is considered business income subject to allocation.[51]

Transactional Test

This test provides that income is business income if it arises from "transactions and activities in the regular course of the tax payer's trade or business."

> **Example 3.4.** The sale of a machine by a machine part manufacturer would not generate business income if the sale was unusual and extraordinary and occurred outside the regular course of the manufacturer's trade or business.

Functional Test

This test provides that income generated from property is business income if the acquisition, management, and disposition of the property constitute integral parts of the taxpayer's regular trade or business operations.

> **Example 3.5.** The sale of a machine by a machine part manufacturer would generate business income because the machine was acquired and used in the manufacturer's regular trade or business.

Income Classification Under the Multistate State Tax Commission Regulations

The Multistate Tax Compact makes it more likely that income will be classified as business income. For example, Multistate Tax Compact Regulation IV. 1.(a) provides that "the income of a taxpayer is business income unless clearly classifiable as non-business income." Under the Compact, the following are business income:

- *Rents from Tangible Personal Property* — If rents are received from property used in or incidental to the taxpayer's trade or business, they are business income.[52]
- *Gains and Losses from Sales of Property* — If a gain or loss is realized from the disposition of property that was used in the taxpayer's trade or business, the gain or loss is business income.[53]
- *Interest Income* — If interest is generated by an asset used, arising from, or acquired and held for a purpose related or incidental to a trade or business, such interest is business income.[54]
- *Dividends* — If dividends come from stock that arose from or was acquired in the regular course of the taxpayer's trade or business, or if the purpose of acquiring and holding the stock is related or incidental to the taxpayer's trade or business, the dividends are business income.[55]
- *Patent and Copyright Royalties* — If a patent or copyright results from or was created in the regular course of the taxpayer's trade or business, or if the purpose of acquiring and holding the patent or copyright is related to or incidental to the taxpayer's trade or business, then royalties from the patents or copyrights are business income.[56]

Example 3.6. How would the following types of activities be classified?

- Dividends received by a manufacturing corporation for stock held as an investment that is unrelated to its business? Nonbusiness.
- Gain or loss from the sale of an office building by a convenience store operator that was previously used as corporate headquarters, but was vacated and rented to an unrelated company over the last 7 years? Nonbusiness.
- Dividends from a minority stock investment in a supplier? Business.
- Interest income from a long-term investment of funds derived from the sale of a subsidiary that management is trying to decide how to invest? Nonbusiness. In most states, the sale

of the subsidiary itself will be considered business income. However, the interest income from the proceeds, when the firm may decide to invest the proceeds in nonbusiness-type assets, is usually considered nonbusiness income.

■ Royalties received from a laser disc technology patent acquired by a book publishing company as the result of the purchase of another company? Nonbusiness.

■ Rents received by a rental car business for the use of its cars? Business.

■ Royalties from book copyrights received by a book publishing company as the result of the purchase of another book publishing company? Business.

■ Interest income from temporary investments in working capital? Business.

■ Gain or loss from sale of manufacturing plant by manufacturer? Business.

■ Dividends received from investment in company that has unrelated business? Nonbusiness.

ALLOCATING NONBUSINESS INCOME

Rather than being divided among the many jurisdictions in which a firm might operate, nonbusiness income is allocated — this also is called "sourced" — to a particular state. That is, all of a firm's nonbusiness income is taxable by this state, and only this state. The allocation rule depends on the type of nonbusiness income. Table 3.2 lists these rules.

> **Example 3.7.** Smithco, a New York corporation, manufactures consumer products that it then sells to wholesalers in a number of states. Due to P.L. 86-272, the company does not have nexus in other states with respect to its sale of products. Usually, it invests its working capital in stocks and bonds, except that last year, it purchased a small office building that it rented until its sale at the end of this year. The building was located in New Jersey. Information on the company's investments follows:

Interest income on certificates of deposit at local banks	$100,000
Dividends from investments in mutual funds	200,000
Net (of expenses) rental income from building	400,000
Gain on sale of building	300,000
	$1,000,000

TABLE 3.2. Allocating Nonbusiness Income Under UDITPA

Type of Income	State Allocated/Sourced	Comments
Rents (realty and personalty)	Location where utilized	If company is not subject to tax in the state where the property is utilized, source becomes commercial domicile.
Capital gains and losses (realty)	Location where utilized	
Capital gains and losses (personalty)	Location where utilized	If the company is not subject to tax in state where the property is utilized, source becomes commercial domicile.
Interest and dividends	Taxpayer's commercial domicile	
Patent and copyright royalties	Location where utilized	If income cannot be allocated or accounting procedures do not reflect the state of utilization, source becomes commercial domicile.

Given the above facts, the four items are nonbusiness income. The interest and dividends are allocated to New York. The rental income and the gain on the sale are allocated to New Jersey.

Example 3.8. If the facts are the same as in Example 3.7, except that Smithco's intention for the building was to hold it for income production as a separate line of business, then the rental income and the gain are both business income subject to apportionment.

APPORTIONMENT RULES FOR BUSINESS INCOME

Under UDITPA, two questions must be answered before income can be correctly apportioned:

1. Is the income taxable by a state other than the state of incorporation?
2. If so, is the business a unitary entity?

If the business is a unitary entity and operates in one or more so-called "unitary" states, then it must use "combined reporting" to apportion its income.

Taxable in Another State

For apportionment purposes, a business is considered taxable by a state other than the state of incorporation if the business is subject to one of the following types of taxes:

- Net income tax
- Franchise tax measured by net income
- Franchise tax for the privilege of doing business
- Corporate stock tax in another state

In addition, a business is considered taxable in another state, even if the other state has the authority to subject the business to a net income tax but chooses not to impose a tax. A business is subject to taxation by another state if it exceeds the protection of P.L. 86-272.[57]

UNITARY TAXATION

States either require separate accounting or the unitary approach. The former is much like the "arm's-length standard" applied under Federal law (e.g., IRC §482) and by most countries (e.g., the members of the Organization for Economic Cooperation and Development).

Generally, states west of the Mississippi River are unitary; states east, except Illinois, are separate accounting states. Tax Management in Action 3.3 lists unitary states versus separate accounting (nonunitary) states.

In states requiring separate accounting, each corporation doing business in a state files a separate return even if it is a member of a group that files a Federal consolidated return. In contrast, under unitary taxation, affiliated corporations that are considered part of the same business combine their results as a unitary group and file a combined tax return. (A combined return is much like a Federal consolidated return, except that combined returns often include foreign subsidiaries, which typically are not included in Federal consolidated returns.)

Tax Management in Action 3.4 reports the permissibility of consolidated returns by state. Of this combined result, business income is partitioned among the jurisdictions in which the group operates based on rough approximations of the companies' presence there. This usually is based on a formula that considers the relative payroll, property, and sales of the group in each jurisdiction.

Tax Management in Action 3.3			
Unitary Status of the States*			
State	**State Code §**	**Nonunitary**	**Unitary**
Alabama	40-18-2	X	
Alaska	No state income tax	N.A.	
Arizona	43-1111		X
Arkansas	84-2003	X	
California	23151; 23501		X
Colorado	39-22-301		X
Connecticut	12-214	X	
Delaware	1902	X	
Florida	220.02	X	
Georgia	91A-3602	X	
Hawaii	235-21 to -35		X
Idaho	63-3025		X
Illinois	201		X
Indiana	6-3-2-1	X	
Iowa	422.33	X	
Kansas	79-32, 110		X
Kentucky	141.040	X	
Louisiana	31	X	
Maine	5102(b), (8)		X
Maryland	288(b); 316	X	
Massachusetts	2; 39		X
Michigan	208.31	X	
Minnesota	290.02, 03	X	
Mississippi	27-7-5	X	
Missouri	143.441	X	
Montana	15-31-401		X
Nebraska	21-306		X
Nevada	No state income tax	N.A.	
New Hampshire	239-A: 139		X
New Jersey	54:10A-2; 54:10E-2	X	
New Mexico	7-2A-3	X	
New York	209		X**
North Carolina	105-130.3	X	
North Dakota	57-38-30		X
Ohio	5733.01	X	
Oklahoma	2355	X	
Oregon	317; 318.020		X
Pennsylvania	402	X	
Rhode Island	44-11-1	X	
South Carolina	12-7-230	X	
South Dakota	No state income tax	N.A.	
Tennessee	67-2702	X	
Texas	No state income tax	N.A.	
Utah	59-13-3; 59-13-65		X
Vermont	5832	X	

Tax Management in Action 3.3 (continued)

Unitary Status of the States*

State	State Code §	Nonunitary	Unitary
Virginia	58-151.03	X	
Washington	No state income tax	N.A.	
West Virginia	4	X	
Wisconsin	71.01	X	
Wyoming	No state income tax	N.A.	

* Nonunitary states include: states without a corporate income tax, states using separate accounting, states with unitary rules but not requiring combined returns by unitary groups, and states with unitary taxation applying only to "nonbusiness" income (e.g., dividends received).

** Although its combined reporting requirements are limited by statute, New York may be a de facto unitary state due to regulations and judicial support.

Tax Management in Action 3.4

Consolidated Returns by State

State	Consolidated Returns Allowed	State	Consolidated Returns Allowed
Alabama	Yes	Nebraska	Yes
Arizona	Yes	Nevada	n/a
Arkansas	Yes	New Hampshire	No
California	Yes	New Jersey	No
Colorado	Yes	New Mexico	Yes
Connecticut	Yes	New York	No
Delaware	No	North Carolina	Yes
Florida	Yes	North Dakota	Yes
Georgia	Yes	Ohio	No
Hawaii	Yes	Oklahoma	Yes
Idaho	No	Oregon	Yes
Illinois	Yes	Pennsylvania	No
Indiana	Yes	Rhode Island	Yes
Iowa	Yes	South Carolina	Yes
Kansas	Yes	South Dakota	n/a
Kentucky	Yes	Tennessee	Yes
Louisiana	No	Texas	No
Maine	Yes	Utah	No
Maryland	No	Vermont	Yes
Massachusetts	Yes	Virginia	Yes
Michigan	Yes	Washington	n/a
Minnesota	No	West Virginia	Yes
Mississippi	Yes	Wisconsin	No
Missouri	Yes	Wyoming	n/a
Montana	Yes		

Typically, states only apportion the business income of a unitary business or part of a multistate business that constitutes a unitary business. To determine whether a business is unitary, states usually treat all activities carried on by a single business entity as one unitary business. In contrast, Multistate Tax Compact regulations apportion the activities of a single business entity, if the activities constitute discrete business activities.

> **Example 3.9.** Jonesco is domiciled in Illinois. Its main operation is a retail clothing store located in Chicago. As a separate, autonomous business, it operates a sporting goods store in Indianapolis. These two businesses do not constitute a unitary business, and thus neither apportions its income among multiple states. The Chicago store is taxed only in Illinois; the Indianapolis store is taxed only in Indiana.

As a practical matter, parts of the same group of companies — whether incorporated or not — usually are considered a unitary group if they are required to be consolidated for financial statement purposes under U.S. generally accepted accounting principles. That is, the corporate group is considered a unitary business. A unitary group must file a combined state income tax return. This return includes the income of affiliated corporations that are members of the same unitary business. The combined income is then apportioned between states. This pooling and apportionment treatment of income occurs only in so-called unitary states.

> **Example 3.10.** Swenco's corporate headquarters are in Nashville, Tennessee. Swenco operates two subsidiary corporations. Both corporations are in the same line of business. Subsidiary A is located in Tennessee, a nonunitary state. Subsidiary B is located in California, a unitary state. Both subsidiaries only do business in their respective states. For Tennessee tax purposes, only Subsidiary A is taxed in Tennessee. For California tax purposes, the incomes of Subsidiaries A and B are pooled, and the pooled income is apportioned to California and Tennessee.

THREE-FACTOR APPORTIONMENT FORMULA

Most jurisdictions use a three-factor formula to apportion a unitary group's multistate business income. They consist of a property factor, payroll factor, and a sales or receipts factor. Each factor is expressed as a fraction. The numerator is the taxpayer's property, payroll, or sales within the taxing state. The denominator is the taxpayer's overall property, payroll, or sales.

The average of these factors is expressed as a percentage and referred to as the apportionment percentage. Some states use a double-weighted sales factor.[58]

Table 3.3 lists each state's weighting of the factors and whether each state has a "throwback" rule for sales. The throwback rule is discussed later in this chapter.

In addition, the following states allow the taxpayer to elect an alternative set of weights: Colorado (0.5, 0.5, 0), Hawaii (0, 0.5, 0.5), Kansas (0.5, 0.5, 0), Missouri (1, 0, 0), and New Mexico (0.5, 0.25, 0.25). Connecticut's set of weights is for manufacturing businesses; other businesses use another set of weights: 1, 0, 0.

Factor 1: Property Factor

According to UDITPA, property is included in the property factor if it is owned or rented, and used, by the taxpayer during the tax period. The property must be used or be capable of being used in the taxpayer's regular course of trade or business, and it must produce business income. The property factor usually does not include intangible property.[59] Property is included in the property factor when it becomes eligible for depreciation.

TABLE 3.3. Apportionment Factor Weighting by State

State	Sales, Property, Payroll (%)	State	Sales, Property, Payroll (%)
Alabama	1/3 each	Nebraska	1, 0, 0
Arizona	0.5, 0.25, 0.25	Nevada	n/a
Arkansas	0.5, 0.25, 0.25	New Hampshire	0.43, 0.285, 0.285
California	0.5, 0.25, 0.25	New Jersey	0.5, 0.25, 0.25
Colorado	1/3 each	New Mexico	1/3 each
Connecticut	0.5, 0.25, 0.25	New York	0.5, 0.25, 0.25
Delaware	1/3 each	North Carolina	0.5, 0.25, 0.25
Florida	0.5, 0.25, 0.25	North Dakota	1/3 each
Georgia	0.5, 0.25, 0.25	Ohio	0.5, 0.25, 0.25
Hawaii	1/3 each	Oklahoma	1/3 each
Idaho	0.5, 0.25, 0.25	Oregon	0.5, 0.25, 0.25
Illinois	1, 0, 0	Pennsylvania	0.5, 0.25, 0.25
Indiana	0.5, 0.25, 0.25	Rhode Island	1/3 each
Iowa	1, 0, 0	South Carolina	1/3 each
Kansas	1/3 each	South Dakota	n/a
Kentucky	0.5, 0.25, 0.25	Tennessee	0.5, 0.25, 0.25
Louisiana	0.5, 0.25, 0.25	Texas	n/a
Maine	0.5, 0.25, 0.25	Utah	1/3 each
Maryland	0.5, 0.25, 0.25	Vermont	1/3 each
Massachusetts	1, 0, 0	Virginia	1/3 each
Michigan	0.9, 0.05, 0.05	Washington	n/a
Minnesota	0.7, 0.15, 0.15	West Virginia	0.5, 0.25, 0.25
Mississippi	1/3 each	Wisconsin	0.5, 0.25, 0.25
Missouri	1/3 each	Wyoming	n/a
Montana	1/3 each		

Example 3.11. A warehouse under construction is not included in the property factor, but a completed warehouse that is temporarily vacant is included in the property factor.

Property is removed from the property factor when its permanent withdrawal is established by an identifiable event such as its conversion to the production of nonbusiness income, its sale, or the lapse of an extended period of time (normally, 5 years) during which the property is held for sale.[60]

Location of Property

The location of property (often called "situs") is an important issue, especially for movable (often called "mobile") property, property in transit, nonjurisdictional property, and intangible property. Mobile property is property that moves from state to state in normal usage, such as construction equipment or trucks. It is sourced to each state based on a ratio of either the time spent in the state to total time or the miles traveled in state to total miles traveled during the year.[61]

Planning

A manufacturer may not be able to move a plant between jurisdictions, but it can reduce its taxes by establishing a warehouse or distribution center in a low-tax location. By shifting its property or payroll to the low-tax state, more income is allocated to the low-tax state and less to high-tax states. The firm's business income will still be taxed but at a lower rate.

Property in transit between a seller and a buyer is sourced to the buyer's destination state. Likewise, property in transit between two locations of the taxpayer-owner is sourced to the destination state.[62] Temporary delays in transportation, as in the time needed to transfer from one truck to another, do not affect sourcing. However, delays relating to specific business needs, such as the further processing or packaging of goods for final delivery, can change sourcing.

Example 3.12. An auto manufacturer's cars were sourced to Maryland. The cars were shipped to Maryland for final preparation before delivery to dealers. The fact that their final destination was outside of Maryland did not matter.[63]

Most states make no special provision for inventory in transit between states. Some states have a "throwout" rule: inventory in transit between states is eliminated from both the property factor numerator and denominator. Other states employ a destination rule: inventory in transit is included in the numerator of the state of destination.[64]

Nonjurisdictional property is property not located within the taxing jurisdiction of any state. For example, airplanes and satellites may spend all of their time outside of every state. This type of property could potentially not be sourced to any state. Inclusion of such property in total assets reduces the denominator of the property factor and thus results in a "dilution of the factor." Consequently, the total of all states' property factor numerators will not equal the denominator, so some portion of business income will be untaxed. States have addressed this issue by adopting special formulas for this type of property.

> **Example 3.13.** Alaska uses a "port day" formula for airlines and steamships. Property is sourced to Alaska based on the number of days it spends in an Alaskan port versus the total number of days it spends in port elsewhere.
>
> **Example 3.14.** Satellites present a difficult nonjurisdictional problem. California sources a portion of a satellite's value to itself via a ratio of California stations served by the satellite to all stations served by the satellite.[65]

Intangible Property

Inclusion of intangible property in special apportionment formulas raises concerns about the location of intangible property for sourcing purposes. Generally, states' rules for sourcing intangible property are arbitrary. Some states may source intangible property according to commercial domicile; others source based on the business location and usage of the property.

> **Example 3.15.** Multistate Tax Compact regulations contain special rules applicable to financial institutions. The special rules include loans and credit card receivables in the property factor of such institutions. These intangibles are sourced to the state where the taxpayer's place of business having the most substantive contact with the intangibles is located.[66]

Valuation of Property

Under UDITPA, owned property is valued at original cost. Generally, this valuation is the same as the original acquisition basis for Federal income tax purposes. Fair market value is not used. In addition, depreciation is generally not considered.

A few states use net book value. An average of the beginning and ending values of owned property is calculated, and is used to represent the value of business property for the tax period. Monthly average values may be necessary if property amounts fluctuate substantially during the year.[67] Weekly or daily averaging may be required to accurately reflect the presence of property in the state.

Leasing versus buying property can change apportionment factors for property, but usually not totally. This is because rented property almost always is included in the property factor. First, the annual rent must be calculated. The annual rent is the amount paid for a year's usage of the property, plus amounts paid in lieu of rent, such as real estate taxes, interest, insurance, and repair costs. Annual rent does not, however, include service charges such as utilities, heating, cooling, cleaning, or security.[68] If the taxpayer subleases the property, the subrents should be deducted from the taxpayer's rental rate, except when the sublease is a transaction producing business income. Part-year rent is not annualized. Next, once the final amount of rent is determined, that amount is multiplied by eight for inclusion in the factor. Leasehold improvements are treated as owned property, and not rental, regardless of the lessee's right to remove the property at the end of the lease term. Therefore, the lessee includes the leasehold improvements in its property factor at original cost.

> **Example 3.16.** A grocery store receives subrents from a pharmacy located in the grocery store. The subrents are not deducted from the rent paid by the taxpayer for the grocery store, since the subrents are business income.
>
> **Example 3.17.** A taxpayer pays the lessor $24,000 a year rent plus taxes of $2,000 and mortgage interest of $2,000. The annual rent is $28,000.
>
> **Example 3.18.** The taxpayer pays $2,000 per month in base rent plus 1% of its gross sales. Gross sales for the year were $100,000. The annual rent is $48,000 + (1% of $100,000) or $49,000.

Factor 2: Payroll Factor

According to UDITPA and the Multistate Tax Compact regulations, the payroll factor includes amounts paid as compensation by the taxpayer in the regular course of its trade or business. UDITPA does not define "employee," so the term is interpreted according to common law rules. Compensation includes taxable wages, salaries, commissions, and any other form of remuneration paid to employees. Compensation does not include any amount paid to independent contractors or any other person not classifiable as an employee. Some states, such as New York, do not include executive compensation in the payroll factor. Payroll costs that are included in the basis of a self-constructed asset are also included in the payroll factor.[69]

Planning

One of the most successful approaches today is locating management (and the related facilities, such as corporate headquarters) in states that do not include executive compensation in the payroll factor. (As of June 1999, six states excluded such compensation: Delaware, Mississippi, New York, Oklahoma, South Carolina, and Vermont.) Instead, a firm might locate management in states that use only a single sales factor (Iowa, Massachusetts, Nebraska). Because management facilities typically have few sales, this results in little or no income apportioned into that state. Similarly, management can be located (as with any part of a company's operations) in states without an income tax.

Payroll related to activities generating nonbusiness income are excluded from the payroll factor. For example, the salaries of treasurer's office personnel who manage investments producing nonbusiness income are not included in the payroll factor.[70]

> **Example 3.19.** Taxpayer corporation owns various stocks and bonds. The corporation holds these investments separate from its business. Ms. A is an employee whose sole duty is management of this portfolio of separately held investments. Consequently, her entire salary is excluded from the payroll factor.

Payroll Sourcing Rules

The numerator of the payroll factor includes compensation paid to employees for services rendered within the state.[71] If an employee works both within and without the state, his or her wages are sourced according to the Model Unemployment Compensation Act (MUCA). MUCA provides four tests to be applied successively:

1. Source wages to the state where a majority of the services are performed, if only incidental services are performed outside the state.
2. If the employee's services outside the state are more than incidental, source wages to the state that is the base of operations for the employee, as long as some services are performed in that state.[72]
3. If the employee has no base of operations, source wages to the state from which the employer exercises direction and control, but only as long as some services are performed in that state.
4. If the employee's wages cannot be sourced under any of the three preceding tests, use his or her state of residence.[73]

The denominator in the payroll formula is total compensation paid every-where during the tax period, including compensation paid in a state where the tax-payer is not subject to tax. When payroll is in a state where nexus does not exist, the payroll is assigned to the state where the taxpayer does not have nexus. The payroll is not "thrown back" to the state of commercial domicile or otherwise.

> **Example 3.20.** A corporation has employees in States 1, 2, and 3. It is only taxable in 1 and 2. The denominator of the payroll formula includes payroll in all three states.

If a partnership has a corporate partner and they are engaged in a unitary business, the corporate partner can generally "flow through" a portion of the payroll of the partnership to their payroll factor, limited to the extent of its own-ership interest in the partnership.

Factor 3: Sales Factor

Under UDITPA, all gross receipts from transactions and activities conducted in the regular course of the taxpayer's business are included in the sales factor. Gross receipts include receipts from the sale of inventory: gross sales less returns and allowances, all interest charges, service charges, carrying charges, and Federal and state excise taxes that are passed on to the purchaser (e.g., sales taxes). Gross receipts also include commissions from the performance of serv-ices, lease payments from the use of real or tangible personal property, proceeds from the disposition of tangible and intangible assets, and payments from the sale, assignment, or licensing of intangible personal property such as patents and copyrights.[74] In sum, all receipts that have the character of business income are included; nonbusiness receipts are excluded.

Excludable Receipts

In addition to nonbusiness receipts, certain business receipts are excluded from the gross receipts factor. For example, capital gains are usually considered part of business income, but not all receipts from capital transactions are included in the sales factor. The sale of a significant asset, such as a plant, may distort the overall apportionment of income by giving undue weight to a particular state.[75] The frequent sale of investments can also lead to distortion.

> **Example 3.21.** One state's Supreme Court held that including receipts from the "churning" of investments in the sales factor would lead to distortion. The Court permitted the state to delete such receipts from the denominator of the sales factor pursuant to UDITPA §18.[76]

Sourcing Sales of Tangible Personal Property

Under UDITPA, sales of tangible personal property are sourced to the state of destination, i.e., where the shipment is destined. However, sales are sourced to the state where the shipment originated if the purchaser is the U.S. government or the taxpayer is not taxable in the state of destination. This resourcing is known as the "throwback rule."[77]

> **Example 3.22.** A corporation has inventory in State 1. This corporation sells $200,000 of its inventory to a buyer with stores in multiple states, including State 2. Buyer placed his order with the seller's central purchasing department in State 3; $50,000 of the inventory was shipped directly to the buyer's store in State 2. The State 2 store is treated as the buyer for $50,000 of the corporation's sales.

States source government sales and apply the throwback rule differently. Table 3.4 lists state throwback rules. A state's lack of a throwback rule may reduce a taxpayer's state tax burden.

TABLE 3.4. Throwback Rules by State

State	Sales Throwback?	State	Sales Throwback?
Alabama	Yes	Nebraska	No
Arizona	No	Nevada	n/a
Arkansas	Yes	New Hampshire	Yes
California	Yes	New Jersey	No
Colorado	Yes	New Mexico	Yes
Connecticut	No	New York	No
Delaware	No	North Carolina	No
Florida	No	North Dakota	Yes
Georgia	No	Ohio	No
Hawaii	Yes	Oklahoma	No
Idaho	Yes	Oregon	Yes
Illinois	Yes	Pennsylvania	No
Indiana	Yes	Rhode Island	No
Iowa	No	South Carolina	No
Kansas	Yes	South Dakota	n/a
Kentucky	No	Tennessee	No
Louisiana	No	Texas	n/a
Maine	Yes	Utah	Yes
Maryland	No	Vermont	Yes
Massachusetts	Yes	Virginia	No
Michigan	Yes	Washington	n/a
Minnesota	No	West Virginia	No
Mississippi	Yes	Wisconsin	Yes
Missouri	Yes	Wyoming	n/a
Montana	Yes		

The Throwback Rule

A principle underlying the taxation of a multistate business income is that approximately 100% of a company's business income should be apportioned to states where the company is taxable, regardless of whether all these states impose income taxes and thus subject to taxation. An issue arises where a firm has apportionment factors — such as sales — in jurisdictions that do not have the right to tax. Many states deal with this with "throwback" rules for sales: sales into a jurisdiction that cannot constitutionally impose an income tax are counted instead as for the state from which the sales originated.

The throwback rule ensures that all sales are accounted for in the numerator of at least one of the states where the entity is taxable. Sales arising from goods shipped to a state where the company is not taxable are "thrown back" to the state from which the goods were shipped. These thrown back sales are included in the numerator of that state's sales factor.[78]

> **Example 3.23.** A corporation has its production facilities and main office in State 1 and operations and inventory in State 2. The corporation's only activity in State 3 is the solicitation of orders by a salesman living in that state. All orders by this salesman are sent to State 2 for approval and are filled by a shipment of inventory from State 2. Pursuant to P.L. 86-272, the corporation is not taxable in State 3, and its sales in State 3 are thrown back, or attributed, to State 2.

Sometimes "nowhere sales" can occur if a state lacks a throwback rule. Creation of such sales is a basic planning technique. Table 3.4 also lists states that do not have throwback rules.

Planning — Creating "Nowhere Income"

"Nowhere income" is income that is not apportioned to any state in which the taxpayer is taxable. The taxpayer locates its production or warehouse facilities in a state without a throwback rule. It sells from this state into a state where the taxpayer does not have nexus, and thus is not subject to the receiving state's tax jurisdiction. Income generated from these sales is not taxed by the receiving state or the originating state. The result is untaxed income.

Double taxation, however, may also occur. Inconsistent throwback rules among states create the potential for throwing the same sales back to more than one state.

> **Example 3.24.** Smithco is headquartered in Massachusetts and has inventory in California. Both Massachusetts and California have throw-

back rules. A Smithco agent makes a sale to Jonesco, located in Utah, and reports the sale to Smithco's Massachusetts sales office. The inventory is shipped from California. Due to the lack of nexus, Smithco is not taxable in Utah. Due to the throwback rules, the sale is thrown back to both Massachusetts and California.

In some states, the throwback rule is supplemented by a so-called "double throwback" rule that applies to drop shipments. A drop shipment occurs when a seller in State 1 fills an order for a customer in State 2 by having its supplier in State 3 ship the goods directly to the customer. This arrangement gives rise to two possible results. First, due to the throwback rule, if the seller is not taxable in State 2, the destination state, and is taxable in State 3, the supplier's state, the sale would be thrown back to State 3. Second, due to the double throwback rule, if the taxpayer is also not taxable in State 3, the Multistate Tax Compact provides that the sale be thrown back to State 1, the state in which the salesman's office is located.[79] Because the double throwback rule is difficult to apply and may produce a windfall for the state where shipment originated, many states do not employ this rule.

Criticism of the throwback rule has led some to suggest the use of a throwout rule. A throwout rule removes sales shipped to customers in states where the taxpayer is not taxable, as there is no nexus, from both the numerator and the denominator of the sales factor. So, full apportionment is achieved by dividing the business income of the multistate enterprise among the states in which the enterprise is taxable.[80]

Sales of goods to foreign countries give rise to two issues: whether the seller is taxable in the foreign jurisdiction, and which state should receive the benefit of the throwback rule if the seller is not taxable in the foreign country. States follow a number of different approaches for determining whether a taxpayer is "taxable" in a foreign country. Some states refer to the foreign country's laws to determine whether the taxpayer is "taxable in the [country] of the purchaser."[81] Some states apply the same constitutional jurisdictional standards used to determine whether a taxpayer is subject to a state's tax jurisdiction. Several of these states do not take into account P.L. 86-272 in making a determination.

In California, *Appeal of Dresser Industries, Inc.* held that if a foreign country were subject to U.S. constitutional jurisdictional standards and it could, pursuant to these standards, impose a net income tax on a taxpayer, then taxpayer's sales allocable to that country should not be thrown back to California.[82] Other states apply the Federal income tax standards used to determine whether the U.S. has tax jurisdiction over non-U.S. entities. As for which state should receive the benefit of the throwback rule, states have come up with many different approaches to this situation, and no widespread approach is discernible.

Sourcing Receipts from Transactions Other Than Sale of Tangible Personal Property

UDITPA provides that sales from transactions other than the sale of tangible personal property (e.g., providing services or leasing property) are sourced to the location of the "income-producing activity." Income-producing activity means "the transactions and activity directly engaged in by the taxpayer in the regular course of its trade or business for the ultimate purpose of obtaining gains or profit. Such activity includes the rendering of services by employees, the utilization of tangible and intangible property by the taxpayer in performing a service, and the sale, licensing, or other use of intangible personal property. The mere holding of an intangible property is not, of itself, an income-producing activity.[83] In addition, such activity does not include transactions and activities performed on behalf of a taxpayer, such as those conducted on its behalf by an independent contractor."[84]

If income-producing activity takes place in more than one state, the receipts are sourced to the state where the greatest portion of the cost of performance is incurred relative to other states. This rule sources receipts to only one state using an all-or-nothing approach. Some states, however, have interpreted this UDITPA rule to require pro-rata sourcing. A pro-rata share of receipts is sourced to each state where income-producing activity occurs based on the costs of performance incurred in each state. Alternatively, other states disregard the UDITPA rule and source receipts based on time spent in the state or the relative value of the services performed in the state compared to others.

> **Example 3.25.** Macroserve provides information services to customers via leased computer terminals in multiple states. The company has a central databank located in the state of its commercial domicile. From satellite offices in multiple states, company employees assist and train customers to use the databank and terminals. Customer calls are typically assigned to the closest satellite offices. The company charges a hook-up charge and receives lease payments for use of the terminals. Neither source of revenue results from the sales of tangible personal property. Consequently, these revenues are sourced to the location of the income-producing activity, that is, the location of the terminals.

Cost of Performance

"Cost of performance" is determined in accordance with generally accepted accounting principles and the company's trade or business conditions and practices.[85] A company will generally look to the cost of employees and property associated with the production of the income. The Multistate Tax Compact

Audit Manual elaborates on the term "direct costs": "wages, taxes, interest, depreciation, and other costs involved with real and personal property." The cost of performance rule is too vague to be of general application, considering the various types of businesses involved. Furthermore, it invites state tax administrators to adopt rules peculiar to the various industries that produce income other than from the sale of tangible personal property.

Effect on Foreign or Other Out-of-State Businesses

The use of double-weighted sales factors and single-factor sales formulas has the opposite effect for out-of-state businesses, because they emphasize the value of sales into the taxing jurisdiction. Single-factor sales formulas can be especially detrimental to out-of-state businesses, as they do not allow any relief despite the company's property and payroll located outside the taxing jurisdiction.

The impact of these formulas on firms' locating decisions is unknown; businesses are usually concerned about tax rates and credits rather than unequally weighted apportionment formulas. This is because low rates *directly* reduce a company's tax bill, as do tax credits (these are discussed in detail in a later chapter of this book). Further, the lack of a throwback rule tends to be viewed as more attractive than a double-weighted sales factor.

APPORTIONMENT AND CONSOLIDATED OR COMBINED TAX RETURNS

Technically, combined and consolidated tax returns are different.[86] Combined returns are mandatory and consolidated returns are voluntary. A combined return must be filed by a corporation subject to taxation in a unitary state; the return must include the pooled information of the corporation and the other members of the unitary group. In contrast, a consolidated return pools the operations of affiliated corporations operating in a nonunitary state or nonunitary affiliated corporations operating in a unitary state.

A consolidated return is beneficial if affiliates having NOLs are combined with profitable affiliates, as the NOLs may be used to offset the profits and thus reduce the total tax liability of the affiliated corporations. As shown in Tax Management in Action 3.4, not all states allow consolidated returns.

With a combined return, the members of the unitary group are treated as a single corporate entity for the purpose of apportionment. Transactions between members of the group are eliminated. Generally, for each of the three apportionment factors, the elements from each corporation in the group are added together to form combined factors. The combined factor is then applied to the unitary group's combined income.

Example 3.26. In some unitary states, combined returns include only members of the unitary group that have nexus with the taxing state, called "nexus combinations."

With a consolidated return, affiliated corporations in a state may elect to file a single return on behalf of the affiliated corporations. A group of affiliated corporations that elects to file a consolidated return is called a consolidated group. In a unitary state, a consolidated group, while consisting of affiliated corporations, may include corporations that are not members of the same unitary group. Two methods are used to apportion the income of a consolidated group: the separate corporation method and the consolidated method. The separate method requires that apportionment be done on a company-by-company basis followed by adding these apportioned amounts together. In contrast, the consolidated method apportions the consolidated group's aggregate income.

Example 3.27. Massachusetts uses the separate corporation method. Each member of a consolidated group must compute and apportion its income on a separate entity basis with no elimination of intercompany transactions.

Combined Returns: Sales Factor Sourcing and the Throwback Rule — Two Approaches

States calculate the combined sales factor using either a separate entity approach or a unitary business approach. Using the separate entity approach, each unitary group member's sales are subjected to the throwback rules before the numerator of the group's combined sales factor is determined. In comparison, using the unitary business approach, all sales into the state are sourced to it regardless of the status of the members. In addition, sales into other states that would be thrown back are not thrown back if any member of the unitary group is taxable in the other state. These approaches arose in California in two unrelated appeals before the State Board of Equalization, an administrative agency that hears tax-payer appeals.

Separate Entity Approach — The Joyce Approach

Appeal of Joyce, Inc. dealt with sales into California by a corporation that was not taxable in California due to P.L. 86-272. It was held that these could not be included in the numerator of the California combined sales factor, though the corporation was a member of a unitary group that had other members taxable in California. To do so, the selling corporation itself must be taxable in California.[87]

In 1999, California incorporated the *Joyce* rule into its tax code. This was affirmed in *Huffy Corporation v. The State Board of Equalization.*

Illinois follows the *Joyce* approach. The Illinois Appeals Court held that certain sales made to customers in jurisdictions in which other members of the taxpayer's unitary group paid taxes were not includible in the taxpayer's Illinois sales factor numerator. The court reasoned that "taxpayer" in the throwback rule applies only to the individual corporate taxpayer and not to its affiliates or to other members of the unitary group.[88]

Unitary Business Approach — The Finnegan Approach

In *Appeal of Finnegan Corp.*, the State Board of Equalization overruled the rule in *Joyce*.[89] Instead, it held that the term "taxpayer" meant all the corporations within the combined unitary group, i.e., the corporations taken together. Thus, sales by a unitary group member could not be thrown back to California, if the sales were into states where the corporation itself was not taxable but other members of the group were.

Maine follows the *Finnegan* approach rule: the term "taxpayer" in Maine's throwback provision means the combined unitary group, and not the individual members of the group, having nexus with Maine.[90] Kansas also follows *Finnegan*. In Kansas, a corporation's nexus with the sales destination state is determined by considering the activities of its unitary group.[91]

ALTERNATIVE APPORTIONMENT FORMULAS

Alternative State Formulas

Some states have alternative formulas for apportionment of multistate business income and thus are exceptions to the standard three-factor formula. Iowa and Texas have a single-sales-factor formula. Missouri has an election for a single-factor formula. Colorado and Hawaii have an election for a two-factor formula. Massachusetts has a single-factor formula for manufacturers.

Industry-Specific Formulas

UDITPA was designed for manufacturers and mercantile businesses, so its provisions are not always well suited to other businesses. In response, states have adopted specialized industry formulas that provide a more effective division of a corporation's income among the states.

The Multistate Tax Compact provides a number of alternative formulas; examples follow. Railroads use a standard three-factor formula of property, payroll, and sales, but the factors are modified to accommodate a miles-based ratio to be included in the factors. Rolling stock (railroad cars and locomotive engine cars) are included in the property factor based on a "locomotive miles" ratio. Similar adjustments are made to account for freight and passenger receipts as well as compensation paid to trainmen.

Radio and television broadcasting companies source receipts from radio, television broadcasting, and film to states based on an audience ratio. The property factor is determined using a throwout rule for film or radio programming. Companies may include payments made to independent contractors (e.g., actors and network analysts) in the payroll factor, if such payments constitute at least 25% of the taxpayer's total compensation. Similarly, publishing companies use a modified three-factor formula that sources advertising receipts based on the ratio of a circulation factor. Financial institutions use modified property and sales factors to take into account their reliance on tangibles.

UDITPA §18 provides both taxpayers and states with the opportunity to use alternative apportionment formulas when use of the traditional three-factor formula would cause distortions. State tax administrators rely on §18 as authority to use specialized industry formulas, such as the Multistate Tax Compact examples above. Corporations also have used §18 to create apportionment factors. To create an alternative factor, a proponent must prove not only that the traditional three-factor formula distorts its income attributable to the state, but also that the proposed alternative factor will more "fairly" apportion income attributable to the state.[92]

COMBINED RETURNS AND UNITARY TAXATION

What Is a Unitary Business?

As noted before, most states west of the Mississippi are unitary states. In these states, combined returns are required for all members of the same unitary group. The question then becomes: what constitutes a unitary business? California cases have led the way by establishing three different tests to determine the existence of a unitary business: the three-unities test, the functional integration test, and contribution dependency test. *Container Corporation of America v. California Franchise Tax Board* (1983) established the functional integration test. This test is met if contributions to income result from functional integration, centralization of management, and economies of scale. *Edison California Stores, Inc. v. McColgan* established the contribution dependency test.[93] This test is met for a member of an affiliated group of companies if it makes a contribution to, or depends on, other members of the unitary group.

The three-unities test arose in large part from *Butler Bros. v. McColgan*. In this case, Butler Brothers was a wholesaler of dry goods and general merchandise.[94] The central office in Illinois provided management and other services to its own distribution houses. It also purchased inventory at a discount and sold it through related unincorporated distribution houses in various states, including California. The Court concluded that Butler Brothers was a unitary business due to the centralized nature of its corporate activities: purchasing of merchandise with resulting volume discounts, advertising, and management decision making.

Many courts now refer to the "three-unities" test set forth by the California Supreme Court in *Butler Bros*:

- Unity of ownership (defined as greater than 50% ownership or control)
- Unity of operation as evidenced by centralized purchasing, advertising, accounting; centralized management, and economies of scale
- Unity of the centralized executive force and system of operation

Multistate Tax Compact Unitary Business Regulations

Multistate Tax Compact regulations provide that the presence of any of the following factors creates a strong presumption that the activities of the taxpayer constitute a single trade or business.

- Horizontally integrated business activities (e.g., multiple corporations which are in the business of selling shoes)
- Vertically integrated business enterprise (e.g., two corporations, one a manufacturer and the other a distributor of automobiles)
- Strongly centralized management, coupled with the assistance of centralized departments for functions such as financing, advertising, research, or purchasing

Note that in a group of affiliated corporations, more than one unitary group can exist.

Example 3.28. Unitary factors exist between Corporation X and Corporation Y's computer manufacturing business. Unitary factors also exist between Corporation Z and Corporation Y's oil distribution business. Two unitary groups exist. Corporation Y is included in both.

Unitary Checklists

Many states, as well as the Multistate Tax Compact, have developed unitary checklists to assist auditors and taxpayers to determine the existence of unitary groups. These checklists are rooted in the numerous U.S. Supreme Court cases and state court cases defining unitary groups. Tax Management in Action 3.5 contains a checklist of factors to be considered when determining whether firms under common control are unitary. This chart is rooted in the Multistate Tax Compact Unitary Group Checklist.

Tax Management in Action 3.5

Unitary Business Checklist

Goal: To determine whether a unitary group exists.

General Business and Organization

1. List all subsidiaries and affiliates including the following information: (a) percentage of stock owned, (b) country or state in which company is domiciled, and (c) brief description of trade or business.
2. Provide a list of officers and directors of the parent company and subsidiaries owning greater than 50% of the parent or a subsidiary.
3. What business activity is conducted in this state and elsewhere? (Detail by division/company)
4. How are the business operations/methods conducted within the state different from the way business is conducted out of state and/or overseas? (Be specific)

Functional Integration

1. Do the parent and subsidiaries sell similar products or services? (Describe)
2. Are there common patents, brand names, trademarks, symbols, or slogans? (Describe and list)
3. Is there a transfer of research or know-how between the parent and subsidiaries?
4. Are there intercompany sales? If so, give detail on: (a) amounts, (b) types of products/services, and (c) prices.
5. Is there centralized purchasing of raw materials? If so, give details on: (a) who does it, (b) what materials, and (c) who approves purchase contracts.
6. Is there common advertising and/or promotions for the parent and subsidiaries?
7. How does the group hold itself out before the public, single company or separate companies?
8. Are there common facilities for manufacturing, warehousing, offices, etc.? If so, give details on: (a) written agreements, (b) terms of leases, and (c) who approves leases.
9. Are there intercompany loans or transfers of money? If so, give details on: (a) amounts, (b) what rate, (c) any written documentation, (d) purpose of loan, and (e) names of parties involved.
10. Does the parent guarantee loans for subsidiaries?
11. Does the parent approve major expenditures of subsidiaries? If so, give details.
12. What is the policy for outside financing?
13. Are there common banking facilities?

Tax Management in Action 3.5 (continued)

Unitary Business Checklist

14. Are the sales functions centralized, and if not, how are the markets penetrated?
15. Are there common customers or similarity of customers?
16. How are the sales forces managed? Give details as to training, hiring, and territorial assignments.
17. Are there common employee benefit plans (i.e., pension plans, stock option plan)?
18. Are there common employee hiring procedures and training manuals or programs?
19. Are key employees hired or approved by the parent?
20. What is the policy for rotation of overseas assignments?
21. Does the parent approve promotions, bonuses, etc., of management personnel of the subsidiaries?
22. Are employees transferred between the parent and subsidiaries or among the subsidiaries? If so, provide details on (a) names, (b) dates, (c) positions, and (d) company.
23. Do the parent and subsidiaries use common labor unions or bargaining units?
24. Are labor contracts of the subsidiaries approved or negotiated by the parent?
25. Are there common insurance policies or a common carrier/broker (e.g., fire, group, liability)? If so, list.

Centralized Management Control

1. Does the parent charge the subsidiaries management fees for services? If so, give details on (a) services provided, (b) amount of fee.
2. Does the parent set goals and/or policies for the subsidiaries?
3. Are there common policy and procedure manuals? List.
4. Are there common officers and directors? If so, who are they and what is their function?
5. Are there transfers of officers between the parent and subsidiaries? Provide details of names, dates, positions, and companies.
6. Do executives of the parent travel to locations of the subsidiaries? If so, why?
7. Do executives of the subsidiaries travel to parent's headquarters? If so, why and how often?
8. Does a committee of the parent's board of directors monitor activities of the subsidiaries?
9. Do the boards of directors of the subsidiaries report directly to the parent?
10. Does the board of directors of the parent control the dividends (amount and/or timing) paid by subsidiaries?
11. How often do the subsidiaries report sales to the parent?
12. How often do the subsidiaries report profits and losses to the parent?
13. Are the budgets of the subsidiaries approved by the parent?
14. What other reports are submitted to the parent? How often?
15. Does the parent approve or sign contracts for the subsidiaries?
16. Do internal auditors of the parent audit the subsidiaries?
17. Is there a common communication system?

Worldwide Unitary

Most unitary states require that domestic and foreign corporations with more than 20% of their activity in the U.S. be included in a domestic or "water's edge" unitary group. Some states require the filing of a worldwide unitary group. For example, California permits a worldwide unitary group to elect to file on a water's edge basis. The constitutionality of worldwide unity was first addressed in *Container*.[95] The Court ruled that foreign-based subsidiaries of a domestic parent comprised a unitary business with their parent and domestic affiliates. This case is discussed in detail later.

Planning — Restructuring

Restructuring is a common tax planning technique. It can involve splitting a corporation and then operating *via* two or more corporations. If a company operates solely in nonunitary states, such restructuring can minimize overall state taxes, as shown in the following example.

> **Example 3.29.** ACDC Corporation operates in States 1 and 2. In State 1, its operations generated $300,000 from $50 million in property; in State 2, its operations generated $200,000 from $350 million in property. The tax rates in States 1 and 2 are 4 and 10%, respectively. Assume that both states use one-factor property apportionment. Note the tax savings that arise from restructuring ACDC.

AC and DC operating as a single corporation, the total tax is:

State 1: $50/400 \times \$500,000 \times 4\%$	$= \$2,500$
State 2: $350/400 \times \$500,000 \times 10\%$	$= \underline{\$43,750}$
Total tax	$= \$46,250$

AC and DC operating as separate corporations, the total tax is:

State 1: $50/50 \times \$300,000 \times 4\%$	$= \$12,000$
State 2: $350/350 \times \$200,000 \times 10\%$	$= \underline{\$20,000}$
Total tax	$= \$32,000$
Tax savings from restructuring	$= \$14,250$

Restructuring also can be done by combining entities. This is useful when one entity operates at a loss and the other at a profit.

Example 3.30. Alpha Corp does business in State 1 using $150 million in property, and in State 2 using $250 million in property. It generated a total profit of $400,000. Beta Corp operates only in State 2 using $300 million in property. It generated a loss of $200,000. The tax rates in States 1 and 2 are 10 and 4%, respectively. Assume that both states use one-factor property apportionment. Note the tax savings that arise from restructuring ACDC.

Alpha and Beta operating as a separate corporations, the total tax is:

Alpha Corp:

State 1: 150/400 × $400,000 × 10%   = $15,000
State 2: 250/400 × $400,000 × 4%   =   10,000

Beta Corp:

State 2: $300/300 × <200,000>   =   0

Total tax   = $25,000

Alpha and Beta operating as a single corporation, the total tax is:

AlphaBeta Corp:

State 1: 450/700 × $200,000 × 10%   = $12,857
State 2: 250/700 × $200,000 × 4%   =   2,857

Total tax   = $15,714

Tax savings from restructuring   = $9,286

TAXATION OF FLOW-THROUGH ENTITIES

Firms often use flow-through entities. There are a variety of reasons for this. Sometimes they are contractual: a flow-through entity may be established in a nonunion state so a unionized parent can operate there free of existing union contracts. Other times it is a matter of financing through sharing tax benefits: a firm starting a new business may joint venture with financing sources, to avoid fixed payment schedules for debt in exchange for specific allocations of start-up losses and other tax benefits. State tax treatment of three flow-through entities — predominantly partnerships, limited liability companies, and S corporations — is much the same as Federal taxation. However, there are some important differences by state.

Partnerships

As note above, most states follow the Federal rules and also do not tax partnerships. Instead, distributive shares of partnership profit or loss are passed through to the partners. Exceptions are the District of Columbia (Unincorporated Business Tax), Illinois (Personal Property Replacement Tax), New Hampshire (Business Profits Tax), New York City (Unincorporated Business Tax), and Michigan (Single Business Tax).

Generally, a partner is subject to state taxation if the partner is either a resident of the state of the partnership or is a nonresident but is doing business in the state. Individual partners are also subject to taxation by their state of residence on their entire taxable income, including their distributive share of partnership income. However, most states provide a resident individual with a credit for taxes paid to nonresident states.[96] Most states do not provide a credit either for a tax paid by the partnership directly or for taxes paid by the partnership on behalf of its nonresident partners.

For corporate partners, the partnership must first separate business and nonbusiness income. The separation is based on the relationship between the asset-yielding income and the partnership's business. The partner must also separate business and nonbusiness income. This separation is based on the relationship between the partnership's business and the corporate partner's business.

States employ three methods to attribute partnership income to corporate partners. One method is partnership-level apportionment. First, the corporate partner's distributive share of partnership taxable income is apportioned at the partnership level. Second, the distributive share is specifically allocated by the corporate partner.[97]

A second way is flow-through apportionment. First, the corporate partner's distributive share is added to the partner's own apportionable business income. Second, this total is apportioned using a formula combining the partner's distributive share of the partnership's apportionment factors and the corporation's own apportionment factors.[98]

The third method is corporate-level apportionment. The corporate partner multiplies its stand-alone apportionment factors to its distributive share of partnership income. Application of this method depends on whether the partnership and the corporate partner are part of the same unitary business.[99]

The lack of uniformity between methods used by states creates a tax-planning opportunity, as flow-through entities may be used to shift nexus and income between corporations and states.

> **Example 3.31.** X Corporation owns 20% of Partnership Y. They are unitary businesses. X's business income is $1 million and Y's, $800,000. Accordingly, X's business income is $1 million + (20% × $800,000) =

$1,160,000. This amount is apportioned among the states in which X and Y do business. Apportionment is based on X's own business factors and its 20% share of factors from Y's business.

Example 3.32. Instead, assume X owns 20% of Y but the two are not unitary. Thus, X is engaged in two businesses. One business earned $1 million and the other, $160,0000. These two incomes must be separately apportioned. X apportions its $160,000 distributive share of partnership income based on Y's factors and only in states where Y does business.

Most states require partnerships to file informational returns if they conduct business or derive income from the state.[100] Even if there is no requirement, a partnership that is treated as a separate taxable entity may want to file in order to document losses incurred. Many states allow composite filings on behalf of their nonresident partners, whereby the partnership return does not disclose individual partners' identities. Generally, certain conditions must be met for composite returns to be filed.[101]

Finally, there are no filing requirements for nonresident partners of investment-type partnerships in two states despite the partnership's presence in the state.[102]

Limited Liability Companies (LLCs)

All states allow LLCs. An LLC is a hybrid entity having the qualities of a partnership and a corporation. The LLC is usually not taxed at the entity level, like a partnership, and its members, shareholder-equivalents, have legal liability limited to the extent of their investments, like a corporation. For Federal tax purposes, the LLC may elect, under the "check the box" regulations, to be treated as a flow-through entity, and thus not itself be directly subject to tax. Similarly, most states recognize LLCs as flow-through entities and do not tax them. Florida, Texas, and Pennsylvania, however, tax LLCs as corporations.[103]

One planning technique using the technique of transforming involves using an LLC when a corporation has NOLs and is located in a nonunitary state.

Example 3.33. X Corp is located in Indiana. Y Corp is located in Ohio. X Corp is a subsidiary of Y Corp. Every year, X Corp generates NOLs and Y Corp has taxable income. Both corporations are located in separate accounting states, so they cannot apply X Corp's NOLs against Y Corp's taxable income and obtain a tax benefit. If X Corp converts to an LLC that is owned by Y Corp, then X Corp's NOLs can flow through to Y Corp, i.e., Y Corp can apply the NOLs against its taxable income and reduce its tax liability.

Subchapter S Corporations

Most states recognize Federal S corporation status for state income tax purposes. S corporation status permits a corporation to be taxed as a flow-through entity. Some states require that the Federal election be attached to the state return; other states, such as New Jersey and Pennsylvania, require a separate election to be filed with the state. Five states impose a tax on S corporations. California, New Jersey, and New York have a small tax (called a "toll charge") that equalizes the rate differential between state corporate and individual tax rate structures.

Michigan imposes its Single Business Tax on S corporations. Texas imposes its franchise tax on S corporations, and Massachusetts, its excise tax.[104] Taxation of S corporation shareholders is similar to taxation of partners in most states. As S corporations cannot have corporate owners, they are less flexibile for use in multicorporate tax planning.

EXCEPTIONS TO THE "NORMAL" RULES FOR TAXATION

Michigan

Michigan imposes a Single Business Tax (SBT) on sole proprietorships, flow-through entities, trusts, and corporations. SBT is tax on a person for the privilege of doing business in Michigan. There are two ways to compute the tax: the gross receipts method and the regular method. The gross receipts method applies the statutory 2.2% tax rate to 50% of gross receipts. The regular method starts with Federal taxable income and adjusts this number. The major adjustments relate to plant and equipment: depreciation is added back and capital acquisitions during the year are subtracted. As shown in Table 3.3, Michigan apportionment factors are weighted 90% to sales. The 2.2% tax rate is applied to the tax base. Consolidated returns are not allowed unless each entity is a Michigan taxpayer, engages in substantial intercorporate transactions, is subject to the same apportionment formulas, and is part of an affiliated group.

Washington

Washington imposes a Business and Occupation (B&O) tax on gross receipts. The 0.484% tax applies only to sales made within the state, regardless of where the good is manufactured. To reduce pyramiding of the tax, a business that buys goods from a manufacturer that has paid the B&O tax (e.g., a wholesaler or retailer) may take a credit to reduce its B&O tax to the extent that the tax was paid by the manufacturer on that good.

Texas

Texas imposes a franchise tax on corporations and LLCs. The tax is the sum of (1) 0.25% times net taxable capital and (2) 4.5% times net taxable earnings, minus (1). If either (1) or (2) is negative, it is given a value of zero in the calculations. Net taxable capital is owner's equity, book value of equity plus retained earnings, multiplied by a single-sales factor, ratio of Texas sales over sales everywhere. Net taxable earnings are net income for the year multiplied by the single-sales factor. The franchise tax will apply if there is net equity or positive income for the year.

Planning

Since the franchise tax does not apply to partnerships, firms and their tax consultants should consider doing business in Texas using a limited partnership.

DISCUSSION QUESTIONS

1. What are the typical criteria for nexus for income/franchise tax purposes?
2. How do we usually distinguish between business and nonbusiness income? How are the two treated?
3. How does double weighting of the sales apportionment factor favor firms located in a state? How does the absence of a throwback rule do the same?
4. What are the common definitions of a unitary business?
5. What are the basic differences between unitary and separate accounting states?

PROBLEMS

Problem 1

Jill Corp is subject to tax in only one state. During the year, it generated the following:

Depreciation for Federal tax (250K allowed for state)	$200,000
State income tax expense	60,000
Refund of state income tax	22,000

Federal taxable income is $1,200,000. What is the corporation's state taxable income?

Problem 2

Trish Corporation operates in State A and State B. Which of the following would be used to modify Federal taxable income, in order to arrive at State A taxable income?

Indicate whether the modification would be an addition or a subtraction, and the amount. Consider each independently.

1. Dividend income received from State B corporation of $5,000. It is eligible for a 70% Federal Dividends Received Deduction.
2. Federal income taxes paid of $15,000.
3. County property taxes paid (deducted on Federal return) of $7,000.
4. Federal depreciation of $15,000 (State A is $10,000).
5. Federal enterprise zone credit of $0; state credit of $2,000.
6. Refund from last year's State A income taxes of $1,000.
7. An asset was sold for $36,000. Original cost of $40,000. Accumulated Federal (State A) depreciation of $22,000 ($8,000).

Problem 3

Pamela Corp has operations in States 1 and 2. Its operations for the year were:

	State 1	State 2
Sales	$600,000	$150,000
Payroll	200,000	50,000
Property: Avg. Cost	250,000	400,000
Avg. Accum. Depr.	150,000	250,000
Rent expense	5,000	17,500

Calculate the apportionment factors for States 1 and 2. Assume that State 1 uses a three-factor apportionment formula, in which sales, property(net), and payroll are equally weighted. Assume that State 2 uses a single factor based on sales. Only State 1 follows UDITPA with respect to rent expense.

Problem 4

Assume the same facts as Problem 3, except both states use a three-factor formula where sales are double weighted. For the property factor, State 1 uses book value, while State 2 uses net book value. Neither state follows UDITPA with respect to rents.

Problem 5

Lyn Corporation has its manufacturing, distribution, and retail operations in State 1. However, sales are made to customers in States 1, 2, and 3. Sales in State 1 are made through retail stores. Sales in State 2 are obtained by Lyn's sales representatives who have the authority to accept and approve sales orders. Customers in State 3 can purchase Lyn's products only if they arrange to take delivery at Lyn's shipping dock. Lyn's sales, by state, were as follows: $650K to residents of State 1; $400K to residents of State 2; and $150K to residents of State 3.

Lyn's activities in the three states were limited to the above. All states use an equally weighted three-factor formula and have a throwback rule. State 1 sources dock sales to the destination state. Determine Lyn's sales factor for all three states.

Problem 6

Cynthia Corp has manufacturing facilities in States 1 and 2. It also owns non-business rental property in State 2. Cynthia had the following payroll costs:

	State 1	**State 2**
Officers' salaries	90,000	40,000
Manufacturing workers	187,500	100,000
Administrative salaries	47,500	32,500

State 1 includes all income in the definition of apportionment income. State 2 excludes nonbusiness income from apportionable income. Both states include officers' compensation in the payroll factor. For the administration employees, 10% of the staff in State 1 and 20% in State 2 are dedicated to the operation, maintenance, and supervision of the rental property.

Problem 7

Jennifer, Inc. has operations in States 1 and 2. Its assets look as follows:

State 1	**Beg. of Year**	**End of Year**
Inventory	150,000	200,000
Plant and equipment	1,100,000	1,250,000
Accum. depreciation	<600,000>	<750,000>
Land	250,000	300,000
Rental property	450,000	450,000
Accum. deprecation	<100,000>	<150,000>

State 2	Beg. of Year	End of Year
Inventory	$100,000	$50,000
Plant and equipment	750,000	600,000
Accum. depreciation	<250,000>	<225,000>
Land	300,000	200,000
Rental property	150,000	150,000
Accum. depreciation	<25,000>	<50,000>

Rental properties were unrelated to the corporation's manufacturing operations. Assume both states use book value of assets. Determine the property factors. How would your answer change if nonbusiness income is apportionable for State 2?

Problem 8

ABC Holding Company, Inc. (ABC) is legally and commercially domiciled in California. ABC is owned in equal percentages by Al, Bob, and Chuck. ABC has two wholly owned subsidiaries: A&B's Golf Clubs, Inc. (A&B) and Chuck's Metals, Inc. (Chuck's). A&B manufactures and distributes high-end golf clubs. Chuck's makes specialty aircraft parts from titanium. A&B was founded by Al and Bob in California during the 1980s. They began manufacturing what was then very advanced golf clubs made from graphite. Up until their new product with ABC, their clubs were considered state-of-the-art. Both Al and Bob were known for their managing and investment skills. Chuck's was founded by an engineer named Chuck. He was known for his skills in developing titanium products.

During 1998, Al and Chuck met while golfing. After a discussion, they realized that A&B could benefit from a new golf club made of titanium, and Chuck could benefit from A&B's management skills. They later formed a holding company, ABC, with each of the three men having a one-third ownership. The transaction was completed in October 1999.

A&B began using Chuck's titanium process in 1999 and it paid a fee to Chuck based on fair market value. However, A&B maintains its own manufacturing facility. The engineers from both companies occasionally meet and share ideas. Additional facts are as follows:

- A&B's corporate headquarters are in Princeton, New Jersey. It has manufacturing facilities in Champaign, Illinois, and Chapel Hill, North Carolina. It also has sales offices in Boston, Chicago, New York, and Los Angeles. It shares a warehouse with Chuck's in Arizona.
- ABC moved into an office in Oceanside, California in October 1999.

- The former Vice President of Marketing at A&B now serves the same role at ABC. No other personnel transfers occurred. As treasurer of both companies, Bob has made changes to the investment strategies of all companies.
- All three companies have completely independent personnel departments.
- The three companies integrated their accounting systems in December 1999.
- Each company has different distribution systems due to product differences.
- ABC and Chuck's use the same insurance company; A&B uses another company.

The companies recently hired you to provide tax services. In 1999, all three companies filed separate California returns. You have been asked to perform a unitary analysis for California, and provide them with the optimal tax-saving supportable structure in terms of unitary versus separate filing. California has a double-weighted sales factor.

Company Information

	ABC	**A&B**	**Chuck's**	**Consolidated**
Federal taxable income	<500,000>	700,000	800,000	1,000,000
California sales	4,000,000	21,000,000	11,000,000	36,000,000
Everywhere sales	4,000,000	50,000,000	66,000,000	120,000,000
California payroll	2,000,000	3,5000,000	500,000	6,000,000
Everywhere payroll	2,000,000	5,000,000	8,000,000	15,000,000
California property	1,000,000	5,500,000	500,000	7,000,000
Everywhere property	1,000,000	11,000,000	16,000,000	28,000,000

ENDNOTES

48. Based on authors' calculations.
49. 112 S.Ct. 2247 (1992).
50. 112 S.Ct. 931(1992).
51. A small number of UDITPA states, notably Kansas and Iowa, have adopted only the transactional test for determining business income. In these states only income that arises in the regular course of the taxpayer's trade or business is considered business income. For these states, the functional test is not applied.
52. MTC Reg. §IV.1.(c)(1).

53. TC Reg. §IV.1.(c)(2).
54. MTC Reg. §IV.1.(c)(3).
55. TC Reg. §IV.1.(c)(4).
56. TC Reg. §IV.1.(c)(5).
57. Note that businesses with activities in states that do not impose income taxes or impose very low taxes could use these rules to their advantage. For example, a state without a throwback rule (e.g., Rhode Island) can be used to reduce total state tax liability.
58. Variations from the standard formula were created as an incentive for businesses to locate within a particular state, or in recognition of the importance of the market state in the production of income.
59. A number of special industry regulations, as well as general equitable adjustment provisions, may require the inclusion of intangible property in the property factor. For example, securities brokers, dealers, and banks deal extensively with intangible property, and the exclusion of such property from their property factors would not fairly reflect the extent of their business operations within the various states.
60. MTC Reg. §IV.10(b).
61. MTC Reg. §IV.10(d).
62. MTC Reg. §IV.10(d).
63. *Mercedes-Benz of North America v. Comptroller of the Treasury*, July 1989 (CCH Maryland Tax Rptr. Par. 201-335).
64. For tax planning purposes, when states make no provision for inventory in transit, taxpayers may be justified in creating "nowhere income" by including such inventory in the taxing states' property factor denominators but excluding it from all states' numerators.
65. See .0722 California UDITPA Manual (1984).
66. MTC Reg. §IV.18. A planning opportunity results from the inconsistency in sourcing rules for intangible property among the states. A taxpayer could create "nowhere income" that is not apportioned to and thus not taxed by any state. However, it also creates the potential for double taxation.
67. MTC Reg. §IV.12.
68. MTC Reg. §IV.11(b).
69. MTC Reg. §IV.13(a)(2).
70. MTC Reg. §IV.13(a)(2).
71. UDITPA §13.
72. The term "base of operations" means a place of more or less permanent nature from which the employee starts his or her work and completes it.
73. State tax auditors generally review Federal forms 940 and 941 and state unemployment insurance contribution forms to verify the payroll factor.
74. MTC Reg. §IV.15(a).
75. MTC Reg. §IV.18 requires that the sales proceeds of a factory or plant be excluded from the sales factor.
76. See *American Tel. and Tel. Co. v. Tax Appeals Bd.*, 787 P2d 754 (Mont. 1990).
77. UDITPA §16(b).
78. MTC Reg. §IV.16(a)(1). The Massachusetts throwback rule is slightly different from the throwback rule employed by other states. In Massachusetts, sales are allocated to Massachusetts when (1) the taxpayer is not taxable in the state of the purchaser or the purchaser is the U.S. government, and (2) the property was not sold by an agent chiefly situated at, connected with, or sent out from business premises owned or rented outside of Massachusetts by the taxpayer. Mass. Gen. L. ch. 63, §38(f).

79. MTC Reg. §IV.16(a)(7).
80. West Virginia has adopted a throwout rule in its version of the UDITPA apportionment factor. W.Va. Code §11-24-7. The Pennsylvania and Kentucky State tax authorities apply the throwout rule to the various factors in their revised or special apportionment formulas. Arguably, this results in a fairer distribution of sales among the states.
81. *Scott & Williams, Inc. v. Board of Taxation*, 117 N.H. 189 (1977).
82. *Appeal of Dresser Industries, Inc.,* California State Board of Equalization, October 26, 1983.
83. MTC Reg. §IV.17(3).
84. MTC Reg. §IV.17(2).
85. MTC Reg. §IV.17(3).
86. In some nonunitary states, such as Massachusetts, a consolidated return is referred to as a "combined return."
87. *Appeal of Joyce,* Cal. SBE, Nov. 23, 1966.
88. *Dover Corporation v. Department of Revenue,* 271 Ill. App. 3d 700 (1995).
89. *Appeal of Finnegan Corp.*, Cal. State Board of Equalization, Aug. 25, 1988.
90. *Great N. Nekoosa Corp. v. State Tax Assessor,* Me. Super. Ct. (1995).
91. Kansas Rev. Rul. 12-9-91 (1991).
92. See *Crocker Equipment Leasing, Inc. v. Department of Revenue*, Oregon S. Ct. No. SC S38059 (1992). The Oregon Supreme Court held that a corporation that not only was engaged in the business of leasing and financing tangible personal property, but also was a member of a unitary group engaged in the financing and banking industry, was entitled to deviate from the traditional three-factor formula by including intangibles in the property factor.
93. 30 Cal. 2d 472 (1947).
94. 17 Cal. 2d 664, 678 (1941), aff'd 315 U.S. 501 (1942).
95. *Container Corp. v. California Franchise Tax Board* (1983).
96. The credit is usually limited to the lesser of the amount of tax computed by multiplying the taxpayer's total tax by a fraction or the amount of tax actually paid. The fraction is the amount of taxable income subject to tax in the nonresident jurisdiction under the resident's state tax laws over the resident's entire taxable income.
97. Examples include Louisiana and California (if the corporate partnership and the partner are not unitary).
98. Examples include Illinois, Pennsylvania, Arizona, and California (for nonunitary partner-partner(s) situations).
99. For example, in California, if a unitary relationship exists, then the partnership items must be combined and apportioned with the partner's other business income. If no unitary relationship exists, the items are considered to have arisen out of a separate trade or business of the partner and must be apportioned separately from the partner's other business income. See §25137-1 of the California Regulations.
100. Failure to file may result in penalties. For example, New Jersey imposes $100 per month; New York, $50 per month per partner; Massachusetts, $5 per day; and California, $10 per month.
101. Typical conditions in most states include: (1) partnership income on the return must be the only in-state source of income for the partner; (2) partnership must notify each partner of the right to elect to participate in the return on an annual basis, (3) each partner must consent in writing to inclusion in the group return, (4) partners and the partnership must agree that the partnership will pay any deficiencies (including penalties) assessed

with respect to the composite return, (5) partnership will act on behalf of the partnership in the proceedings, (6) no deductions or credits unrelated to the partnership may be taken into account when determining the amount to be withheld, (7) taxes for each electing nonresident must be paid at the highest state marginal tax rate, and (8) partnership must ensure that estimated tax payments and returns are filed.

102. In California, a partnership that exclusively conducts investment activities in the state is not doing business in the state, and thus the state is not entitled to tax the nonresident partners on partnership income. *Appeal of Robert M. and Ann T. Bass, SBE 1989 Cal Rptr CCH Para. 401-709*. In New York, nonresident partners are exempt from tax if the partnership's activities are limited to trading for its own account. N.Y. Tax Law §631d; *Matter of Singer, TSB-A-92-(2)I,1992)*.

103. In Pennsylvania, certain types of professional services LLCs (attorneys, CPAs, engineers, etc.) are not taxed.

104. Many states impose the equivalent of the IRC §1374 Built-In Gains Tax and the IRC §1375 Excess Passive Income Tax.

Free value-added materials available from the
Download Resource Center at www.jrosspub.com.

4

SALES AND USE TAXES

INTRODUCTION

Sales taxes first came into being in the U.S. around the time of the Great Depression to overcome the shortfall in revenues from income and property taxes. In 1932, Mississippi was the first state to enact a sales tax having most of the features of sales taxes as we know them today. Many states quickly followed Mississippi's lead and enacted sales taxes of their own. Today, forty-five states and the District of Columbia have a tax that can be classified as a sales tax. The five states currently without a general retail sales tax at the state level are Alaska, Delaware, Montana, New Hampshire, and Oregon. However, throughout the 1990s, initiatives have been put forward before the electorates in these states to enact some type of a sales tax. For example, in November 1994, Oregon considered eliminating all state taxes in lieu of adopting a 2% "trade levy," which is more similar to a value-added or gross receipts tax. The proposal was defeated.

Although sales taxes typically are levied at the state level, many municipalities and other local subdivisions also impose sales taxes and these taxes are being used increasingly to supplement revenues from property taxes, the traditional source of revenues for local governments. An interesting example is Alaska, which does not have a state-level sales tax but has an extensive system of sales taxes at the local level. Many cities, such as Atlanta, Chicago, Los Angeles, New York, and Phoenix, also impose sales taxes of their own, which then are added on top of the state-level sales tax. From an administrative standpoint, local sales taxes usually are integrated with the state sales tax so that collection is consolidated at one point. The state then distributes the local government's share of the tax for a fee.

TYPES OF SALES TAXES

Sales taxes imposed by state and local governments can be classified along many different dimensions. They could be grouped by who bears the legal liability for the tax, who bears the ultimate incidence of the tax, or the type of transactions on which it is imposed. The three major types of sales taxes that currently are employed by the various states are the retail consumer tax, the seller privilege tax, and the gross receipts tax. The most prevalent of these taxes is the retail sales tax and hence the focus of this chapter will be on this tax. Before discussing this tax in detail, it is useful to know the difference between each of these types of taxes, and they are briefly described below.

Retail Sales Tax

At the outset, it is important to distinguish a "sales tax" from a "use tax." A use tax is the equivalent of a sales tax imposed on retail sales of out-of-state vendors. The tax is imposed by the state where the consumer resides, or "uses" the product. The sales tax applies to retail sales by vendors to customers within the same state. For example, if a California store sells goods to its customers in California, the California sales tax applies. If the California store sells goods to customers in Arizona, an Arizona use tax applies. It is important to note that a use tax only applies if a vendor has nexus in the state where the good is used.

As shown in Table 4.1, each state's sales and use tax is essentially the same. However, for sales tax purposes, cities and counties add on additional taxes. For example, the 6% California sales tax is increased to 8.25% for sales in Los Angeles. For this reason, an out-of-state vendor has a slight price advantage (even if it has nexus) over an in-state vendor.

The most common form of sales tax, as well as the most significant in revenue terms, is the retail sales tax. This tax typically is imposed on the sale of tangible personal property at retail to the final consumer. However, the term "sales tax" refers to a broad category of levies that have different names and cover different types of transactions. In some states, each of these levies is indeed a different tax, but collectively they are referred to as sales taxes.

Seller Privilege Tax

The seller privilege tax is imposed on a seller for the privilege of doing business in the state. The seller may or may not be able to shift the tax to the consumer, depending on state law. Alabama, Arizona, Hawaii, Kentucky, Missouri, and Nevada are some of the states that impose a seller privilege tax. However, these states use different labels for the tax and also operationalize it in different ways.

TABLE 4.1. Sales/Use Tax Rates by State

State	Sales/Use Tax Rate	State	Sales/Use Tax Rate
Alabama	4	Nebraska	4.5
Arizona	5	Nevada	6.5
Arkansas	4.625	New Hampshire	0
California	6	New Jersey	6
Colorado	3	New Mexico	5
Connecticut	6	New York	4
Delaware	0	North Carolina	4
Florida	6	North Dakota	5
Georgia	4	Ohio	5
Hawaii	4	Oklahoma	4.5
Idaho	5	Oregon	0
Illinois	6.25	Pennsylvania	6
Indiana	5	Rhode Island	7
Iowa	5	South Carolina	5
Kansas	4.9	South Dakota	4
Kentucky	6	Tennessee	6
Louisiana	4	Texas	6.25
Maine	5.5	Utah	4.75
Maryland	5	Vermont	5
Massachusetts	5	Virginia	3.5
Michigan	6	Washington	6.5
Minnesota	6.5	West Virginia	6
Mississippi	7	Wisconsin	5
Missouri	4.225	Wyoming	4
Montana	4.5		

For example, Arizona's tax is labeled the "transaction privilege tax" and is imposed on the person engaged in the taxable business activity. In Arizona, the seller has a choice whether to pass on the tax to the end consumer or not; hence, the amount of the sales tax can be used as a point of negotiation on the selling price. Further, it is optional for the seller to separately state the amount of the tax on the invoice.

In contrast, Alabama's seller privilege tax requires that it be shifted to the consumer and separately stated on the invoice. Thus, the Alabama tax in reality is a retail sales tax on the consumer that the seller is required to collect, even though it is labeled a seller privilege tax. Finally, Nevada, like Alabama, requires the seller to shift the tax to the consumer but only "insofar as it can be done." Thus, the burden of the tax is not really on the consumer, and the seller is not relieved of the liability to pay the tax.

Gross Receipts Tax

A gross receipts tax has the essential elements of both the retail sales tax and the seller privilege tax. Like a retail sales tax, a gross receipts tax typically is levied on the sale of property. However, the tax base in a gross receipts tax is broader than a retail sales tax, and usually includes sales of professional services and in some instances the sale of intangibles as well. Like a seller privilege tax, the gross receipts tax is imposed on the seller with no requirement for shifting the tax to the consumer. Hawaii and New Mexico are examples of states that employ a gross receipts tax.

Importance of Sales Taxes

Currently, sales taxes are the number one source of total (business plus individual) state tax revenues, accounting for approximately one-third of total tax collections, closely followed by state income taxes. Considering that sales taxes became popular only in the 1930s, their share of the total state revenues underscores the tremendous importance of this tax for state governments.

In addition to the importance of sales taxes at the state level, this tax is also becoming increasingly important at the local level. Although property taxes continue to be the mainstay, the growing importance of sales taxes at the local level can be gauged from the fact that currently there are over 6,000 local sales tax jurisdictions in the U.S.

THE RETAIL SALES TAX — THE BASICS

An Overview

The general retail sales tax is the most common form of sales taxation in the country. As mentioned before, this tax is imposed on the sale of tangible personal property at retail to the consumer. Certain criteria must be satisfied for this tax to apply. Specifically:

- The sale must take place within the territorial boundaries of the taxing jurisdiction, i.e., the state or local jurisdiction must have power to impose the tax.
- The sale must be of tangible personal property, in contrast with the sale of services or intangible property, and the sale must be at retail.

The first criterion is concerned with constitutional limitations on the power of the state or local jurisdiction to impose the tax. At a very basic level, this criterion simply lays out the first condition that must be satisfied before the tax can be imposed, and that is the sale must have been consummated within the boundaries of the state or the locality seeking to impose the tax. However, this seemingly simplistic criterion has spawned a long debate of considerable importance which the U.S. Supreme Court has weighed on numerous occasions. This issue is discussed at some length later in the chapter.

Assuming that the constitutional requirements are satisfied, the next criteria concern the two fundamental questions that must be answered to gain a sound understanding of the retail sales tax. These questions are (1) What is "tangible personal property"? and (2) What is a "retail sale"?

What is "Tangible Personal Property"?

Black's Law Dictionary defines "tangible property" as property that has physical form and substance and is not intangible; it may be either real or personal. Following this definition, most state tax codes define "tangible personal property" as personal property that can be seen, weighed, measured, felt, or touched, or is in any other manner perceptible to the senses. See, for example, Arizona Revised Statutes §42-5001(16) and California Revenue and Taxation Code §6016.

In most states, the sale of tangible personal property does not include the sale of services or the sale of intangible property. However, distinguishing the sale of tangible personal property from the sale of services or intangible personal property is not an easy task since most sales involve a mixture of both property and services.

Sale of Services

Traditionally, retail sales taxes have been imposed on the sale of tangible personal property; hence, services typically have been exempt from the tax base. However, the steady growth of the service sector in the U.S. economy has prompted more and more states to add selected services to their tax bases, resulting in most states taxing at least some services. Among the services most frequently exempt from sales tax are professional services (e.g., those provided by accountants, lawyers, dentists, and physicians) and personal services (e.g., hairdressing, house cleaning, laundry, and dry cleaning). Services that are most frequently taxed include repair and maintenance type services and transportation services. Some states such as Hawaii, Iowa, New Mexico, and South Dakota have taken this trend to the other extreme by taxing most or all services.

In view of the differing tax consequences associated with the sale of tangible personal property compared to the sale of services, the question often arises whether the transaction involves the sale of one or the other. In reality, however, most transactions are mixed and involve both tangible personal property and service components.

Example 4.1. A shoeshiner provides the service of shining shoes, but in doing so uses shoe polish, cream, and other ingredients to shine the shoes. Similarly, a hairdresser might use shampoo and conditioner in washing hair prior to performing whatever service the client might want, such as a haircut or a perm.

In trying to resolve whether such transactions involve the sale of tangible personal property or the sale of a service, some courts have considered the relative cost of the tangible personal property compared to the total amount charged to the consumer. To the extent the price of the materials was an inconsequential element of the total consideration, these cases held that the sale would be considered primarily that of a service. However, this test proved quite problematic because, as pointed out by the North Dakota Supreme Court in *Voss v. Gray*, "[t]here is no article, fabricated by machine or fashioned by the human hand, that is not the fruit of the exercise and application of individual ability and skill."[105]

Consequently, courts have tried to use other rationales for differentiating between whether the transaction is a sale of tangible property or services. Many state courts have adopted what is referred to as the "true object" test for making this distinction. The Supreme Court of Ohio in *Accountants Computer Services, Inc. v. Kosydar Inc.*[106] stated that:

In determining whether a mixed transaction constitutes a consequential personal service transaction, a distinction must be made as to the *true object* of the transaction contract; that is, is the real object sought by the buyer the service per se or the property produced by the service. [Emphasis in original]

In a later decision, the same court in *Federated Department Stores, Inc. v. Kayda* considered the question of whether advertising materials, consisting of radio and TV commercials and free-lance artists' sketches used in newspaper and magazine compositions, constituted tangible property or personal service.[107] The taxpayer argued that the property it acquired was the end product of an individual's personal or professional skills and that it was unsuitable for anyone other than the taxpayer. The court held that, with respect to the radio and TV commercials, the taxpayer's real object was to acquire possession of the radio and TV tapes and films and not merely the services performed in producing them. Similarly, the court held that the taxpayer's real object in hiring the artists was to acquire the sketches themselves. Thus, the advertising materials in question were considered to be tangible property rather than a personal service.

Planning

Businesses engaged in a mixed activity, which may involve partly taxable activity and partly nontaxable services, inevitably face some vexing decisions in the matter of sales taxes. If there is any doubt as to the sales tax liability in a given transaction, the business would be well advised to collect the tax. Consultants provide this advice because, if subsequently found liable, the business must not only bear the sales tax burden itself but also the interest and any penalties. That is, the business usually cannot go back to the buyer and collect sales taxes after the sale. If the issue is material, the business would be well advised to seek a letter ruling from the state's Department of Revenue clarifying the business's tax liability in such transactions.

Sale of Intangible Property

Given that retail sales taxes are imposed on tangible personal property, a key distinction that must be made is whether the property is tangible or intangible. If the property is intangible, then sales taxes generally would not be imposed on its sale. However, a comprehensive definition of this term does not appear to exist. Thus, it is not surprising that state statutes seldom define the term intangible property, except in a negative sense as a complement to tangible property — intangible property is property other than tangible property.

Generally, intangible property is property that is a "right" rather than a physical object. Thus, for purposes of the tax laws, intangible property may be defined to include property that is not itself intrinsically valuable, but that derives its value from what it represents or evidences (see *Black's Law Dictionary*).

In the current business environment, the lines between tangible and intangible personal property are becoming increasingly blurred. Some of the more valuable assets of many businesses are their intellectual property rights. Also, with the advent of the information age, one type of transaction that has created much consternation with regard to its taxability is the sale of computer software.

Sale of Computer Software

Numerous courts across the country have dealt with the question of whether computer software is tangible or intangible property for the purposes of sales, use, and property taxes. In *District of Columbia v. Universal Computer Associates., Inc.*,[108] which is generally regarded as the first case on this issue, the court held that software was intangible, and therefore not taxable. However, two cases decided only one day apart in the early 1980s — *Comptroller of the Treasury v. Equitable Trust Company*[109] and *Chittenden Trust Company v. King*[110] — found computer software to be tangible personal property for the purposes of sales, use, and property taxes.

A Louisiana Supreme Court's decision in *South Central Bell Telephone Company v. Barthelemy*[111] provides an elaborate discussion of the rationale underlying the conclusion that computer software is tangible personal property:

> In its broadest scope, software encompasses all parts of the computer system other than the hardware, i.e., the machine....In its narrowest scope, software is synonymous with program, which in turn is defined as "a complete set of instructions that tells a computer how to do something."...When stored on magnetic tape, or computer chip, this software, or set of instructions, is physically manifested in machine-readable form. [Further], [t]he software itself, i.e., physical copy, is not merely a right or an idea to be comprehended by the understanding. The purchaser of computer software neither desires nor receives mere knowledge, but rather receives a certain arrangement of matter that will make his or her computer perform a desired function....That the software can be transferred to various media, i.e., from tape to disk, or tape to hard drive, or even that it can be transferred over telephone lines, does not take away from the fact that the software was ultimately recorded and stored in physical form upon a physical object.

Because of the considerable controversy surrounding the taxability of sales of computer software, many states have passed specific legislation or administrative regulations to address this issue. The trend among the states has been to tax "canned" software and exempt "custom-made" software. In fact, as of 1997, all states with a sales tax impose a tax on canned software, while only about one-half of those states tax modified canned software and approximately one-third tax custom software.

> **Example 4.2.** Under *Arkansas Code Ann. §26-52-304*, computer software is specifically defined as tangible personal property. Thus, in Arkansas, sales taxes are imposed on the sale of all software — canned, customized, and custom alike. [See generally *Ark. Code Ann. §26-52-101 et seq.* (sales tax) and *§26-53-101 et seq.* (use tax).] The specific implementing regulations are found in *Arkansas Gross Receipts Regulations GR 25.*

The predominant practice of taxing canned but not custom software raises some fundamental questions, such as:

1. Is there any valid reason for drawing the distinction between canned and custom software?
2. Is this distinction any different for software than it is for any other type of property?
3. Is there a clear distinction between canned and custom software? It has been argued that the line between custom and canned software often is so thin that reliance on it creates uncertainty, controversy, and difficulties in administration.[112]

What is a "Retail Sale"?

Apart from obtaining a clear understanding of the term tangible personal property, it is equally important to understand what is meant by the terms "sale" and "retail sale," and when does a "sale" take place to truly understand the scope of retail sales taxes.

Definition of "Sale"

Webster's Dictionary defines "sale" as "the act of selling; specifically, the transfer of ownership of and title to property from one person to another for a price." As this definition makes clear, technically a sale involves both an ownership transfer and consideration. Recognizing that these dual requirements would limit the scope of a sales tax to only certain transactions, most state legislatures define the term "sale" more broadly in their own statutes.

> **Example 4.3.** Arizona's sales tax statutes define "sale" to mean any transfer of title or possession, or both, exchange, barter, lease or rental, conditional or otherwise, in any manner or by any means whatever, including consignment transactions and auctions, of tangible personal property or other activities taxable under this chapter, for a consideration, and includes:
>
> a. Any transaction by which the possession of property is transferred but the seller retains the title as security for the payment of the price.
> b. Fabricating tangible personal property for consumers who furnish either directly or indirectly the materials used in the fabrication work.
> c. Furnishing, preparing, or serving for a consideration any tangible personal property consumed on the premises of the person furnishing, preparing, or serving the tangible personal property.

[A.R.S. §42-5001(13)].

Thus, depending on the specific state statute, many transactions that would not normally be considered sales may be subject to sales taxes. For example, most state sales tax statutes consider "leases" of tangible personal property as a sale of such property and subject to the sales tax.

Scope of a "Retail Sale"

The basic principle underlying the retail sales tax is that it should apply to sales made at retail, which usually mean sales made to the final consumer. Based on this principle, this tax should be structured such that it is imposed only once during the entire chain of events starting from the point where the goods are manufactured and culminating with their eventual sale to the retail customer. To make their sales tax laws faithful to the basic principles of a retail sales tax, states' statutes typically provide an exemption for the following types of transactions:

- Sales-for-resale
- Casual or occasional sales
- Sales of items used in manufacturing, processing, or fabricating
- Sales of machinery or equipment
- Sales of certain essential items, such as food, medical devices, and prescription drugs
- Sales to certain organizations or entities, such as governmental agencies

THE RETAIL SALES TAX BASE

As with any taxing statute, the first step in determining the sales tax liability of a taxpayer is ascertaining the base on which the tax is to be imposed. For purposes of the retail sales tax, this process can be divided into two steps. In the first step, one must identify transactions that are exempted from sales tax for whatever reason. In the second step, for transactions that are taxable, one must identify the amounts that must be included in the retail sales amount.

Exemptions from the Retail Sales Tax

Sale-for-Resale Exemption

Given the objective of the retail sales tax, a sale of tangible personal property that will be resold should not be included in the retail sales tax base. Indeed, this "sale-for-resale" exemption is the most common kind of exemption provided by state sales tax statutes. Under this exemption, property that will be resold as well as property that is incorporated into another product to be resold (e.g., raw materials) are exempt. If an exemption were not allowed for these transactions, tax would be assessed with each sale, resulting in a pyramiding of the retail sales tax faced by the ultimate consumer.

> **Example 4.4.** Typical examples of transactions that would qualify for the sale-for-resale exemption are

> ■ Wood purchased by a furniture manufacturer to make furniture.
> ■ Food, drinks, or condiments purchased by a restaurant business.
> ■ Purchase of equipment by a business for rental to third parties. (The rationale for this exemption is that in most states the rental or lease receipts are subject to sales taxes. Thus, the exemption from sales tax on the sale of equipment prevents the pyramiding of the tax.)

Problems in Determining If a Sale Is for Resale

Although the sale-for-resale exemption may appear to be logical and its application straightforward, in practice it is not always clear whether an item purchased is intended for resale. This problem occurs especially when purchases are made by businesses.

> **Example 4.5.** Consider the purchase of disposable wrappers, cups, napkins, and plastic eating utensils by fast-food restaurants. The courts have been split as to whether these restaurants can purchase these disposable items free of sales tax under the sale-for-resale exemption.
>
> In *Burger King, Inc. v. State Tax Commission*,[113] the New York Court of Appeals held that the purchases of disposable hamburger wrappers, beverage cups, and French fry "sleeves" were indeed for resale. The court reasoned that the packaging is a "critical element of the final product" and thus "as much a part of the final price as is the food and drink item itself. It would be exalting form over substance, therefore, to hold that resale of these paper products does not take place merely because Burger King does not list a separate price."
>
> In contrast, the Illinois Supreme Court in *Sta-Ru Corp. v. Mahin*[114] held that the purchase of the disposable plastic and paper containers was taxable and not exempt as a resale. The court's reasoning was that "Sta-Ru [a Dairy Queen franchisee] is in the business of selling food and beverages, not disposable containers, and it is the food or beverage which its customers come to purchase." The court analogized that just as the purchase of permanent dinnerware would not be exempt but rather be considered a cost of doing business, so should the disposable containers be viewed.

Example 4.6. Questions similar to the ones above arise in many other situations, such as in the case of hotel amenities (e.g., writing pads, stationery, postcards, pens, matches, sewing kits, shoeshine cloths, and other toiletries) or the institutional purchase of food (e.g., by airlines, hospitals, and schools).

Planning

Many businesses routinely overpay sales and use taxes on their purchases by not notifying vendors of their exemption. This particularly is the case if the business is a manufacturer that buys materials and machinery for production. One of the ways to deal with this is to perform a "reverse sales tax audit": an overpayment of sales and use tax can be determined by examining invoices, and subject to the statute of limitations, the firm can apply for a refund of sales/use taxes paid. Such reverse audits can be performed with respect to all other exemptions or exclusions on which the firm may have incorrectly paid sales/use taxes. Also, to avoid such overpayments in the future, the attorneys, accountants, and other outside consultants can consult with the client's accounts payable employees, perhaps revising the client's software, to rectify the system, including notifying vendors of the client's exemption status.

Resale Exemption Certificate

Proper documentation is required to get the sale-for-resale exemption. In general, this documentation is referred to as the "resale exemption certificate." To be valid, states generally require that the following conditions be met:

- The certificate is accurate, complete, and applicable to the transaction.
- The seller has accepted the certificate in good faith.

The exemption certificate is prepared by the purchaser and should be retained by the seller (vendor).

Occasional or Casual Sales Exemption

Most states provide an exemption for occasional or casual sales that would otherwise be classified under the state statutes as a taxable sale. This exemption is provided primarily for administrative convenience and to eliminate the overwhelming task of enforcing the sales tax statutes for persons who are not engaged in making taxable sales on a regular basis.

Example 4.7. Transactions that typically are exempt under this provision include garage sales, sale of a used automobile, and sale of a business.

Consider the compliance nightmare for both the taxpayer and the state revenue agency if the above transactions were considered taxable.

The problem, of course, is in defining what constitutes a "casual" or occasional sale. Does it mean only a single sale or does it cover more than one sale? Does it matter whether or not the seller is engaged in the business of selling? Most states have tried to resolve this problem by setting a threshold (typically of three or more sales in a single 12-month period), which if exceeded would require compliance with the state sales tax statutes.

Example 4.8. In Texas, the occasional sale rule is written such that the third sale qualifies the person as a retailer. Consequently, tax would have to be collected on the third sale and on every subsequent sale thereafter, unless the sale qualifies for an exemption. In California, if a taxpayer makes a third sale, tax becomes due on all three sales and every subsequent sale thereafter unless it is specifically exempt under some other provision.

Business Asset Transfers

Often the state statutes concerning the casual or occasional sales exemption are written such that sales or transfers of business assets qualify under the exemption. Given the frequency with which mergers, acquisitions, and reorganizations take place in the business world, this exemption can provide practitioners with a useful planning tool. However, states usually impose strict conditions under which this exemption is available. For example, it is common for states to require that:

- The entire operating assets of the business be sold
- The sale be made in a single transaction
- The sale be made to a single purchaser

Thus, even in transactions involving the sale of all of the operating assets of a business, an exemption from sales tax may not be available if the sale is structured through several transactions or if several purchasers are involved.

Planning

When purchasing a business, the acquirer usually is engulfed with many important issues, such as what the business is worth, how to finance the purchase, which employees to retain, etc. One of the issues that does not receive as high a priority is whether the seller has any unpaid sales taxes. In most jurisdictions, the purchaser of the business steps into the shoes of the seller or succeeds the seller with regard to any unpaid sales taxes. The acquirer can protect himself by requiring the seller to obtain "good standing letters" from the appropriate departments of revenue and local governments. These letters certify that no sales or use taxes are due from the seller in those jurisdictions. If the acquirer armed with these letters is subsequently audited and deficiencies are assessed, the department would be required to collect the sales taxes from the seller.

The occasional sales exemption also applies when there is a transfer of all or substantially all of the property held or used in the regular course of business, if after the transfer there is no real or ultimate change in the ownership of such property. Thus, incorporation of a sole proprietorship would be exempt from sales taxes. Likewise, the transfer of assets by partners to a partnership would be exempt under the casual sale rule. These provisions are similar to those found in the Internal Revenue Code that exclude the gains on such transfers from being included in gross income.

Manufacturing, Processing, and Fabricating Exemption

All states imposing a sales tax provide an exemption from sales tax for purchases of materials used in the manufacturing, processing, or fabricating of tangible personal property for sale. This exemption also is referred to as the ingredient or component part exemption. The rationale underlying this exemption is similar to that for the sale-for-resale exemption — the materials purchased are in fact resold in the form of the final manufactured product rather than being used for ultimate consumption by the purchaser. Although the rationale appears straightforward, there is much disagreement over what each of the terms — manufacturing, processing, and fabricating — means. To make matters more complicated, state statutes contain different definitions of these terms, and the revenue agencies and courts seem to differ in their interpretations.

In general, manufacturing is comprised of all stages in the production process commencing with the acquisition of raw materials and culminating with the completed tangible personal property. Processing normally involves applying materials and labor to modify or alter the characteristics of tangible personal property. Thus, repairs and maintenance generally are not included within processing because typically those acts simply result in restoring the property to its original form. Finally, fabrication usually consists of a procedure or series of procedures whose aim is to make the property function better or differently.

Although one should carefully review the statutes, administrative regulations, and court cases to fully understand the scope of this exemption in any given state, some of the key issues to consider are (1) Is the process really "manufacturing"? and (2) Is the product "used" in the manufacturing process?

With regard to the first question, examples of processes that may not qualify are those that merely reshape or repackage an item or are ancillary to the actual manufacturing process. For example, the freezing of food that has already been prepared may or may not be considered part of the manufacturing process. Depending on the answer to that question, a freezer purchased for use in the freezing stage may or may not be exempt.

With regard to the second question, one has to identify the start and the end of the manufacturing process. In addition, proximity of the property to the process may be relevant. Thus, acts associated with the preparation for production and not the production itself may be excluded from the term manufacturing, but purchases made for those acts may not be exempt. Testing equipment and transportation equipment are examples of items that may not qualify for exemption.

There are numerous court cases specifically dealing with this exemption that can provide some insights to the practitioner when advising a client. However, these cases often reach different conclusions with seemingly identical fact patterns, underscoring the paramount importance for the practitioner to fully understand the facts in the client's case before rendering advice.

Planning

Firms, and their outside consultants, should look to see if some part of the process can be moved closer to the manufacturing process. For example, a finished goods facility, if moved immediately next to the manufacturing center, may then become an integral part of the manufacturing process. If this occurs, items that the client purchases that are related to finished goods (e.g., packaging materials) may be exempt from sales or use tax.

Machinery or Equipment Exemption

Most states provide an exemption for machinery or equipment purchased to be used in the manufacture, production, or processing of tangible personal property that is to be sold. The rationale for this exemption is the same as mentioned for the two previous exemptions — the sale-for-resale and the manufacturing exemptions, i.e., business inputs should be exempt to prevent the pyramiding of sales taxes. In addition to that rationale, states provide an exemption for machinery and equipment to encourage business investment and location within their boundaries. That, in turn, provides a basis for increased employment and other economic benefits.

Although the specifics of this exemption vary greatly by state, industrial or manufacturing machinery typically is exempt and many states also exempt farm machinery. However, office machinery is not exempt in any state. For example:

- Some states do not exempt the machinery used in manufacturing but either tax it at a lower rate (e.g., Alabama) or provide an investment credit (e.g., New Mexico).
- Some states exempt purchases of machinery up to a certain dollar amount (e.g., the exemption for farm machinery in Louisiana applies to the first $50,000 of the purchase price).

An important aspect of this exemption is that states typically restrict the exemption to machinery used "directly" or "predominantly" in the manufacturing or processing of tangible personal property. So in addition to the controversy associated with first determining whether the activity constitutes manufacturing or processing discussed above, the second issue is whether the machinery or equipment is being used directly or predominantly in such activity.

Planning

For most states, capital acquisitions of personalty (such as machinery and equipment) are subject to sales/use taxes. Most states allow no sales/use taxes for purchases made from the Federal government, "casual sales," or for personalty which will become part of the manufactured product. Additionally, many states allow credits for personalty purchased in enterprise zones. Also, some allow no sales/use taxes for personalty sold within these zones.

Another method for postponing sales/use taxes on equipment is by leasing, instead of purchasing. Here, the above tax incentives typically do not apply. However, significant tax savings can occur by delaying sales/use taxes, by using a leasing company. Normally, if a company is planning on purchasing equipment, it should expect to pay sales/use tax. One way to postpone tax is by forming a leasing company, as follows:

| **Equipment Purchase** | **Equipment Leased** |
| (1st transaction) | (2nd transaction) |

VENDOR ⟶ LEASING COMPANY ⟶ COMPANY

$ purchase price   Lease payments (over time)

In this setting, the first transaction is not subject to sales/use tax, since the equipment is for ultimate resale. The second transaction is subject to sales/use tax, but over time, i.e., as payments are made. Thus the tax savings flows from the present value of tax savings. Of course, the consultant should check with local tax law to see if the above tax planning method is legitimate.

Status Exemptions or Exempt Organizations

Most states allow the purchases of certain organizations to be exempt from sales and use tax purchases. These organizations include:

- The U.S., its unincorporated agencies and instrumentalities, and organizations fully owned by the U.S.
- The state along with its counties, cities, and special districts
- Charitable organizations
- Educational organizations
- Religious organizations
- Youth athletic organizations
- Organizations which qualify for exemption from the Federal income tax under IRC §501(c)(3)

As one might expect, to qualify for exemption from the sales and use tax, the organization must be organized or formed solely to conduct one or more exempt activities, and it must devote its operations exclusively to one or more of the exempt activities. Further, private shareholders or other individuals should not profit or gain from such activity.

MEASURE OF THE SALES AND USE TAX

The measure or base of sales and use taxes generally is the consideration paid for goods and services or the gross proceeds for which the taxable item is sold, leased, or rented. The exact definition of the terms and what is included or excluded from the tax base varies by state.

> **Example 4.9.** In Kansas, as in most other states, the sales tax is imposed on the "gross receipts" from the sale of tangible personal property *(Kan. Stat. Ann. §79-3603)*. "Gross receipts" are defined in the statutes as "the total selling price or the amount received as defined in this act, in money, credits, property or other consideration valued in money from sales at retail within this state" [*Id. §79-3602(h)*]. The term "selling price" is defined as "the total cost to the consumer exclusive of discounts allowed and credited, but including freight and transportation charges from retailer to consumer" [*Id. §79-3602(g)*].

As a general principle, gross receipts do not include the following:

- Cash discounts allowed on the sale — Some states distinguish between cash discounts and "early payment discounts," with the latter usually not excluded from the sales tax base.
- Returns and allowances — The amount charged for tangible personal property returned by a customer if the total amount charged is refunded by cash or credit.
- Transportation charges if stated separately — These are excluded to the extent they occur after the sale. Thus, freight charges when the sale is made under the terms FOB shipping point would be excluded, while freight charges under the terms FOB destination would be included in the sales price.
- Trade-ins — Many states allow trade-ins to be excluded from gross receipts, thereby imposing a tax only on the net invoiced value. Some states allow trade-ins to be excluded only on certain property (e.g., Alabama and Connecticut exclude trade-ins only on motor vehicles and certain agricultural equipment).
- Finance and service charges or interest from credit extended on sales of taxable items.
- Bad debts — Some states allow gross receipts to be reduced by the amount of bad debts actually written off.

The above is by no means an exhaustive list of the issues one has to consider in determining what constitutes "gross receipts." Some of the other questions that must be resolved in this regard include:

- Should taxes paid be included in taxable receipts for the purpose of sales taxes? Does (should) the answer depend on the type of taxes paid?
- What should be the impact of discount coupons issued by a retailer on the sales tax base?
- Are tips and service charges includable in the sales tax base?
- When should the tax be collected in an installment sale — when the goods are delivered, when the cash is collected, or when the final payment is received?

USE TAX BASE

Although not mentioned above, most state statutes adopt the same measure for both the use and sales tax bases. However, some of the terminology might be changed to reflect the nature of the transaction. For example, "cost price" might be used instead of "sales price."

CONSTITUTIONAL ISSUES IN IMPOSING SALES AND USE TAXES

At the outset it was mentioned that the first condition that must be met before a state's sales and use tax statutes apply to a given sale transaction is that the transaction must take place within the state's borders. Only then does the state have jurisdiction to impose tax. When the entire transaction takes place within a state's borders, such as when both the buyer and the seller are located in the state and the property changes hands within the state, there is no question that this condition is satisfied. However, the issue is not so straightforward when the transaction involves more than one state, that is, an interstate sale. In such transactions, the question, of course, is where did the sale take place and therefore which state has the jurisdiction to impose its sales tax on that transaction? The answer depends on one word — nexus.

"Nexus" literally means attachment or connection. Depending on the extent of the taxpayer's presence in or proximity to the taxing jurisdiction, the taxpayer may be considered to have sufficient nexus with that jurisdiction for the purposes of its sales and use tax. Although, as mentioned before, sales taxes in the U.S. are a state- or local-level levy, the U.S. Constitution plays an overarching role in limiting the power of states to impose this tax. The specific provisions in the U.S. Constitution that do so are the Commerce Clause and the Due Process Clause.

These provisions serve as a watchdog to guard against the possibility of taxpayers being subject to multiple taxation in interstate sales transactions. In this section, we discuss some of the major cases decided by the U.S. Supreme Court that consider these constitutional limitations in the context of sales and use taxes. These cases are discussed in chronological order to help trace the evolution of the court's position in this matter.

The Key U.S. Supreme Court Decisions

The U.S. Supreme Court's fundamental analytical framework for evaluating the constitutionality of state sales and use taxation of interstate retail sales transactions was set out in three companion cases — *McLeod v. J. E. Dilworth Co.*, *General Trading Co. v. State Tax Commission*, and *International Harvester Co. v. Department of Treasury*.[115] In *Dilworth*, the Court considered whether Arkansas could impose its sales tax on a Tennessee corporation's sales made in Arkansas. The corporation, which had its home office and principal place of business in Memphis, solicited orders in Arkansas by mail, telephone, or by regularly sending solicitors, but accepted the orders in Tennessee and delivered the goods to a common carrier there for shipment to the purchaser in Arkansas. The Court held the Arkansas tax to be invalid because the sale was made in Tennessee. "For Arkansas to impose a tax on such transaction would be to project its powers beyond its boundaries and to tax an interstate transaction."

The decision in *Dilworth* reflected the Court's early interpretation of the Commerce Clause that states could not impose a tax on interstate sales because such a tax would amount to a tax on, and thus a regulation of, interstate commerce that only Congress was authorized to do. However, the Court stated that while the Arkansas sales tax was invalid, the state's use tax might be sustained in the same situation. The reasoning for this conclusion is that the Commerce Clause and Due Process Clause do not forbid the imposition of the use tax on property involved in the interstate sale because the tax is imposed on the use of the property, which certainly takes place within its territorial boundaries. The only question is whether the state can require the out-of-state seller to act as a vendor charged with the obligation of collecting the use tax from its in-state consumers. This has not been an easy question for the Court to answer, as the following cases demonstrate.

In *Miller Brothers Company v. Maryland*,[116] the question was whether a Delaware department store that sold merchandise to customers residing in Maryland was liable to collect Maryland's use tax on the sales to its residents. The store delivered goods to some of the customers at its store, whereas other customers were sent goods either by common carrier or by the store's own trucks. The Court held that Maryland could not have imposed its sales tax on these sales since they were made in Delaware. Based on that reasoning, the Court's conclusion on the question of use tax collection obligation was that "[i]t would be strange law that would make appellant more vulnerable to liability for another's tax than to a tax on itself."

In *Scripto Inc. v. Carson*,[117] the Court addressed the question of whether the presence of independent contractors in the state was a valid basis for imposing a use tax collection obligation on an out-of-state vendor. In this case, a Georgia corporation, which had no office or regular employees in Florida, employed wholesalers to solicit sales on its behalf in Florida. The Court held that, even though the wholesalers were independent contractors and not employees of the seller, these representatives gave the seller enough presence in the state to require it to collect use taxes.

In *National Bellas Hess, Inc. v. Department of Revenue*,[118] the issue before the Court was whether Illinois could impose a use tax collection obligation on an out-of-state mail-order seller that had no physical presence in the state and communicated with its customers through the mail or common carrier. The Court held that the Commerce Clause and Due Process Clause precluded Illinois from making such an imposition. This decision is widely believed to have been one of the most important decisions in the Court's history of dealing with the issue of nexus in the context of taxing interstate transactions.

The Court again dealt with an out-of-state mail-order business that had an in-state presence, although unrelated to the mail-order business, in *National Geographic Society v. California Board of Equalization.*[119] The taxpayer was a District of Columbia corporation that made mail-order sales of maps, atlases, and books to customers in California. Although the corporation maintained two offices in California strictly for the purpose of soliciting advertising for its magazine, it conducted none of its mail-order business from those offices. The Court held that the taxpayer's offices and activities in California adequately established a relationship or nexus that made it valid for California to impose a use tax obligation.

In the most important case on this issue, the Court in *Quill Corp. v. North Dakota*[120] reaffirmed its *Bellas Hess* decision that an out-of-state mail-order business with no physical presence in the state could not be required to collect that state's use taxes. However, in *Quill*, the Court distinguished its *Bellas Hess* decision in a very important way. The Court stated that the nexus standards under the Due Process Clause and the Commerce Clause are different, and that while the *Bellas Hess* conclusion is valid under the substantial nexus requirement of the Commerce Clause, it is not valid under the minimum connection requirement of the Due Process Clause.

States' Responses to the Court Decisions

As the above discussion demonstrates, a majority of the nexus cases have revolved around mail-order businesses. In *Quill*, the Court categorically referred to the tremendous growth in the mail-order industry "from a relatively inconsequential market niche" to a "goliath," that was in part due to the substantial reliance placed by the industry in its *Bellas Hess* decision, as a reason for not overturning that decision. However, the Court was careful to limit its holding to mail-order sales. The Court also reminded Congress that this was an area where it alone had the power under the Commerce Clause to enact legislation that could regulate such transactions.

In response to the *Quill* decision, legislation was introduced in Congress that would authorize states to collect use taxes on mail-order sales (*The Consumer and Main Street Protection Act of 1995*). However, the states and the mail-order industry could not agree on the specifics, and the bill was not enacted into law. This was not the first time Congress attempted to act and it is unlikely to be the last. Notwithstanding the lack of Federal legislation in this area, many states have tried to specify their own rules under which mail-order sales would be taxable.

Example 4.10. In Arizona, a mail-order business is liable for use tax if solicitations are substantial and recurring and if retailer benefits from banking, financing, debt collection, communication system, or marketing activities in Arizona or authorized installation, servicing or repair facilities in Arizona.

Example 4.11. In Indiana, liability attaches if an out-of-state retailer regularly solicits sales in Indiana (makes at least a hundred retail transactions from outside Indiana during any 12-month period or makes at least ten retail transactions totaling more than $100,000 from outside Indiana to destinations in Indiana during a 12-month period).

Planning

If practical, a business may want to avoid the use tax by severing nexus with a state. Instead of having a sales force and offices in a state, the firm can consider moving the sales force and office out of state and making sales by direct mail, perhaps by use of the Internet.

ADMINISTRATION OF SALES AND USE TAXES

Managing compliance with the sales and use tax laws is a nontrivial issue, especially because there are over 6,000 state and local tax jurisdictions. Depending on how and where a business operates, it might have compliance obligations in many jurisdictions. Moreover, businesses typically enter into numerous separate taxable transactions. Thus, the burden of complying with sales and local tax laws can be very significant, especially if not properly managed and planned. The primary compliance obligations include reporting requirements, record-keeping requirements, and preparing for and handling audits.

Reporting Obligations

Retailers have a fiduciary responsibility to properly collect and remit sales and use taxes. To discharge this responsibility, they must (a) register their business and (b) file tax returns.

Registration

States with sales and use taxes require all retailers engaged in the business of selling a taxable item for storage, use, or consumption to register their business with the state in which they conduct their business operations. If a retailer has multiple business locations within a state, it will usually be required to register each location separately. The registration results in the taxpayer receiving an identification number.

Returns

Once registered, the taxpayer is required to file a sales and use tax return each period. In addition to filing returns, the taxpayer must also collect the taxes on a timely basis, and remit those taxes to the state authorities.

1. Due dates: Due dates for tax reports vary by state and depend on the amount of the taxpayer's tax liability.
2. Content: As one might expect, a sales or use tax report typically will require information about:
   - The total receipts of the seller during the reporting period (or total purchases for use tax purposes)
   - Sales to other retailers for resale
   - Sales of exempt property
   - Sales to the U.S. government
   - Sales in interstate or foreign commerce
   - Sales returns
   - Uncollectible accounts written off
   - Cash discounts

If local taxes are reported to and collected by the state, the return may also include lines to allow for that computation. Some states also allow for a vendor tax collection discount or fee to help offset the cost of collecting the tax. If allowed, the return might provide for its calculation as well. For example, Georgia allows a 3% discount of the first $3,000 of sales and use taxes collected and 0.5% of the excess. In contrast, Arizona, California, and Massachusetts are among the states that do not allow any collection discount to the seller.

- Accounting methods: Most states allow taxpayers a choice in the accounting method (e.g., cash or accrual basis) that they can use to report their gross receipts for purposes of the sales and use tax returns. Although a choice may be allowed, some states require that taxpayers use the same method as they used for their books. Once the taxpayer makes a choice for a particular method, states require consistency in its use, with changes in the method requiring a formal petition to the taxing authority.

Rates

Table 4.1 summarizes statutory sales/use tax rates by state, as of June 1999. The rates do not include additional sales tax rates added on by local governments (counties and cities).

As can be seen, there is a high variability across states, with some states having no sales/use taxes at all. An obvious planning consideration is to try to establish nexus in 0% rate states, so that sales will be taken out of the tax base in higher rate states.

Record Keeping

Proper documentation is of paramount importance for taxpayers to be able to support their sales and use tax liabilities. Apart from the regular books of account maintained by a business, some of the following documents can help establish the correct amount of the liability:

- Invoices to document any taxes paid or collected
- Contracts and purchase orders to support dates of transactions
- Bills of lading to support delivery destinations
- Support for credits for returns and write-off of bad debts
- Exemption and resale certificates to support exempt transactions

Audits

Audits are the primary mechanism available for state tax agencies to evaluate the extent to which taxpayers are complying with the tax laws. Because the number of taxable transactions tends to be voluminous, sampling techniques are used extensively in sales tax audits to minimize costs and make the task manageable.

Sampling simply consists of drawing inferences about the population from a smaller set of observations. Thus, it is absolutely essential that great care be taken in identifying the procedures that would yield an appropriate sample. For example, care should be exercised to make sure that the sample captures as closely as possible the normal conditions under which the business operated during the period under audit. Typically, taxpayers have the right to be involved in developing the audit program and technique. Hence, they should ensure that the sample does not consist of unusual or nonrecurring transactions and that such transactions are identified and dealt with separately.

Generally, there are two types of sampling procedures used most frequently in sales and use tax audits — block samples and random or statistical samples.

Block Samples

Under this method, the auditor first picks a block of time, such as one or more months in a year. For that block, the auditor then usually examines all transactions for compliance accuracy. Based on the error rate in the sample, the auditor extrapolates to the entire population. For example, if the auditor chooses 1 month in the year as the sample for examination, he must multiply the errors found by 12 to get the number of estimated errors in the population.

The biggest drawback of the block sample procedure is that the time block selected for the sample may not reflect normal operations of the taxpayer in the remainder of the year. Thus, extrapolating from the sample results may lead to either over- or underestimating the errors for the entire year.

Random or Statistical Samples

To ensure that the sampling procedure results in unbiased inferences about the population, a simple random or stratified random sample may be required. In a simple random sample, the auditor picks a sample of transactions purely at random (usually identified using a random number generator) or by employing some random sampling rule.

> **Example 4.12.** The auditor may choose to verify every tenth transaction.

However, for many businesses, a simple random sample may not be appropriate; instead, the nature of the business might call for a stratified random sample. In this technique, transactions are first classified into strata or groups based on some characteristic that is suitable given the nature of the business activities. Thus, the strata might be based on the dollar amount of the sales or the geographic regions in which the taxpayer conducts business or the vendors to whom the sales are made or some combination of these and other criteria. Once the strata are created, then transactions are chosen at some rate from within each stratum.

The sampling rate might differ for each stratum, depending on its importance or the frequency of transactions. Given the different strata and likely difference in the sampling rates within each stratum, care needs to be exercised when using this technique in drawing inferences about the population. Since the use of this technique can quickly become complicated, an appropriate understanding of stratified statistical sampling is recommended.

Statute of Limitations

Most states provide a 3-year statute of limitations within which the audit must be performed or the claim for refund must be filed. The 3-year period runs from the date the return is filed or the date the return is due, whichever is later. If the taxpayer does not file a return or files a return that is false or fraudulent, usually there is no statute of limitation, i.e., the audit can be performed up to an indefinite time.

Tax Management in Action 4.1

Additional Secondary Sources for Sales Taxation

1. William F. Fox, Ed., *Sales Taxation: Critical Issues in Policy and Administration*, Westport, Conn.: Praeger (1992).
2. John F. Due and John L. Mikesell, *Sales Taxation: State and Local Structure and Administration*, Washington, D.C.: Urban Institute Press (2nd ed., 1994).
3. Robert J. Fields, *Understanding and Managing Sales and Use Tax*, Chicago, Ill.: CCH Inc. (3rd ed., 1994).
4. Jerome R. Hellerstein and Walter Hellerstein, *State and Local Taxation: Cases and Materials,* chap. 9, St. Paul, Minn.: West Publishing Co. (6th ed., 1997).
5. Matthew N. Murray and William F. Fox, Eds., *The Sales Tax in the 21st Century*, Westport, Conn.: Praeger (1997).

DISCUSSION QUESTIONS

1. What are the different types of sales taxes currently in use in the U.S.? Specifically, how do they differ from each other?
2. What are the key criteria that must be satisfied for a retail sales tax to apply?
3. Discuss what is meant by the term "tangible personal property."
4. In determining whether an asset is tangible or intangible personal property for the purpose of sales and use taxation, do the following play any role? If yes, why?
   a. The taxpayer's treatment of that asset on its Federal income tax returns
   b. The taxpayer's treatment of that asset on its financial statements
5. What is the rationale, if any, for states to generally exclude services from their sales tax base?
6. What is the "true object" test? In what connection has this test been used? How have the courts operationalized this test? Apart from the cases discussed in the text, locate one or more cases in your state that have used this test.
7. With regard to the taxation of the sale of software:
   a. Is there a clear distinction between canned and custom software? Is there any valid reason for drawing the distinction between canned and custom software?
   b. Is this distinction any different for software than it is for any other type of property?
8. Define the term "sale." Discuss what exactly the term "retail sale" means.
9. What are some of the principal exemptions from the sales tax base typically found in most state statutes? Explain the rationale of some of these exemptions.
10. What is a resale exemption certificate? Who provides this certificate to whom?

11. Is the sale of an entire business exempt from sales tax? Under what circumstances might such a sale be exempt?

12. The base of the sales tax is either "sales proceeds" or "gross receipts." In general, discuss whether the following are included or excluded from the sales tax base:
    - Returns and allowances
    - Bad debts
    - Tips and service charges
    - Trade-ins
    - Transportation charges

    What is the rationale for the inclusion or exclusion of the above from the sales tax base?

13. What is (are) the basic principle(s) underlying a retail sales tax? How do the state statutes attempt to be faithful to these principles?

14. Define "nexus." What is the minimum nexus standard for sales and use tax purposes? After reviewing the U.S. Supreme Court cases mentioned in the chapter, do you think that the Court's opinion has changed over time regarding what the minimum nexus standard for sales tax purposes is?

15. Does a reading of the Court's opinion suggest that the nexus standard for sales tax imposition is different from the nexus standard for use tax collection obligation?

16. What are the basic reporting obligations of the taxpayer for sales tax purposes?

17. Suppose you were advising a new client who is just starting a business in a state that imposes a sales tax. What type of records would you advise this client to keep so as to help in meeting the client's sales tax obligations?

18. For purposes of sales tax audits, auditors use either the block sampling method or the random or statistical sampling method.
    a. What is the difference between the two sampling methods?
    b. If you were asked to represent a client in a sales tax audit, which method would you advocate that the auditor use and why?

19. What is meant by the term "statute of limitations"? What is the typical statute of limitation for sales tax purposes?

20. Sales and use taxes raise many important public policy questions that have been part of the national political debate and several recent presidential elections. Some of the key questions in this debate are
    a. Should there be a national sales tax in lieu of an income tax?
    b. Should there be a national sales tax in addition to an income tax, which is then imposed at a reduced rate?

    Prepare a brief one-page argument in support of and against each of these questions.

PROBLEMS

Problem 1

Examine the sales and use tax statutes of your home state and determine the following:

a. What is the type of sales tax imposed by the state?
b. On whom is the legal imposition of the sales tax?
c. How is sales price defined? What is included and what is excluded from this term?
d. What are the principal exemptions from the sales tax base?
e. Does the state have a machinery exemption? If so, how is machinery defined?
f. Are monies received for warranties subject to sales tax? What about extended warranties?

Problem 2

Read the full decision of the U.S. Supreme Court in *Quill Corp. v. North Dakota*, 504 U.S. 298, 112 S.Ct. 1904 (1992).

a. Does the Court's decision imply that there is a different nexus standard for different taxes (e.g., sales tax versus income tax)?
b. In the absence of the Court's ruling in *National Bellas Hess*, would the Court have reached the same conclusion in *Quill*?
c. In your opinion, is the Court's decision limited to one industry (the mail-order industry) or does it have broad applicability to all businesses?

ENDNOTES

105. *Voss v. Gray* 298 N.W. 1 (1941).
106. *Accountants Computer Services, Inc. v. Koysdar*, 35 Ohio St.2d 120, 298 N.E.2d 519 (1973).
107. *Federated Dept. Stores, Inc. v. Koysdar*, 45 Ohio St.2d 1, 340 N.E.2d 840 (1976).
108. 465 F.2d 615 (D.C.Cir., 1972).
109. *Comptroller of the Treasury v. Equitable Trust Co.*, 296 Md. 459, 464 A.2d 248 (1983).
110. *Chittenden Trust Co. v. King,...* 143 Vt. 271, 465 A. 2d 1100 (1983).
111. *South Central Bell Telephone Co. v. Barthelemy*, 643 So. 2d 1240 (1994).
112. Jerome R. Hellerstein and Walter Hellerstein, 2 State Taxation ¶ 13.05[2] (2d ed. 1993).
113. *Burger King, Inc. v. State Tax Comm'n*, 51 N.Y. 2d 614, 416 N.E.2d 1024 (1980).
114. 64 Ill.2d 330, 356 N.E.2d 67 (1976).

115. 322 U.S. 327, 64 S.Ct. 1023 (1944); 322 U.S. 335, 64 S.Ct. 1028 (1944); 322 U.S. 340, 64 S.Ct. 1019 (1944), respectively.
116. 347 U.S. 340, 74 S.Ct. 535 (1954).
117. 362 U.S. 207, 80 S.Ct. 619 (1960).
118. 386 U.S. 753, 87 S.Ct. 1389 (1967).
119. 430 U.S. 551, 97 S.Ct. 1386 (1977).
120. 504 U.S. 298, 112 S.Ct. 1904 (1992).

5

PROPERTY TAXES

INTRODUCTION

As noted previously, property taxes account for approximately 65% of all state and local tax payments made by businesses. Property taxes generate over $250 billion in revenues per year. In general, there are three methods of valuation: cost, income, and market. In tax planning, it is important to consider all elements that affect value, as well as these three approaches to value, to ensure that property is correctly valued so that a taxpayer is not paying more than his/her fair share of property taxes.

The property tax is primarily a local tax that is levied and administered by local jurisdictions rather than the states. Throughout the history of the U.S., this tax has contributed the lion's share of revenues for local jurisdictions. However, as the U.S. economy has undergone significant changes, with services accounting for an increasingly larger share, the relative importance of the property tax as a source of local revenues has declined. For example, whereas in the years up to World War I property taxes constituted over 90% of the tax revenue base of local governments, that proportion declined to less than 80% in the 1990s. As a percentage of total revenues of local governments, the change has been even more dramatic — property taxes now constitute roughly 40% of the total revenues compared with 80% up to the 1940s.[121]

Property taxes pay for all kinds of local services, such as schools, fire stations, parks, and libraries. They are also used to provide public safety and health, transportation, and emergency services. As such, the governing body of each county, school district, city, and town levies property taxes.

The property tax generally is imposed on real property and, in most states, on tangible personal property used in business. Some states, such as New Jersey, New York, and Pennsylvania, exempt personal property from the state's property tax base. The tax is imposed on the value of property, which is usually defined as some measure of fair market value. Property values are determined by qualified appraisers, who are employed by the Assessor's Office. In many jurisdictions, Assessors are elected to their office.

Because property taxes are levied to meet projected expenditures of local jurisdictions, their amount is determined as the residual required to meet those expenses after considering the revenues from all other sources. The required property tax levy is divided by the final assessed values of the properties to compute the tax rate. Administratively, this tax rate is applied to each parcel of property on the tax rolls in proportion to its value. Statements are issued to the property owners and tax is collected usually according to a statutory schedule.

The reasons why the property tax is the mainstay of local jurisdictions and for its longevity lie in the inherent advantages of this tax. Perhaps the most significant advantage of this tax is that its base — the property on which the tax is imposed — can be easily located and identified. Further, the site where the property is located is also not very controversial most of the time, reducing concerns about which locality has the jurisdiction to impose its tax. At least for real property, it is also true that the tax base is fairly stable in that real estate is not easily moved in response to taxation. Of course, in the long run, business and personal investments in real estate can and do respond to tax impositions, but usually with a fairly long time lag. Another advantage of the property tax is that unpaid taxes can easily attach to specific property, thereby providing greater surety of their eventual collection, even if the taxpayer were to become insolvent or bankrupt. More importantly, the services financed by property taxes are overwhelmingly local: education, fire and police, street maintenance, and the like.

Of course, the property tax is not without disadvantages. Its biggest advantage — the certain and determinable tax base — can turn out to be its most significant disadvantage. Specifically, economic downturns inevitably are accompanied with declines in property values, which cause the tax base to shrink. Theoretically, the local jurisdiction can continue to raise the same amount of tax revenues by simply adjusting the tax rate, but in recessionary times such actions are at best political suicide and at a minimum of questionable economic prudence. Thus, the limitation of the property tax to a specific asset, which makes it so attractive as a local levy, also can contribute to its biggest difficulty. In view of this problem, it is not surprising to see local governments seek a more diverse tax base as evidenced by the declining share of property taxes as a percentage of the local tax base.

THE PROPERTY TAX BASE

Property taxation can be divided into three categories. These basic types are real property, tangible personal property, and intangible property.

For *realty*, real property taxes are imposed on land and its related structures. The value is determined by the local Assessor.[122] Once the value is determined, it is constant until there are changes in market conditions, or periodic revaluations, or changes due to modifications of the size or quality of the property. There are three general valuation systems used by the states. Under the first, used by the District of Columbia and twenty states, real property is valued at "market value." Under the second system, used by twelve states, all taxable realty is assessed at a single percentage of market value. Under the third system, used in sixteen states, "classified assessment level" is used, under which the state divides the property tax base into two or more uses or other categories, and establishes a particular level of assessment for each.[123]

Tangible personal property is "valued" annually as of a specific assessment date. Tangible property is taxed in every state and the District of Columbia.[124] Taxpayers file annual property tax reports which show, by class of property, the original cost of their assets by year of acquisition. After the base value is determined from the review of comparables, adjustments are made to arrive at the final value.

For state and local property tax purposes, the distinction between real and personal property is made on a state-by-state basis. It is important to properly classify property according to the local jurisdiction's standards to ensure that assets are not taxed twice and the proper tax is paid. This process is known as *cost segregation.*

As mentioned above, property taxes typically are levied on real property and personal property. However, in most jurisdictions, different tax rates are applied to the two types of property. Further, it is common to have multiple classes within each of these two property types, with different tax rates applied to each class. Hence, taxpayers wishing to ensure that they pay the correct amount of property tax must examine carefully the following:

1. The property is correctly classified.
2. The property is not specifically exempt from the tax base.
3. The property is correctly valued.

Real Property versus Personal Property

The first issue to be resolved is whether the property is real or personal. Apart from the different tax rates that might be applied, the tax on personal property usually is limited to tangible property used in business. Real property (and real estate generally) includes land, buildings, and other improvements on the land. Personal property usually is defined as all property that is not real property.

Example 5.1. Arizona statutes define personal property to include "property of every kind, both tangible and intangible, not included in the term real estate" [A.R.S. §42-11002(7)].

The Arizona Department of Revenue's Personal Property Manual (January 1, 1997) further explains that property is personal property if it can be removed without damaging itself or the property to which it is attached, and it is only temporarily attached, or it is interchangeable with other items, or the real property to which it is affixed can function without it [Table 2.1, p. 2.12].

The following are examples of items that might be classified as real property or personal property:

Examples of Real Property	Examples of Personal Property
Wall-to-wall carpets	Window air conditioners
Ceiling fans	Blinds
Electrical wiring	Laboratory equipment
Built-in furnishings	Machinery
Lighting fixtures	Movable or detachable partitions
Sprinkler systems	Printing press

Source: Arizona Department of Revenue, Personal Property Manual (Jan. 1, 1997), Table 2.2 at pp. 2.14–2.20.

Although tangible personal property is taxed in most states (Delaware, New York, and Pennsylvania are some of the exceptions), inventories are not taxed in most states (Alaska, Georgia, and Indiana are some of the exceptions). The amount reported for inventories varies from state to state. In some states, the amount reported is the average of 12 months preceding the assessment date, whereas in others it is as of the assessment date.

Exempt Property

Even though there is great variation among the local jurisdictions in terms of specific exemption from their property tax base, listed below are some of the common types of exemptions from property tax:

- Agricultural land
- Government property
- Education and library property
- Health care property
- Religious property

- Cemeteries
- Property of widows, widowers, veterans, homeowners, the elderly, and disabled persons
- Observatories
- Animal control and humane societies
- Property of arts and science organizations
- Volunteer fire departments
- Property of veterans organizations

TANGIBLE PERSONAL PROPERTY

Personal property includes everything except intangibles that are not realty and/or not permanently attached to realty. There are four major classes of personal property: machinery and equipment, inventories, leasehold improvements,[125] and intangibles. The exact composition and taxation of these classes vary depending on statutory and jurisdictional guidelines. Each of these categories is discussed next.

Types of Property

Machinery and equipment, in addition to encompassing the common definition, also includes supplies, consigned goods, and goods in-transit. *Inventories* are the stock in the trade of the business. Frequent issues associated with the valuation of inventory include associating all accrued costs with the goods at the level where the goods are resting, tracking goods in-transit, and identifying who bears the tax burden in the case of consigned property. *Leasehold improvements* typically take the form of walls, ceilings, carpeting, and lighting. The most significant issue associated with the valuation of leasehold improvements is their classification as real or personal property. The appropriate treatment is determined by local jurisdictional guidance.

Machinery and equipment includes a wide variety of items, including plant machinery and equipment, office furniture and equipment, computers/data processing equipment, motor vehicles, aircraft, mobile homes and boats, leased equipment, construction in progress, and tools. Although each state and class of machinery and equipment has some specialized rules, they are typically more general rules. Machinery and equipment can be difficult to classify depending on how much detail is recorded in the asset records. Depreciation and obsolescence can both significantly reduce taxable values; here, detailed records are critical. As an example, computers and related peripheral equipment are often grouped with office furniture, but such equipment has a much shorter useful life than most other items included in that group.

Inventory, in every stage of production, is subject to tax in about seventeen states. For manufacturers, inventory includes raw materials, work-in-progress, and finished goods. For merchandisers, inventory is goods held for sale.

Valuation of Property

There are a number of important issues to consider in the valuation of tangible personal property. One such issue is an Assessor's identification of property, or "verification." Normally, the Assessor will identify a business's personal property by either the self-declaration or the rendition prepared by the business on or after the annual assessment date.

The Assessor may also use less common methods. One such method is a review of government filings, including income tax returns, business license lists, airport and marina lists, corporate charters, and business permits. Other methods less commonly used by the Assessor may include desk, telephone, or correspondence audits and physical inspections or discovery reviews.

Three methods of valuation — cost, income, and market — are used to determine the assessed value of personal property. (These methods are detailed in *Realty*, below.) Use of these approaches depends on the availability of reliable data.

Property Classification

The proper classification of tangible property is an important issue. Such misclassification often leads to overpayments. One such misclassification is overstated value due to understated depreciation or missed obsolescence. Another is double taxation due to property classified as tangible personal property on the fixed asset records and included in the value of the real property to which it is attached. In addition to classification, keeping detailed and accurate property tax records is very important.

Planning

One of the most fruitful approaches is to review fixed asset inventories, leases, and other property records. This often results in finding improperly recorded disposals, double recording of property, and misclassification of property. Outside accountants, attorneys, and other consultants can be very effective here, because the very reason for these errors often makes a company blind to correcting them. The consultant can significantly decrease a company's property tax bill.

Situs

There are a number of issues relating to situs. Generally, stationary property is subject to taxation where it is located. On the other hand, movable property (such as vehicles, boats, aircraft, and construction equipment) generally requires a more or less permanent situs from which it operates in order to be taxed. Property temporarily removed from the business premises does not necessarily lose its taxable situs there. Two issues must be considered under the local jurisdiction's guidelines: how long is temporary and what happens if the property crosses state lines such as railroads, utilities, pipelines, and airlines?

For in-transit property that moves by common carrier or private conveyance in interstate commerce, only property in-transit on the assessment date is affected. Although Assessors may attempt to tax property physically in-transit, court rulings have generally held that this is generally not allowable.

REALTY

The term "real property" includes all interests, benefits, and rights inherent in the ownership of physical real estate, and physical land and structures affixed to the land.

Valuation

All valuations are market driven. The three most common methods of valuation are the *income method*, *cost method*, and *market method*.

The Income Method

Under the income method, property valuation is based primarily on the net cash flows expected to be derived from the property. There are two ways this can be determined. The first is "yield capitalization," which is used if the cash flow from the property is unstable. The cash flow is projected into the future and discounted. The capitalization rate is determined by examining market trends in sales, investment (e.g., debt to equity ratios), and industry sources.

If the property's cash flow is stable and is expected to stay that way, then the income method uses "direct capitalization." Here, income valuation is based on the formula:

$$Value = Income/Rate$$

The income method is frequently used for apartments, hotels, shopping centers, and strip malls.

Property that generates income can be valued using an income capitalization approach. Basically, this approach consists of deriving the present value of the income stream expected from the property. Operationally, this approach calls for two main data items: the "net income" from the property and the capitalization or discount. The calculation can be performed as follows:

Total Estimated Income from Property

Less:	Vacancy and collection loss
Add:	Other income property
Equals:	Effective gross income
Less:	Operating expenses
Equals:	Net operating income
Divide by:	Capitalization rate
Equals:	Property value

Care should be taken to deduct only those expenses that actually are related to the operations. Expenses typically allowed for accounting purposes, such as depreciation and interest expenses, and certain taxes, such as Federal income taxes or property taxes, usually are not deductible as operating expenses.

Example 5.2. An office building typically generates net income of $100,000 per year. Assuming the appropriate discount rate is 10%, the direct capitalization value is $1 million. This is computed as $100,000/10%.

Example 5.3. Assume the same facts as above except that the rents are irregular. Current year (2003) net income is $70,000, and management's best forecast is that net income will increase by approximately $5,000 per year, peaking at $90,000. Assuming a 10% discount rate, the property's value, based on the present value of the income stream, is:

2003: $70,000 × (0.9091)	=	$63,637
2004: $75,000 × (0.8264)	=	$61,980
2005: $80,000 × (0.7513)	=	$60,104
2006: $85,000 × (0.6830)	=	$58,055
2007–?: $90,000 × (8.51–5.165)	=	$301,050
Present Value of Cash Flows		$544,826

(As noted above, present value tables are provided in Appendix B.)

Basically, under the *comparable sales* method of market valuation, property is valued by comparing it to recent sales of similar property. The market value method is referred to by different names in the various states. For example, in Arizona, property is taxed on its "full cash value." This term is defined in the statutes as being synonymous with market value, which means the estimate of value that is derived annually by the use of standard appraisal methods and techniques [A.R.S. §42-11001(5)].

Market value of a property is the most probable price that a property would bring in a competitive and open market, in which the price is not affected by undue circumstances. Implicit in this definition of market value are several conditions:

- Both the buyer and seller are motivated.
- Both buyer and seller are well informed and acting in their own best interests.
- A reasonable time is allowed for exposure of the property to the open market.
- The price represents the normal consideration for the property and is unaffected by special financing or other terms granted by anyone associated with the sale.

The Cost Method

The cost method attempts to find the value or cost to replace an improvement with a new improvement. Items to be considered when estimating value under the cost approach include replacement cost, reproduction cost, and either physical, functional, or economic depreciation (the latter can be deducted from "gross" value). Land that is added is valued at market value.

Under the cost approach to valuing property, care should be taken to include only those costs that have an effect on value of the property. The basic formula for determining the cost is:

Cost of Improvements
Less: Depreciation/obsolescence
Add: <u>Land (valued as if vacant)</u>
Equals: <u>Cost value</u>

Cost of improvements should include:

- Direct costs (such as materials and labor)
- Indirect costs (such as architect fees and sales tax on materials)
- Reasonable profit

Depreciation is the straight reduction in value from wear and tear. Obsolescence is more comprehensive and encompasses:

- Physical obsolescence
- Functional obsolescence
- External obsolescence

Physical obsolescence is essentially synonymous with depreciation. However, functional obsolescence goes beyond wear and tear to include obsolescence due to technological advances or changes in the nature of the business activities being conducted.

When using the cost method, care should be taken to include only those costs that actually increase the property's economic value. Thus, rather than just take the book balance from the real property account, that account should be examined to ensure that only value-enhancing items are included. In other words, costs that have limited or no resale value should not be included in the cost amount for property tax.

> **Example 5.4.** The following costs, typically included in the building account for accounting purposes, should be eliminated for property tax purposes:
>
> - Demolition costs of an old building
> - Costs of land surveys conducted before site selection
> - Costs incurred to overcome construction problems

The Market Method

The last method of valuing real property is the *market* or "comparable sales" method. Applying a market approach to valuing real property, an Assessor will investigate and analyze sales of comparable properties.

> **Example 5.5.** Assume the same facts as in Example 5.3, and that similar office buildings (in terms of location and square footage) have been selling for $1.2 million. Using the market method, a property tax assessor may assess a value of $1.2 million, instead of $1 million.

Other Valuation Issues

Overarching the application of all of the above valuation methods are the concepts of "contribution," "highest and best use," and "substitution." Regarding "contribution," the value of a particular component is measured in terms of its contribution to the value of the whole, or as the amount that its absence would detract from the whole. For example, when an appraiser examines a home, the value of that extra bathroom or fireplace is already determined. This is because the value does not necessarily relate to its cost to build, but more to the fact that it is there already.

Appraisers often look to the reasonable (physically possible and financially feasible) and legal use of a property that results in the highest value, or "highest and best use." This concept can apply to vacant land as well as a building or facility. Finally, the appraisal process is based largely on the principle of "substitution." This principle presumes that a prudent purchaser will pay no more for any real property than the cost of acquiring an equally desirable substitute on the open market.

> **Example 5.6.** A taxpayer owns a vacant lot that it purchased for $1 million. It is zoned for either residential or commercial use. If subdivided, similar lots used for house construction are worth $2 million. Similar lots used for office building sites sell for $1.8 million. Under the "highest and best use" concept, an Assessor would value the land at $2 million.

Planning

Planning in this area can add value to the firm in a number of ways, as is illustrated in the following planning examples. Again, due to the very reasons that such opportunities have been overlooked by entrepreneurs, managers, and in-house accountants, this is a very fruitful area for outside accountants, attorneys, and other consultants to help clients.

1. After reviewing a company's personal property tax renditions, the consultant discovers that machinery that had been retired is still listed. By removing the machinery, the consultant can save the firm property taxes.
2. A consultant discovers that local county officials assess realty based on prior year's value, increased by general market trends in the county. The consultant discovers that in the client's part of the city, property values have actually declined. The consultant hires an appraiser who establishes that the client's property has not increased as much in value as has the rest of the county. The consultant files an appeal with the County Assessor to have the value (and tax) reduced.
3. It is not uncommon for an outside consultant, on review, to find that for a client's office building, improvements such as draperies and carpeting have accidentally been included both in the personal property tax rendition and in the real estate tax value. The resulting advice is straightforward, and often significant: take steps to remove the property from one of the tax rolls.

INTANGIBLES

A number of states impose taxes on intangible property such as stocks and bonds. Some states also include in the overall value of property the value of intangible property such as copyrights, trademarks and patents, goodwill, exploration rights, an assembled workforce, and the intangible portion of business enterprise value.

The following are assessment dates and type of taxable intangibles by state: Alabama—Oct. 1 (stocks/bonds); Florida—Jan. 1 (stocks/bonds); Iowa—Jan. 1 (credit union reserves); Kentucky—Sept. 1 (deposits), Jan. 1 (stocks/bonds); Louisiana—Jan. 1 (bank stock, premiums on loans); Maryland—Jan. 1 (most exempt); Michigan—(phased out Jan. 1, 1998); Mississippi—March 1 (notes with usurious interest); Pennsylvania—Jan. 1–15 (stocks/bonds); Rhode Island—Dec. 31 (bank and credit union deposits); Tennessee—Jan. 1 (stock of loan, investment and cemetery companies; capital stock of insurance companies); Texas—Jan. 1 (limited); West Virginia—July 1 (bonds, stocks of banks, industrial loan companies, building and savings and loan companies).

Some states exempt intangible property from the property tax, even though a specific exemption is not provided for such property. For example, in Arizona, neither the Constitution nor the statutes specifically exempt intangible property. The Arizona Constitution §1 states, in part, "[a]ll taxes shall be uniform upon the same class of property within the territorial limits of the authority levying the tax, and shall be levied and collected for public purposes only."

Nevertheless, the Arizona courts have long held that intangible property is not subject to the state's property tax because of the absence of (1) a method of equalizing intangibles and (2) an adequate procedure for collecting the tax on intangibles [*Maricopa County v. Trustees of Arizona Lodge No. 2*, 52 Ariz. 329, 80 P.2d 955 (1938)].

Administrative Issues

In the case of real property, the property owner generally is not required to file any reports. In contrast, taxpayers are required to file annual personal property tax returns based on values established on the annual assessment date.

When the taxpayer receives a notice of value, he is allowed a certain number of days to make an administrative appeal, usually to the Assessor. If the meeting with the Assessor does not result in a resolution of the dispute, the taxpayer must file an appeal against the proposed value shown in the notice. The State Board of Equalization (or equivalent body) usually hears this appeal. If agreement is not reached, the next stage is the courts.

CONSTITUTIONAL ISSUES

State-Level Constitutional Issues

Most state constitutions contain a uniformity or equality clause that limits the state's power to impose taxation. For example, Article 9 of the Arizona Constitution provides:

> The power of taxation shall never be surrendered, suspended, or contracted away. All taxes shall be uniform upon the same class of property within the territorial limits of the authority levying the tax, and shall be levied and collected for public purposes only [Ariz. Const. art. 9, §1].

These uniformity and equality clauses vary considerably among the different states. Some state constitutions require only that the taxes be uniform (e.g., Arizona's constitutional provision cited above), whereas other state constitutions may require taxes to be both equal and uniform or proportional and uniform. Some state constitutions, such as New Hampshire's, go even further to provide that the state may "impose and levy proportional and reasonable assessments, rates, and taxes" [*New Hampshire Const.* Part II, Article 5].

Regardless of the specific language used, the uniformity or equality requirement in most state constitutions pertains to the property tax as stated in the Arizona Constitution above. However, some states' constitutions extend the uniformity or equality issue more generally to cover all taxes. Wisconsin requires that "[t]he rule of taxation shall be uniform" [*Article VII*, §1].

The basic concern with these uniformity or equality provisions is how the state's specific provision impacts its ability to impose taxes. In addressing this concern, one must first consider the following two preliminary questions (which have been discussed previously in another context):

1. Is the levy being imposed a tax or a fee?
2. If the levy is a tax, is it a property tax or an excise tax?

Tax versus Fee

Ascertaining whether a state or local levy is a "tax" or a "fee" is relevant because the state equality and uniformity provisions typically apply only to taxes. Thus, state or local governments may structure fee schedules that are not uniform or equal. The issue of course is what makes a levy a tax rather than a fee. Also, does it matter whether the levy is labeled a tax or a fee?

Example 5.7. In two West Virginia cases, the courts reached very different conclusions for two levies, neither of which was labeled a tax — a solid waste assessment charge was determined to be a "regulatory fee" rather than a tax,[126] whereas a fire service fee was held to be an *ad valorem* property tax.[127] Thus, the latter levy was subject to the state constitution's uniformity and equality clause, but the former was not.

Property Tax versus Excise Tax

Criteria for Distinguishing Between a Property Tax and an Excise Tax

Assuming the levy at issue is determined to be a tax, the next question is whether this tax is a property tax or an excise tax. Again, resolution of this question is necessary because most states' constitutional requirements about equality and uniformity apply only to property taxes. However, determining whether a tax is a property tax or an excise tax is not easy. The fundamental distinction between the two types of taxes lies in whether the tax is imposed on all of the privileges of owning a property or only on some of the privileges. A property tax does not usually impose any condition or place any restriction on the use of the property. If the tax is imposed simply because the person is the owner of the property and not because he exercises some privilege that the property entitles him to, then the tax would be considered a property tax.

Other factors that can distinguish between a property tax and an excise tax are whether the tax is recurring or it is a one-time imposition and whether the tax is imposed on a fixed day or on the happening of some event. Property taxes tend to be recurring in nature and assessed as of a fixed date each period, usually annually, even though they may be payable quarterly or semi-annually. In contrast, fees tend to be one-time charges imposed on the privilege of exercising some right.

Federal-Level Constitutional Issues

As mentioned before, there are several provisions in the U.S. Constitution that have a bearing on state and local taxes. The most frequently raised challenges to state and local tax levies are based on the Due Process and the Commerce Clauses in the U.S. Constitution. With much less frequency, state and local taxes have also been challenged under the Equal Protection and the Privileges and Immunities Clauses, which have much in common with the uniformity and equality provisions in the state constitutions.

The Fourteenth Amendment to the U.S. Constitution provides:

[N]or shall any State…deny to any person within its jurisdiction the equal protection of the laws [U.S. Const. amend. XIV, §1].

Although the Equal Protection Clause makes no mention of taxation, the context in which it has been invoked is very similar to the state-level equality and uniformity provisions, and that is whether the tax being imposed treats different "persons" equally.[128] To be sure, the U.S. Supreme Court's position in matters of taxation has been that state legislatures should be allowed a high degree of flexibility in classifying taxpayers as long as there is some reasonable basis for their position. The following statements from the decision in *Lehnhausen v. Lakeshore Auto Parts Co.*[129] are illustrative of the Court's approach in attacks on a state or local tax on equal protection grounds:

> The Equal Protection Clause does not mean that a State may not draw lines that treat one class of individuals or entities differently from the others. The test is whether the difference in treatment is an invidious discrimination. *** Where taxation is concerned and no specific federal right, apart from equal protection, is imperiled, the States have large leeway in making classifications and drawing lines which in their judgment produce reasonable systems of taxation.

Further, the Court grants "a presumption of constitutionality" on the state's classification scheme, while placing the onus on the person raising the equal protection challenge to overcome that presumption. The Court's rationale for doing so is that it is not possible to acquire knowledge of local conditions without elaborately cataloging those conditions. The legislature is in a unique position to have intimate knowledge of such factors and must be presumed to have used that knowledge to devise its taxing scheme. As long as there is any conceivable basis for treating classes of taxpayers or members of a class differently, the taxing scheme would be able to withstand the equal protection challenge.

Example 5.8. California's Proposition Thirteen dealing with the state's real property tax system is perhaps one of the most widely known and controversial state tax initiatives that imposed differential tax burdens. This measure amended the state constitution to limit property taxes to 1% of 1975–76 valuations and to cap annual increases in valuations at 2%, unless the property underwent a change in ownership (e.g., sale) or was a new construction. Thus, under this system of assessing property values based on date of acquisition rather than current value, a taxpayer continuing to live in the same property might have a substantially different property tax burden from a taxpayer who newly buys a virtually identical property in the same neighborhood. (As suggested above, the constitutionality of Proposition Thirteen was challenged under the Equal Protection Clause, but the Supreme Court upheld the California scheme on the ground that the difference in treatment of newer and older owners rationally furthered a legitimate state interest of preserving and stabilizing local neighborhoods.)[130]

From a substantive point of view, the basic question of course is what are the permissible distinctions between taxpayers, property, and activities for state tax purposes? Finally, from a practical standpoint, the inevitable question is whether the above questions are relevant today. Are they ever relevant in practice? We will provide some perspective on these issues next.

Relation Between the Federal Equal Protection Clause and State Uniformity and Equality Provisions

As with all matters concerning Federal and state jurisdictions, Federal statutes dominate the state statutes. Thus, state constitutional provisions regarding equality and uniformity cannot go beyond the Federal Equal Protection Clause or expand it in any way. As mentioned before, state equality and uniformity provisions typically target the state's taxing powers, whereas the Federal equal protection requirement is more general and extends to all laws. In many state constitutions, this taxing power is further limited in a variety of ways. Thus, state constitutions tend to provide stricter tests that state tax statutes must pass with regard to equal protection. Finally, the U.S. Supreme Court's decisions, such as in *Lehnhausen* mentioned above, allow state legislatures a great degree of flexibility in devising taxing statutes that would pass muster under the Federal equal protection requirement.

Permissible Distinctions Between Taxpayers, Property, and Activities for State Tax Purposes

The fundamental question, of course, is to what extent is the state legislature allowed to distinguish between taxpayers, property, and activities without violating the Federal equal protection right and its own equality and uniformity standards. This is a much more difficult question to answer unequivocally. The answer would, however, depend in large part on the specific language used in the state constitution. Depending on that language, one might arrive at different answers to questions such as the following:

- Can taxes be imposed at different rates on different taxpayers, property, or activities?
- Does providing an exemption to a taxpayer, property, or activity amount to differential taxation within the purview of the uniformity and equality clauses?

- Does providing a tax credit to a taxpayer, property, or activity amount to differential taxation within the purview of the uniformity and equality clauses?

DISCUSSION QUESTIONS

1. What are the advantages and disadvantages of a property tax?
2. Most individual taxpayers view a property tax as being a tax on real estate. Discuss what other types of property can be subject to the property tax. Discuss also the problems, if any, in distinguishing between these types of property.
3. For five of your neighboring states, identify all of the different types of property that are subject to taxes in those states.
4. What are three main methods of valuing property for property tax purposes?
5. What is the constitutional significance of the equality and uniformity clause found in state constitutions?
6. Research the state constitutions of your five neighboring states and find the exact language of their equality and uniformity clauses. Discuss how each state's clause differs from the others and what the implications of those differences are.
7. Why is it important to distinguish between a tax and a fee? What characteristics are associated with these two levies?
8. Why is it important to distinguish between a property tax and an excise tax? What characteristics are associated with these two levies?

PROBLEMS

Problem 1

For your state, list realty that is exempt from property tax, e.g., realty owned by a church.

Problem 2

For your state, list if inventory is subject to property tax, and if so, the valuation method used and assessment date.

Problem 3

Assume that an office building typically yields net income of $1.5 million per year. The county has assessed the building at $20 million, based on the price of comparable buildings sold in the area. Assuming a discount rate of 10%, what alternative value might you assert for property tax purposes?

Problem 4

Your client is in the process of building a new factory. What sort of detail would you suggest the client keep on its costs?

Problem 5

Your client, who owns several factories, has for years paid the property tax assessed without question. What sort of information might you request from the client in an attempt to reduce the client's property taxes?

ENDNOTES

121. Total local revenues here means all revenues of local governments other than intergovernmental transfers from the state or Federal government. Source for these statistics is the U.S. Bureau of the Census, various series, available on the World Wide Web at http://www.census.gov/govs/qtax.
122. Assessors are local valuing officials; some appointed, some elected. The exception to local Assessors is in Maryland, where Assessors work for the state. An Assessor's job is to discover, list, and value each taxable property in their jurisdiction, using the value level established by law.
123. The remaining two states are California and Indiana. California uses a market value approach, unless the property was acquired by the current owner prior to the passage of Proposition in June 1979. In Indiana, the law since 1986 says that "true tax value" is not "fair market value."
124. Exceptions are Delaware, Hawaii, Illinois, Iowa, Minnesota, New Hampshire, New Jersey, New York, North Dakota, Pennsylvania, and South Dakota.
125. Leasehold improvements are sometimes classed as real estate; see later discussion under real property.
126. *Wetzel County Solid Waste Auth. v. West Virginia Div. of Natural Resources*, 195 W. Va. 1, 462 S.E.2d 349 (1995).
127. *City of Fairmont v. Pitrolo Pontiac-Cadillac Co.*, 172 W. Va. 505, 308 S.E.2d 527 (1983), *cert. denied*, 466 U.S. 958, 104 S. Ct. 2169 (1984).
128. As an aside, the term "person" has been held to include certain legal entities, such as corporations, but not, as yet, nonhuman life forms (in particular, trees).
129. 410 U.S. 356, 93 S. Ct. 1001 (1973).
130. *Nordlinger v. Lynch, sub nom Nordlinger v. Hahn*, 505 U.S. 1, 112 S. Ct. 2326 (1992).

 Web Added Value™

Free value-added materials available from the
Download Resource Center at www.jrosspub.com.

6

UNEMPLOYMENT TAXES

INTRODUCTION

Employment taxes are one type of payroll tax that can be important in state and local tax planning. Wage withholding is the largest. The major employment taxes paid by the employer at the Federal level are Social Security taxes. These come in two parts, one that finances old age and disability benefits at 6.2% up to a maximum indexed by inflation (for 2002, $84,500) and the other that finances Medicare at 1.45% of compensation. In addition to these taxes, employers are subject to a Federal unemployment tax (also called FUTA) of 6.2% on the first $7,000 of compensation paid to an employee.

BACKGROUND ON UNEMPLOYMENT TAXES

Unemployment taxes are used to fund unemployment insurance. Unemployment insurance is a Federal and state program established to provide unemployment benefits to qualifying employees when employment is terminated. State unemployment benefits are governed under both Federal and state law. Unemployment insurance is funded almost entirely by direct taxes levied on employers.

Under FUTA, the Federal government has provided some uniformity for the various state unemployment laws. However, state unemployment programs still are administered under state law. State law prescribes the tax structure, qualifications, limitations, and benefit requirements. While this module describes the general concepts under unemployment tax law, it is very important to review the individual state tax laws to determine each state's applicable rules. Even seemingly minor differences can be important.

Unemployment tax rates are applied to a wide base, which varies by state. The rates also vary by employer. The state wage base cannot be less than the Federal specified wage base of $7,000 per employee. State unemployment rate bases range between $7,000 and $25,800. The state unemployment rates are determined through unemployment rating systems and can be as high as 11% and as low as 0%. New employers are subject to tax at a "new employer" rate. Other employers' rates are based on "unemployment experience." There are four methods used to calculate tax rates: reserve ratio, benefit ratio, benefit wage ratio, and payroll decline. These methods vary by state and are beyond the scope of this text.

In general, rates increase based on unemployment benefits claimed by the company's former employees. When a terminated employee qualifies for unemployment benefits, the benefits are charged to the employer's account. The amount of benefits charged to an employer's account is used to determine the "unemployment experience," which is used to determine such employer's tax rate. States use different methods to calculate unemployment experience and rates.

PLANNING WITH UNEMPLOYMENT TAXES

Planning, typically most effective if initiated by an outside consultant such as an accountant or an attorney, can add value to a company. There are a number of planning techniques; the following have proven most effective.

Avoiding Employee Classification[131]

Employment tax savings can be obtained by having workers classified as self-employed contractors, instead of employees. There is an employer/employee relationship if there is a right to control and direct the services-performing individuals, by the firm for which the services are performed. Only the right to control, not actual control, is required. The control must extend to the outcome of the work and to the details and means by which the work is accomplished. Factors commonly referred to in testing for employee status are furnishing a place to work, furnishing tools, and right to terminate. These rules apply regardless of whether an individual also is a partner in an organization, an officer or manager, or a substitute for a person normally considered an employee. Note that corporate directors are not considered employees.

Although the firm may pay less in *direct* taxes for independent contractors, it may pay more in *implicit* taxes. To see this, suppose a person has a choice between working as an independent contractor or as an employee. Suppose as an employee he would get a salary of $60,000, plus one-half of his Social Security taxes would be paid by his employer (the employee would of course have to pay the other half himself). How much would he require to be self-employed? He would require $60,000 plus the one-half of the Social Security tax he would have to pay as self-employment tax. Whether a firm hiring him as a contractor would actually pay this amount depends on a variety of factors, including negotiating skills and the relative market power of labor versus industry.

Alternatively, certain professionals are almost always considered employees. Included are professionals who offer their services to the public: auctioneers, contractors and subcontractors, dentists, doctors, free-lance professional models, lawyers, public stenographers, veterinarians, and the like. Note that professional status like this actually works to ensure payroll taxes if the firm is in the business of providing these and other services. So, firms providing clients technical personnel such as engineers, computer programmers, and systems analysts will likely have even temporary workers classified as employees.

Employee Leasing

One way to reduce employment costs, and also transactions costs related to employment, is through employee leasing. Here, a company hires whom it wants, but leases the employees from a company that specializes in employee leasing. Here, the firm pays only (tax-deductible) leasing fees to the leasing firm, and is not responsible for employee benefits or payroll taxes. The manager should bear in mind that while leasing may be cost effective, it may not make good business sense (especially if done to an extreme) since there is potentially less control over employee availability, effort, and skill.

Operating in a New State

Any business commencing operations in a new state will be assigned a "new employer" unemployment tax rate. However, if a company maintains a nominal number of employees in the new jurisdiction for an initial period of time before commencing full operations, the unemployment experience and rates may be lowered. This lower rate would then apply to all employees when the corporation commences full operation in the new state.

> **Example 6.1.** Smith Corporation, based in Kansas, begins operations in Oklahoma. Normally, it would be assigned the new employer rate of 6%. If, instead of immediately starting full-scale operations, it operates a scaled-down office and has no layoffs, it may qualify for a rate below 6% (because of zero unemployment insurance claims) when it begins operations the next year.

Acquisition of Another Company

Qualification as a "successor employee" in an acquisition can have advantages. First, a successor may inherit the predecessor's favorable unemployment experience. Second, qualifying as a "successor employer" in an acquisition or merger, the successor may be able to transfer the predecessor's wage base limitations.

Alternatively, not qualifying as a successor employer in limited circumstances may be advisable. That is, it may be best to avoid a predecessor's experience rating if it is unfavorable.

> **Example 6.2.** Jonesco, located in State A, purchases the stock of Barnesco, located in State B. Barnesco has been under financial stress, and due to numerous layoffs has an unemployment tax rate of 11%. Jonesco will probably want to apply for new employer status, which would have a much lower rate.

Qualifying for a successor employer status also means that the successor becomes liable for contributions and unemployment taxes owed (but not paid) by a predecessor. Through negotiation and proper review, the successor can ensure that the predecessor pays for this obligation. Qualifying for successor employer status usually requires that proper notification and other conditions are met.

Business Restructuring

One method of restructuring is downsizing. Downsizing is an employer's reduction in workforce. Such reductions can have a significant effect on unemployment experience and rates. Proper planning can reduce or eliminate the related tax costs. One effective strategy is to add entities by way of a spin-off or other divisive reorganization. A business entity may spin off a segment of the business with a *favorable unemployment experience prior to downsizing*. The corporation created by the spin-off will usually maintain its favorable unemployment experience. This favorable tax rate for the new corporation may lead to savings since it will be absolved from any increase in rate on the existing corporation.

Additionally, the spin-off of a segment of the business with projected *favorable experience* may also lead to savings because the existing corporation could likely be isolated from the negative impact of downsizing in the newly formed spin-off corporation. In addition, the spin-off company may be able to achieve savings through the use of a new employer rate.

Finally, a spin-off that isolates the segment of the business that is *to be eliminated* may lead to savings to the extent that unemployment benefits are charged to the new corporation and do not affect the rate for the existing corporation in future years.

Of course, all other tax and nontax aspects should be examined before a restructuring.

> **Example 6.3.** Davisco is planning on downsizing one of its unproductive product lines. Prior to the downsizing, it spins off the unprofitable product line to a newly created subsidiary, Unemco. After the spin-off, it downsizes the workforce in Unemco. After the layoffs, the unemployment rate (experience rating) increases for Unemco, but not for Davisco.

> **Example 6.4.** Assume the same facts as in Example 6.3, except that 1 year following the spin-off, Unemco is liquidated due to low profitability. The layoff of all employees will have no effect on the unemployment experience rating of Davisco.

Selling Off Part of the Business

A favorable unemployment experience rating is an asset and should be considered when valuing a division or subsidiary for sale. In some cases, the selling corporation may wish to retain the favorable rating when it sells a segment of business. Also, a reduction in workforce by a successor may lead to a higher unemployment tax rate for the predecessor.

> **Example 6.5.** Guptaco has a subsidiary, S_1, which it would like to sell. S_1 has had very low employee turnover, and has a very low unemployment tax rate. Rather than sell the entire company, Guptaco sells all of S_1's assets and retains S_1 as a corporate shell.

DISCUSSION QUESTIONS

1. How is an employer's unemployment tax rate determined?
2. What methods can be used to reduce a client's unemployment tax rate?
3. What is the lowest rate in your state? The highest?
4. What industries typically have the higher rates, and which the lower?
5. What is the likely impact of e-commerce on unemployment taxes?

PROBLEMS

"*Dog Delight* must go" declared Mary Gold, Chief Executive Officer (and majority shareholder) of publicly traded PET Publications, at the quarterly Board of Directors meeting last night. PPI is the industry-leading publisher of electronic magazines for pet owners, and you were at the meeting to brief the board members on sales trends.

"Our shareholders expect a 20% return on sales. All of our titles — *Bird World, Feline Fancy*, and *Reptile World* — clear the 20% hurdle. But *Dog Delight* only makes 10%. Sure, it generates $2 million in NOLs per year, which partly offsets the $20 million of taxable income from the rest of the organization. I think we should sell it to Animal Publications."

Animal Publications is your major rival, comparable in sales and assets ($30 million and $150 million, respectively) but consisting of twenty smaller publications that did not have the brand recognition of PPI's four publications. Data on public 10K reports indicate that the rival was paying taxes at a 34% rate.

As the firm's tax advisor, you are asked for your opinion. First, you point out to the board that it should consider that:

- *Feline Fancy* was the "flagship" publication with a circulation double any of the other three magazines.
- Advertising revenues have declined significantly over the last 3 years.
- If the magazine is sold, it will sell for about a $20 million profit.

Next, you outline the Federal income tax implications of the various ways the transaction could be structured. One of the board members then asks about the impact on payroll. After discussing the direct impact, you are asked to prepare an outline, not to exceed three double-spaced pages, about how payroll taxes can be minimized.

ENDNOTE

131. Karayan, Swenson, and Neff, *Strategic Corporate Tax Planning* (Wiley: 2002) contains an extensive analysis of tax planning to reduce Federal taxes on employee compensation.

Free value-added materials available from the
Download Resource Center at www.jrosspub.com.

PART III:
SELECT APPLICATIONS

7

MERGERS, ACQUISITIONS, AND RESTRUCTURING

INTRODUCTION

To evaluate the state and local income tax consequences of a transaction or effectively recommend alternative transaction structures to taxpayers involved in mergers and acquisition (M&A) activities, business decision makers must understand the business and legal constraints on the transaction structure of the multistate operations of the entities involved. They also must understand the Federal income tax treatment of the transaction. This is important for entrepreneurs and managers, but vital for outside accountants, attorneys, and management consultants.

Although consultants typically focus on the Federal tax consequences of M&A transactions, state and local taxes also are very important. One of the primary reasons for this is that managers and other people inside business organizations rarely have more than a rudimentary knowledge of taxation in jurisdictions other than the one in which they work.

GENERAL STATE INCOME TAX ISSUES RELATED TO M&A

Before discussing the specific state income tax treatments of common M&A, it is best to make sure that there is a firm understanding of the following general state income tax issues: state tax conformity or nonconformity with Federal tax treatment, nexus changes, filing status changes, apportionment/allocation changes, and compliance issues.

Conformity with Federal Tax Law

As discussed previously, states often deviate from Federal income tax treatment. There can be a wide variety in their approach from state to state. It thus is important to carefully analyze any M&A transaction to identify the appropriate state tax treatment.

Nexus Changes

Organizational changes can affect the amount and type of contact a company or group of companies has with a state.

Filing Status Changes

The insertion of a new member into a vertical corporate chain may fill a gap, creating a unitary business where none existed before. This change could require the group to file on a combined or unitary basis in states where separate reporting had been appropriate. Conversely, in some instances, the disposition of an existing member of a unitary business could break a combined group and require separate returns.

Apportionment/Allocation Changes

When a corporation acquires the assets of an on-going business, the target's property, payroll, and sales must be taken into account in computing the buyer's apportionment formulas.

Compliance Issues

Common transaction compliance issues include short period filings and due dates, additional registrations or withdrawals, and obtaining corporate clearance certificates.

> **Example 7.1.** Smithco is a calendar year–end Illinois company with operations in Iowa. On June 30, 2003, it buys Jonesco, an Arkansas corporation. Jonesco has all of its operations in Arkansas, except for a warehouse in Tennessee. Smithco integrates its operations and management with Jonesco. After the acquisition, Smithco has (through unitary taxation rules in Illinois) nexus in Illinois, Iowa, Arkansas, and Tennessee. A combined return is required in Illinois, and separate returns in Iowa, Arkansas, and Tennessee. Short period returns (such as that covering

January 1 to June 30) are required for Arkansas and Tennessee. Although Smithco's apportioned business income will include Illinois in 2002, its apportioned (taxable) Illinois income may or may not increase, since the apportionment factors will change as well.

Note that in the above example, the consultant may wish to assert the so-called "rebuttable presumption." That is, it can be argued that it takes at least a year for operations to be integrated. With this argument, Jonesco would not be included in Smithco's combined return for at least a year. It would instead file separate returns.

Overview

The four most common M&A transactions are taxable stock purchases/sales, taxable asset purchases/sales, tax-free reorganizations, and complete liquidations. The remainder of the chapter summarizes the Federal tax rules, and contrasts these with the state tax issues, associated with each of these four types of transactions, in that order. For each of the four types of transactions, there first is review of a basic transaction scenario, and then discussion of the tax treatment of both the seller and buyer. Following this, there are discussions of complete liquidations, other issues related to M&A, and tax planning opportunities.

TAXABLE STOCK ACQUISITIONS

The Transaction

In this example of a taxable stock acquisition, the stock of subsidiary T is sold by seller (S) company to the purchaser (P) in exchange for cash.

$$S \longrightarrow T\ stock \longrightarrow P$$
$$\longleftarrow \quad cash \quad \longrightarrow$$

Tax Treatment of Seller

Federal Treatment

Sales of securities like common stock and bonds are taxable like sales of any other asset, unless they fall under a specific exclusion. Gain or loss results from the difference between the adjusted basis in the stock and the amount realized. The gain or loss is usually capital in character.

Stock Basis — Generally

The seller's adjusted basis in the stock is ordinarily cost plus contributions to capital less return of capital distributions.

Stock Basis — Consolidated Return Regulations

The basis of the stock becomes more difficult to define when the parent and the subsidiary file a consolidated Federal return. Under Treas. Reg. 1.1502-532, the parent's tax basis in subsidiary stock is cost adjusted by the subsidiary's taxable income or loss, dividends, and other items. Since the parent is being taxed on or obtains a benefit due to the income, loss, or distributions of the subsidiary through the use of a consolidated return, its basis in the stock of the subsidiary should be adjusted to reflect this detriment or benefit.

Intercompany Gains

A sale of subsidiary stock outside the group is a "triggering event" with respect to deferred intercompany transactions. As such, any deferred intercompany gain or loss associated with that subsidiary will be recognized.

State Treatment of Seller

For state purposes, the seller also will recognize gain or loss on the sale of stock resulting from the difference between proceeds from the sale and the adjusted basis in the stock. State and Federal gains or losses will usually be equal unless the parent and target filed a consolidated Federal return. In such cases, the consultant must determine whether the state follows the Federal investment adjustment rules (either specifically or by implication).

States That Do Not Follow Federal Consolidated Rules

Most states do not follow the Federal consolidated investment adjustment rules. In these states, the seller's adjusted basis would be determined under Federal nonconsolidated tax principles.

Example 7.2. Assume that S and T were incorporated January 1 of 1999. S contributed a negligible amount of capital to T on incorporation. In 1999, S and T filed a Federal consolidated tax return. S files an income tax return in a state that does not permit consolidated reporting and does not follow the Federal consolidated return regulations. S's 1999 taxable income is $0; T's 1999 taxable income is $80. On January 1,

2000, S sells T to P for $200. S's Federal and state gains on the sale are $120 and ($200), respectively.

An analogous situation exists if S and T file combined state income tax returns but separate Federal returns. The states do not permit a parent corporation to adjust its state tax basis in the stock of its subsidiary for subsidiary income or loss taxed in the state combined return.

> **Example 7.3.** Assume the same facts as the example above but S and T file separate Federal returns and a combined state income tax return. For Federal tax purposes, S's stock gain is $200 (since S and T did not file a consolidated Federal income tax return). For state tax purposes, S's tax gain is $200. In essence, the S and T combined group has paid state income tax twice on the same $80 of T earnings (once in the combined state income tax return and once on the sale of stock).

Planning

The consultant may wish to consider the following two planning strategies to minimize the risk of double taxation. One is to recognize the stock gain in a nonunitary member that is in a low-rate or no-tax state. This is done to break the unitary relationship. The following example illustrates this method.

> **Example 7.4.** Prior to the sale in Example 7.3, S establishes a holding company, T_1, which is located in Nevada. T_1 owns the stock of T, and S then sells the sock of T_1 to P. The gain is tax free insofar as Nevada has no income tax.

Another approach is to have T dividend its earnings to S followed by a capital contribution of the earnings back to T. Absent a challenge based on the "business purpose" or "substance over form" doctrines, the capital contribution would increase S's stock basis in T while the dividend should be nontaxable to S. To accomplish the desired result, it should be confirmed that the state allows a full or partial dividends received deduction. It also should be confirmed that the state will not disallow a portion of S's expenses as being allocable to exempt dividend income. If these issues arise on audit, or in another setting (such as in tax footnote disclosure in SEC filings), a firm should urge that state to use its discretionary powers to prevent an unjust result. This latter approach often is most successfully pursued by a firm's outside attorney or accountant, rather than by in-house tax or legal staff.

Characterization of Gain or Loss

The seller must also determine whether the gain on the stock sale is business or nonbusiness income. The U.S. Supreme Court held in *Allied-Signal, Inc. v. Director, Division of Taxation*, 504 65 868 112 S. Ct. 2251 (1992), that income from the sale of subsidiary stock could be business income if the investment in subsidiary stock served an "operational" rather than an "investment" function.

> **Example 7.5.** Assuming that T is a manufacturing subsidiary, gain on the sale is business income. As such, the gain is subject to apportionment by S. If, instead, T is a finance subsidiary whose sole function is to invest S's working capital, the gain is nonbusiness and is allocated to one state.

Tax Treatment of Buyer

Federal Treatment of Buyer

In a taxable stock acquisition, the purchased corporation remains in existence and therefore maintains its historical assets, liabilities, and tax attributes. The utilization of the purchased corporation's attributes may be limited, however, under various provisions of the Internal Revenue Code (IRC) (such as IRC §269, §382, §383, or §384). Special consolidated return antiabuse rules, known as separate return limitation years (SRLYs) and consolidated return change of ownership (CRCO), also may limit the use of an acquired NOL.

The purchased corporation's historical "inside" (asset) basis is carried over unless a §338 election is made (see below). Section 382 limits the annual utilization of NOLs following a greater than 50% change in ownership of a 5% or greater shareholder to the value of the corporation times the long-term tax-exempt rate at the date of acquisition.

State Treatment of Buyer: Basis

For state income tax purposes, the target's "inside" state tax of assets and liabilities also remains the same. Regarding other issues, the answers may not be so clear-cut.

State Tax Attributes

The determination of whether the acquired corporation's state NOLs and other tax attributes survive the stock acquisition varies by state. In the states that have adopted the Federal NOL provisions by statute (e.g., those set forth under IRC §172 and §382) or by reference to Federal taxable income (found on Line 30 of

Form 1120), it may be possible to carry over the entire NOL without limitation. For states that have their own state NOL statutes, an analysis should be conducted to ensure the NOL remains in existence following an ownership change. Note that, similar to the Federal, there are some states that will disallow the carryover of the NOL if the principal purpose of the acquisition was to obtain the NOL (e.g., New Jersey).

Planning

When acquiring another firm, it is important to consider whether the state (of the acquired corporation) requires allocation of acquisition year NOLs. Most states require such allocation. The states that do not are Delaware, Maine, Maryland, Massachusetts, New Jersey, New Mexico, New York, Rhode Island, and Virginia.

Perhaps more important is the carryover of state tax credits (many of these credits are discussed in the following chapter). For example, suppose T is a California firm that has unused manufacturers incentive credits (MICs). The availability of these credits to P effectively lowers P's purchase price.

Interest Deduction

Most states provide that in order for interest to be deductible it must be *bona fide* debt (and not a substitute for equity). Further, some states, which do not tax dividends or interest received from subsidiaries, do not permit a purchasing corporation to deduct interest on debt incurred to purchase subsidiary stock under the theory that it, in effect, is an expense incurred to generate tax-exempt income. For example, New York disallows interest expense directly debt attributed to subsidiary capital whether or not a dividend is paid.

Filing Status Changes

To determine whether to file a group return with the new subsidiary, the purchaser will have to consider whether the group is conducting a unitary business, whether a combined/unitary filing is optional or mandatory in the states in which the corporations do business, and whether a combined/unitary filing is beneficial to the group on a going-forward basis. Ideally, the tax consequences of group reporting should be projected over a number of years since it will be difficult to change filing methods in the future. With respect to instant unity, either the taxpayer or the state may argue that creating a unitary business requires time to integrate the operations of the corporations; refer back to Example 7.1.

Section 338 Elections — Federal Rules

There are two basic §338 elections: §338(g) and §338(h)(10). To illustrate the effects of both elections, refer back to the basic stock transaction where S sells stock of T to P in a taxable stock sale.

IRC §338(g) Election

If we assume P makes a §338(g) election, T will be treated as if it sold its assets at fair market value in a taxable asset sale to "new" T. The transaction will be reported on a separate 1-day return for T. The result is that P now owns T and T's assets have a tax basis equal to fair market value.

From the seller's perspective, the transaction is treated as a taxable stock sale on which the seller recognizes gain or loss by reference to the amount received less the seller's basis in the stock sold. In addition, the target is treated as having sold all its assets to a "new target" at fair market value in a taxable transaction. The gain or loss on this transaction is reported on a separate 1-day return of the target. Note that, unless the target has NOLs or credits that can shelter the Federal tax reflected on the 1-day return, the purchaser would never make a §338(g) election.

The "new target" is treated as purchasing all of the assets as of the beginning of the day after the acquisition date. Therefore, the "new target" does not inherit any tax attributes of the selling corporation. Section 338(g) elections are made by the purchaser only and do not affect the seller; the purchaser must, within a 12-month period, purchase 80% or more of the stock of an unrelated target in a taxable transaction. Section 338(g) elections are seldom made because the present value of the step-up in "inside" asset basis does not exceed its cost: current recognition of the step-up as income.

IRC §338(h)(10) Election

To illustrate the effects of a §338(h)(10) election, start again with the basic stock transaction outlined above. Under §338(h)(10), this stock sale/purchase is ignored for tax purposes; however, it is respected for corporate law and other legal purposes. Under the §338(h)(10) election, the target is deemed to have sold its assets at fair market value to a new subsidiary of the purchaser. The shell of the target is then deemed to be liquidated (tax free) into the seller. As a result, the seller retains the target's tax attributes, and the new subsidiary owns assets with a basis equal to fair market value.

The effects of a §338(h)(10) election are the following: the target is treated as having sold all its assets to "new target" (while still a member of the selling group) and then liquidating into the seller in a tax-free §332 liquidation; the tax liability for the inside asset step-up is the sole responsibility of the selling group; and the selling group is not treated as having sold target stock in a taxable stock sale.

IRC §338(h)(10) Election Issues

The acquirer must purchase, within a 12-month period, 80% or more of the stock of an unrelated target, provided target was, prior to the purchase, a member of an affiliated group or an S corporation.

Purchase Price Allocation

If a §338(g) or §338(h)(10) election is made, the purchase price is allocated among the target's assets based on their relative fair market values. Any amount of the purchase price that exceeds the fair market value of the assets is allocated to goodwill. This can be advantageous, because intangible assets like goodwill that are obtained in an acquisition typically can be amortized over 15 years for Federal income tax purposes.

State Tax Issues Related to §338 Elections

Section 338 (g) Elections

Most states honor §338(g) elections because the consequences of the election can be readily isolated at the target level.

Section 338(h)(10) Elections

State treatment of a §338(h)(10) election is far less certain. Few states have statutes or regulations that address §338(h)(10) transactions. The filing status of the selling parent and the target (i.e., separate, unitary, or consolidated) often plays a significant role in the determination of whether §338(h)(10) election will be respected in a state.

Summary of State Treatments

States treat §338(h)(10) elections in four different ways:

1. Recognize the §338(h)(10) election regardless of the selling parent (or S corporation shareholder) and target's filing status in that state
2. Recognize the §338(h)(10) election only if the seller and target file combined or consolidated on the state

3. Recognize the §338(h)(10) election but allocate target's deemed asset sale gain based on target's filing status
4. Recognize the §338(h)(10) election unless the parties specifically opt out of the election at the state level (e.g., Wisconsin)[132]

In states that do not permit consolidated or combined return filings, it may be possible to get a ruling that the Federal §338(h)(10) election nevertheless is allowed. Outside consultants typically should be used to accomplish this. The general planning strategy should be to limit the §338(h)(10) election to those situations where all members of the selling group file combined or consolidated state income tax returns, but disregard the underlying §338(g) election if the §338(h)(10) election is not recognized.

Section 338(h)(10) Election Triggers a Gain

Because the §338(h)(10) election triggers a gain to the seller, the seller may either request a higher selling price or use planning to reduce the gain. One planning technique is described in the following example.

> **Example 7.6.** Assume T's basis in its assets is $30. Suppose that 1 year prior to the acquisition, T acquires T_1, which generates annual tax NOLs of $70. In the sale year, the §338(h)(10) election triggers $100 − $30 = $70 gain to T, but the gain is entirely offset by the T_1 NOL. And T's assets are stepped up to $100, which benefits P.

Other State Tax Issues

The purchase price allocation can significantly affect state apportionment, the amount and type of income (business or nonbusiness income) to the target, and future Federal and state tax depreciation and amortization. This most commonly happens now due to lack of state conformity with IRC §197, which allows intangibles acquired by purchase to be amortized, albeit only straight line and over 15 years.

In some states, the deemed asset sale will be treated as an asset sale subject to state sales tax and/or state bulk sale notification requirements as discussed above.

TAXABLE ASSET ACQUISITIONS

The Transaction

In the example of a taxable asset acquisition, seller T Corporation sells its assets to purchaser P for cash in a fully taxable transaction.

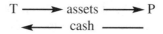

$$T \longrightarrow \text{assets} \longrightarrow P$$
$$\longleftarrow \text{cash} \longrightarrow$$

Treatment of Seller

Federal Treatment

The seller will recognize gain or loss on the sale of assets. The character of the gain or loss is determined by reference to the type of asset in the hands of the seller. The amount of gain or loss is determined on an asset-by-asset basis.

The amount realized is determined based on a purchase price allocation under IRC §1060(a). State nonconformity in this area is quite rare. Section 1060 requires the purchase price to be allocated among the different asset classes according to the fair market value of the assets in each class. Tax authorities rarely challenge contractual allocations based on bona fide negotiations. This is because tax advantages to the seller usually result in tax disadvantages to the buyer.

Like U.S. generally accepted accounting principles (GAAP), the purchase price is allocated to identifiable assets in proportion to their relative fair market value. Purchase price is first allocated to cash, and at its face amount. Allocation to any particular asset cannot exceed its respective fair market value. If the purchase price exceeds the total fair market value of all of the identifiable assets, the excess is allocated to goodwill. Unlike U.S. GAAP, goodwill typically is amortizable.

State Treatment

The state gain or loss on the sale of assets is often the same as the Federal gain or loss. Many states do not have special depreciation rules or they simply incorporate, by statute or by default, the Federal gain or loss into the state income tax base.

Some states do have depreciation rules that are different from the Federal rules. In these states, the state gain or loss will be different from the Federal because the state adjusted tax basis of the asset will be different from the Federal adjusted tax asset basis (examples include North Carolina and Wisconsin).

In addition, state tax adjusted asset basis can differ from Federal tax adjusted asset basis as a result of the following:

1. Sales tax on the purchase of fixed assets that was deducted for state income tax purposes but capitalized for Federal tax purposes (e.g., Pennsylvania)
2. Special state rules concerning the effect of investment tax credits on asset basis; inconsistent prior Federal and state §338 elections (discussed above)
3. Inconsistent prior Federal and state treatment of a reorganization (e.g., taxable versus tax free)

4. Inconsistent Federal and state tax treatment of asset basis reduction for cancellation of indebtedness income (COD)
5. Time lags in adopting Federal depreciation and amortization tax rules (e.g., California)
6. State incentives that reduce or increase property basis for state income tax purposes

Similar to a taxable stock sale, the seller must determine whether the gain or loss on the sale of assets is apportionable business income or allocable non-business income. Classifying the gain is important because it will serve as a basis for determining how to source the income from the sale to the specific states. When making this distinction, it is important to remember two significant distinctions between a stock and an asset sale:

1. The gain or loss on the sale of assets is recognized in the corporation that sold the assets, while a gain or loss on the sale of stock is recognized in the corporation that owned the stock.
2. The sale of assets usually consists of a "mixed bag" of assets (tangible and intangible), while the sale of stock is the sale of an intangible asset.

Gains or losses that are treated as business income are apportioned under the normal apportionment methods. Ordinarily, receipts from asset sales are included in the sales factor, although some states provide the following exceptions: substantial gross receipts from an incidental or occasional sale of a fixed asset used in the regular course of the taxpayer's trade or business may be excluded from the sales factor.

Note that insubstantial gross receipts from incidental or occasional transactions may be included or excluded at the taxpayer's discretion. Sales of intangible property are excluded from the sales factor if the receipts cannot "readily be attributed" to any particular income-producing activity of the taxpayer.

Gains and losses that are nonbusiness income are allocated based on the nature of the property. Gains and losses from the sale of real or tangible personal property are ordinarily allocated to the state in which the property is located. Gains and losses from the sale of intangible property are ordinarily allocated to the taxpayer's commercial domicile.

Example 7.7. Assume that S sells its assets for $270 in total, with the following tax bases and fair market value: inventory $100 and ($120), machinery $80 and ($50), and raw land held for investment $200 ($100). The $100 gain on land is nonbusiness, and is apportioned to the state in which it is located. The net loss of $30 on the other assets is business, and is subject to apportionment by S.

Example 7.8. Assume the same facts as in Example 7.7, except that the fair market values of the three assets have ranges as follows: inventory, $100–$140; machinery, $40–$60; and land, $80–$120. If the inventory and machinery are located in California and the land in Nevada, it makes sense to allocate $120 to the land and the remaining $150 sales price to the other two assets.

Regarding asset acquisitions accomplished through a limited partnership or other pass-through entity, the states are very diverse in their laws concerning how the apportionment factors of the pass-through entity flow through to the corporate owner.

Example 7.9. In Texas, a limited partnership's factors do not flow through to the corporate limited partner if the corporate limited partner does not have any nexus with Texas other than the partnership interest.

Treatment of Buyer

Federal Treatment

For Federal purposes, the buyer will be mainly concerned with the purchase price allocation. The purchase price allocation is often a significant point of contention between the buyer and the seller because of their distinct tax situations. It is generally to the buyer's advantage to maximize the allocations to assets with short depreciable tax lives (e.g., inventory, machinery, and equipment) and minimize allocations to long-lived assets (§197 assets and buildings). Because it is nondepreciable, buyers almost always find it best to minimize the allocation to nondepreciable assets like land and fine art.

On the other hand, it generally is to the seller's advantage to maximize the allocations to nondepreciable assets like land, nonreacapturable assets like goodwill, and limited recaptureable assets like realty. As alluded to above, §197 provides that, for all applicable asset acquisitions occurring after August 10, 1993, most, but not all, intangible assets (such as goodwill, going concern value, noncompetitive agreements, franchises, trademarks, trade names, and other customer/supplier or workforce-related intangibles) are amortizable over a 15-year period regardless of economic life.

State Treatment

For state tax purposes, the buyer is interested in the purchase price allocation and successor liability. For state income tax purposes, the states will generally follow the purchase price allocation made at the Federal level. Some states do not use Federal depreciation rules (generally using longer-lived or nonacceler-ated methods). In these states, the buyer should seek to minimize purchase price allocated to assets with long depreciable state income tax lives or required nonaccelerated state depreciation methods. The purchase price allocation can affect the property apportionment factor. For example, allocating more purchase price to property located in a low (or no) income tax rate state may decrease the corporation's apportionment percentage in high tax rate states.

A number of states have not adopted §197 (e.g., Michigan, Oregon, Texas, and Minnesota). Particularly for state sales tax purposes, the state's acceptance of the purchase price allocation is a facts and circumstances evaluation of whether the purchase price allocation was arrived at by arms-length negotiation. Arms-length negotiation is best shown by the taxpayer by substantiating non-sales tax effects of the purchase price, such as the conflicting interests of the buyer and seller in the purchase price allocation for Federal and state income tax areas and for state property taxes.

Successor Liability

Almost all states impose some type of successor liability on the purchaser of business assets, unless the state receives prior notification of the sale and issues a tax clearance certificate to the seller. Under these rules, the buyer withholds amounts from the purchase price to satisfy the seller's unpaid taxes. Failure to file the required documentation and withhold subjects the buyer to liability for the seller's unpaid states taxes. The consultant should ensure that the purchase agreement requires the seller to obtain state tax clearance certificates prior to closing. This is frequently waived by the parties because the notification often triggers a sales tax audit. Indemnification is sometimes a solution. Alternatively, the purchaser should obtain full indemnification from the seller.

> **Example 7.10.** P purchases the assets of T for $10 million. Unknown to P, T owes back property taxes of $15 million. Unless P obtains indem-nification, the value of T's assets is *negative* $5 million.

In addition to issuing tax clearance certificates to sellers, some states require the purchaser in an asset acquisition to notify the state of the transaction prior to the closing date. Absent the pretransfer notice, the purchaser may be held liable for the seller's pre-existing liabilities.

Nexus

The effect of the asset transaction on the purchaser's nexus position must be reviewed to determine what additional filing and registration requirements exist.

In addition to the additional filings due directly to the assets acquired, the entire purchasing group could experience increased filing requirements if it is conducting a unitary business or is filing in consolidated, combined return states.

> **Example 7.11.** P, which operates exclusively in East Coast states that use separate accounting, purchases a warehouse in Utah. This establishes nexus in Utah and, because Utah is a combined reporting/unitary state, a Utah tax return is required that includes all of P's operations that are part of the unitary business (related to the warehouse).

The purchaser must also adjust its apportionment percentages in states where it, or the group, is already doing business.

Planning

If the purchaser's apportionment percentages will be adversely affected, it may be preferable to structure the transaction as a taxable stock purchase with a §338 election. This structure would not affect the purchaser's state tax apportionment percentages in states that do not follow §338(g) or §338(h)(10) elections or respect the state election at the taxpayer's option (such as in California or Wisconsin). Similarly, a firm may want to consider an asset purchase into a special purpose entity (e.g., acquiring Texas assets into a Texas limited partnership).

Filing Status Changes

Filing status changes will depend partly on the form of the acquisition and the type of assets purchased. The consultant must investigate whether the acquisition affects filing, for example, by creating a unitary business where one previously did not exist.

NOLs and Tax Credits

In taxable asset acquisitions, the seller's NOLs do not become available to the purchaser. This is because the selling corporation remains in existence (and thus IRC §381 does not apply). However, in some cases, credits and incentives do follow the assets in a taxable purchase.[133]

TAX-FREE REORGANIZATIONS

Introduction

This section discusses the state tax issues associated with Federal reorganization provisions and other state tax issues associated with M&A activity in general.

The Federal tax reorganization provisions are very complex and should be thoroughly reviewed during each transaction. The following discussion is at a very general level, and is meant to highlight the state versus Federal treatment of reorganization transactions.

Federal Tax Treatment = State Tax Treatment (The General Rule)

The Federal reorganization provisions are contained in §368. They generally are referred to by their subparagraph letter (that is, mergers are called "A" reorganizations). The four most common acquisitive reorganization forms are

1. IRC §368(a)(1)(A): statutory mergers or consolidations
2. IRC §368(a)(1)(B): stock for voting stock reorganizations
3. IRC §368(a)(1)(C): "substantially all" assets acquired for voting stock reorganizations
4. IRC §368(a)(1)(F): mere changes in identity, form, or place of organization

The requirements for tax-free status vary depending on the form of the transaction. In general, tax-free status cannot be obtained unless a substantial part of the consideration is stock of the acquiring corporation or its parent.

Section 368 is buttressed by a number of judicial doctrines. These contain requirements for tax-free treatment that may not be spelled out in statutory law. The key judicial doctrines are

1. Continuity of interest
2. Continuity of business enterprise
3. The step transaction doctrine
4. The business purpose requirement
5. The substance over form doctrine

The step transaction doctrine and the substance over form doctrine are less well developed at the state level than at the Federal. This particularly is the case for sales tax purposes. Accordingly, there are ways to use the Federal step transaction doctrine to obtain a better sales tax result on a reorganization.

Acquisition Year NOLs

IRC §381 provides for the carryover of certain tax attributes to the acquirer in certain asset acquisitions. The target's tax attributes carried over under §381 to the acquirer include NOLs, earnings and profits, capital loss carryovers, methods of accounting, depreciation methods, credits, and other items. Transactions to which §381 applies are A, C, D (divisive reorganizations), F, and G (bankruptcy) reorganizations under §368(a)(1). It also applies to complete liquidations under §332 (parent-subsidiary liquidations). Section 381 does not apply to B reorganizations under §368(a)(1).

Section 381(c)(1)(B) limits the acquirer's utilization of the target's premerger NOL for the acquisition year. The NOL that can be used is limited to the taxable income earned by the acquirer after the transaction. In states that do not follow §381, this limitation may not apply provided the state does not have any other limitations on the utilization of an acquired target's NOL in the year of the transaction.

Similarly, there are limits on the ability of a regular (i.e., a "C") corporation to carry back or carry forward an NOL. Under IRC §172(h), a loss carryback is limited if there is a "Corporate Equity Reduction Transaction" (called a "CERT"). A CERT occurs if $1 million or more of interest expense is incurred in a "major stock acquisition" of another corporation (or an "excess distribution"). The limitation is the lesser of the interest expense attributable to the CERT, or the excess of interest expense over the annual average for the 3 years prior to the CERT. Similarly, under IRC §§382–384, operating and capital loss carryforwards from an acquisition can be limited to the net fair market value of the acquired company multiplied by the Federal long-term exempt interest rate.

Accumulated NOLs

Generally, §382 provides that if there is a greater than 50% ownership change of a 5% or greater shareholder, then the preownership change NOL utilization will be subject to an annual limit based on the value of the loss company times the long-term tax-exempt rate at the date of acquisition. For all reorganizations, the consultant must analyze the shareholder's ownership percentage before and after the transaction to determine if a §382 ownership change has occurred. Section 382 does not apply to a reorganization under §368(a)(1)(F).

Other NOL Provisions

In addition to §381 and §382, a number of other provisions of the code could also restrict the use of the NOLs (such as §269, §384, and the SRLY rules of Treas. Reg. §1. 1502-2).

State Tax Treatment

The primary state tax income tax issues to be addressed in a tax-free reorganization are state conformity with Federal tax-free reorganization treatment and state treatment of tax attributes. On the first issue, most states automatically adopt the Federal treatment under the general conformity provisions.

Tax Attributes — NOLs

State NOL treatment varies by state. Some states adopt §381 and §382 treatment by direct reference.[134] Other states adopt the IRC because of conformity with Federal law.[135] Many states prescribe their own limitation on the utilization of losses following a reorganization or change in ownership. Then again, some states require that in order for the losses to survive in a merger or reorganization, the loss company must have had nexus in that state in the loss year. Other states provide that the target's NOLs are extinguished if it merges into another corporation without regard to common ownership.[136] Some states have their own version of §382[137] or SRLY (e.g., Illinois).

> **Example 7.12.** P acquires T in a tax-free reorganization for $100 million. T has a $1 million NOL carryover. Assuming the applicable Federal interest rate is 10%, §381 and §382 allow the $1 million to carry over, but only $100,000 can be used each year. If the corporations are based in a state that limits the use of carryovers to 50%, only $500,000 of the NOL carries over for state tax purposes.[138]

State Credits

As alluded to previously, some states grant taxpayers various income tax credits. Most are unique to a state while others are patterned after Federal credits. In the states that do not adopt state variations of the Federal credits, a separate analysis should be done to determine whether these state tax credits carry over under the particular state's law concerning those credits. In the absence of a specific state limitation on the utilization of credits, there may be a filing position that no limitation applies to such credits. This particularly is the case where the state-allowed NOL carryovers are limited. Because reorganizations can dramatically impact the calculation of state taxable income, the utilization of available excess credits can be a material factor.

> **Example 7.13.** P acquires T in a B reorganization. Both are California corporations. T has Manufacturer's Investment Credit (MIC) carryovers of $10 million. Under California law, the credits carry over for up to 8 years unless the underlying assets are sold. Here, the credits would carry over to P. However, if instead P purchased the assets of T, the credits would not carry over.[139]

Other State Taxes

If the reorganization is stock for stock, the reorganization is not a transfer of tangible personal property. Hence, no sales or use tax should attach to such reorganizations.

COMPLETE LIQUIDATIONS

The state tax treatment of complete liquidations usually follows Federal treatment.

Federal Tax Treatment

IRC §331 Taxable Complete Liquidations

When a corporation distributes its assets to its shareholders in complete liquidation, two tax effects occur. First, the liquidating corporation is treated as if it sold its assets at fair market value to the distributee. Second, the amount received by the shareholder in complete liquidation is treated as being received in exchange for the shareholder's stock.

IRC §332 Tax-Free Complete Liquidations

An exception to the above treatment occurs if the liquidating corporation is an 80%-owned (based on both voting power and value) subsidiary. In that instance, the transaction is tax free to the liquidating corporation and the distributee under §332 and §337. The tax attributes of the liquidating corporation carry over to the shareholder under §381.

OTHER STATE TAX ISSUES RELATED TO M&A TRANSACTIONS

Introduction

In addition to evaluating the state and local *income* tax consequences of an M&A transaction, one should also consider the effects of *nonincome*-based taxes. These taxes include sales and use taxes, real property transfer/gains taxes, net worth/franchise taxes, gross receipts taxes, property taxes, and payroll taxes. The transaction costs resulting from these taxes can be significant. Proper transaction structuring and exemption utilization can significantly reduce the tax burden associated with these taxes.

Sales and Use Taxes

Whenever assets are transferred, the transaction must be evaluated to identify any sales tax issues. The following are some considerations: Which states have jurisdiction to tax the transaction? Is the transaction considered a "sale" as that term is defined in the states? What exemptions apply: resale, casual or occasional, or manufacturing? How will intangible assets be transferred? How can the transaction be restructured to minimize tax and still obtain the desired business, legal, and Federal and state income tax results? What compliance issues must be addressed?

Generally, for an M&A transaction to trigger sales/use taxes, there must be a purchase of tangible personalty. Thus, purchase of a target's stock (either as a taxable or a tax-free transaction) is not a taxable transaction. On the other hand, an asset purchase using stock (e.g., a "C" reorganization) is subject to sales/use tax.

As a general rule, even if the transaction involves the purchase of assets, the purchaser may be able to avoid sales/use taxes if the transaction qualifies under bulk sales rules, §351, or other tax-free reorganization rules. Bulk sales exemptions apply in some states if the business does not sell the assets (other than in the M&A transaction) more than once during the year.

As noted above, judicial doctrine — particularly the doctrines of substance over form and step transaction — are less developed in the sales tax area. In addition, the doctrine of continuity of interest and ownership may or may not be relevant in some states. This presents a number of sales tax planning opportunities with respect to the transaction structure.

Planning

One planning technique relates to an asset purchase. A purchase of assets will generally be taxable. However, if a triangular transaction was used (i.e., the assets were transferred to a subsidiary and then the subsidiary's stock was sold), a number of states will not recharacterize this transaction as an asset sale for sales tax purposes. For state and Federal *income* tax purposes, however, both transactions would be collapsed as a taxable asset sale under the substance over form and step transaction doctrines.

> **Example 7.14.** P (a California corporation) wishes to sell assets from one of its divisions to S. Many of the assets in the division are personalty that would be subject to sales taxes. Instead of selling the assets, P forms a wholly owned subsidiary, T, then sells the shares of stock of T to S. Under California law, the sale of the shares will not be subject to sales/use taxes.

Another planning technique relates to the fact that some states exempt "statutory mergers" from sales tax. Rather than purchasing assets, the consultant may want to put cash into a new subsidiary and then merge the new subsidiary into the target. For Federal and state income tax purposes, this will be a taxable event either way. However, the cash merger would meet the statutory merger definition in these states.

Example 7.15. P wants to purchase T. A cash purchase of the stock would cost 6% more, however, due to sales/use taxes on the underlying personalty owned by T. Instead, P forms P_1, by contributing cash and receiving P_1 stock. Next, P_1 and T merge in a statutory "A" merger. Due to state law, it is exempt from sales/use tax.

A final planning idea relates to IRC §351. If a contribution to a controlled subsidiary (§351) is tax free for sales tax purposes in a state, then a firm can contribute the assets to be sold into a subsidiary and then sell the stock of the subsidiary (instead of selling assets directly).[140]

Example 7.16. P wants to buy the assets of T, some of which consist of personalty potentially subject to sales/use taxes. In T's state, §351 transactions are not subject to sales/use taxes. Accordingly, T forms T_1, then sells T_1's stock to P.

Bulk Sales

As discussed earlier, most states require that either the buyer or seller give the state notice of a bulk sale of business assets. Although the seller remains primarily liable for any of its unpaid sales taxes outstanding at the time of the sale, failure to give proper notice or to obtain a tax clearance certificate generally makes the buyer jointly liable for certain of the seller's unpaid state taxes. An indemnification for state taxes should be obtained if there is insufficient time to notify the state and receive a tax clearance certificate prior to the closing. Because the buyer stands to lose in the absence of a tax clearance certificate, it is generally the responsibility of the buyer's state and local tax advisor to raise this point, especially since purchase agreements frequently contain a waiver of bulk sale notification requirements.

Real Property Transfer and Gains Taxes

Approximately thirty-five states, and numerous localities, impose a transfer tax on the sale, assignment, or transfer of interests in real property. When a corporate merger, acquisition, or reorganization involves the transfer of real property, these taxes can apply.

Transfer Tax Rates

Transfer tax rates are generally low (e.g., the New York State transfer tax rate is $2 for each $500 of consideration). However, the taxes could be significant if substantial consideration is given. In addition, some localities (such as New York City) also impose real estate transfer taxes. New York City's rate can be as high as 2.625% of the consideration if the consideration exceeds $500,000.

Gains Taxes

Although gains taxes are usually imposed at a higher rate (e.g., 10% of the net gain), only a few states (like Vermont) impose special gains taxes.

Transfers Subject to Tax

Real property transfer taxes can apply to two different types of transactions: direct transfers (a simple transfer of the real property itself by deed or otherwise) and indirect transfers (a transfer of an ownership interest, e.g., stock or a partnership interest, in an entity which owns an interest in real property).

Indirect Property Transfers

Certain states and localities also tax the transfer of an ownership interest (e.g., stock, partnership interest) in an entity that owns interest in real property. A transfer of a stock or partnership interest or a merger where the underlying company owns real property could trigger transfer or gains taxes. Most of the states that tax transfers of stock or partnership interests (e.g., New York, Connecticut, District of Columbia, Pennsylvania, Washington) generally require that a certain percentage interest in the entity be transferred before a tax is triggered. Some of these states also require that the entity derive a certain portion of its income from the ownership of real property before the tax applies. The consultant must review the rules of each state in which property is located to determine if a transfer or gains tax is triggered.

Exemptions

If a transaction is subject to a transfer tax, the consultant should determine the location of the real property and ascertain whether any exemptions apply. Many states will exempt the transfer of real property that occurs as part of a §351 transaction or a tax-free merger or reorganization. In addition, some states exempt transfers of real property when the ultimate beneficial owners of the real property do not change. This exemption is known as the "mere change in identity" exemption in New York. But even with the exemption, New York gains and transfer tax returns still need to be filed.

Calculating the Tax Due

If exemptions do not apply, the parties must then determine the consideration paid for the transfer to calculate tax due. In many states, consideration includes not only the amount of money paid for the transfer, but also any mortgages or other encumbrances assumed or remaining on the property at the time of sale. Few states, notably California, exclude mortgages from the definition of consideration. In these states, it may be possible to encumber the property prior to the transfer to reduce transfer taxes. In addition, parties often have to rely on appraisals of real property to determine the consideration attributable to the real property where a purchaser is acquiring both tangible and real property in a single transaction. If a bargain purchase is contemplated, however, it may be possible to allocate less than market value to the real property to reduce transfer taxes.

Leasehold Interests

Even if a corporation has less than full ownership of real property, transfer taxes could still apply. For example, a transfer of a leasehold interest in real property could be subject to tax. Most states tax leasehold interests only if they are equivalent to full ownership of property (i.e., leases of sufficiently long duration). Some states, like New York, however, may tax both the original grant of leases and the assignment of leases.

Reporting Requirements

While most states require that transfer taxes be paid at the time title to the property is recorded, some states (e.g., New York) have pretransfer filing requirements. States that impose transfer taxes on indirect transfers of real property often impose pretransfer filing requirements because these types of transfers do not result in the property being recorded. The consultant must ensure that returns are properly filed to avoid delaying the closing for the transaction. Actual recording of deeds is generally handled by a title company.

Franchise or Capital Stock Taxes

Several states impose franchise or capital stock taxes either as an alternative to or in addition to state net income taxes. These taxes are often measured by a corporation's net worth or by its authorized or outstanding shares of capital stock. Accordingly, depending on the structure of the transaction, mergers, acquisitions, and reorganizations can result in significant increases or decreases in these taxes.

Property Taxes

The consultant must also determine if the transaction causes any unexpected property tax results. For example, California reassesses real property when a change in ownership or new construction occurs. Mergers or other reorganizations can cause re-evaluations of California real property.

> **Example 7.17.** P purchases the assets of T. Both P and T are California corporations. T's real estate assets have been assessed at $1 million, although their fair market value is $2 million. After the purchase, California will assess the assets at $2 million.

Unemployment Taxes

Most states levy an unemployment tax based on the employer's wage base. An employer also has an "experience rating" that generally determines the rate at which the employer pays unemployment tax insurance premiums to the state. Frequently, state unemployment taxes are ignored during asset purchases, mergers, or liquidations. However, as noted in the previous chapter, substantial tax savings can be achieved if the acquiring company is able to succeed to the target's favorable experience rating. Another way is to get the new owner's rating transferred to the acquired business. In some cases, the state's "new employer" rating may also result in tax savings.

ADDITIONAL PLANNING OPPORTUNITIES

Introduction

After analyzing the actual state and local tax costs of the acquisition and alerting the taxpayer to other tax considerations, the next step is to focus on how the consultant can best assist the buyer, seller, or new organization in preparing for future operations. Important planning ideas should include use of special purpose entities, restructuring intercorporate debt, performing an income tax filing review, performing a reverse sales and use tax audit, and performing a property tax diagnostic.

Special Purpose Entities

Where appropriate, consider special purpose entities to reduce state and local income taxes. For example, an intangibles holding company established either in a tax haven state (such as Delaware or Nevada) or in a combined return state should be considered when valuable intangibles (e.g., copyrights, trade names, etc.) are acquired. In cases where a parent performs management functions, management fees could also be considered. Properly structured, the use of such entities can significantly reduce state and local income taxes in separate return states by creating a deduction for affiliated operating companies and isolating income to the special entity in a low- or no-tax jurisdiction. A good time to address these issues is when the acquisition takes place. It may be more difficult to transfer assets or create entities after the acquisition is completed.

> **Example 7.18**. P, a Georgia company, acquires T, a California company. T holds valuable patents that it will continue to use and share with P. As part of the acquisition, T forms subsidiary T_1 that holds the patent. After the acquisition, T_1 charges P a royalty for the patent's use. The royalty is deducted on P's Georgia tax return (Georgia is a separate accounting state), and the royalty income received by T_1 does not really increase T_1's California tax, because the combined incomes of P, T, and T_1 are taxed (in part) by California due to California's unitary/combined return requirements.

> **Example 7.19**. X, an Arizona company, acquires Y, a Mississippi company. Both are in the same line of business, and X assumes overall management responsibilities for Y. X sets up a management subsidiary, X_1, also located in Arizona. It charges management fees to Y, which Y can then deduct on its Mississippi return (Mississippi is a separate accounting state). The management fee income has little impact on X_1, since X, X_1, and Y must file a combined return in Arizona (a unitary state) anyway.

Financial Restructuring

As part of the M&A process, decision makers may want to consider debt/equity restructuring to achieve tax savings. One financial restructuring method is by "pushing down" debt from a holding company to an operating company. If the operating company is located in a high-tax jurisdiction, this would optimize the use of an existing interest expense deduction. Another method is the creation of intercompany debt through a "debt/equity swap," which is the conversion of existing equity in a subsidiary to debt.

Other Issues

When dealing with a merger or other acquisition, there should be a review of the buyer's ability to file combined/unitary returns with newly acquired subsidiaries to achieve tax savings. Also, from the due diligence review (discussed below) decision makers should have a good view of the target's various sales, use, and property tax issues. This is an excellent time to perform a reverse sales/use tax audit (as discussed in Chapter 4) or a property tax analysis (as elaborated upon in Chapter 5) to quantify additional refund opportunities.

DUE DILIGENCE

This section discusses the purpose and objectives of conducting a due diligence review, with special emphasis on the associated state tax issues. For many years, state and local taxes were ignored or addressed too late in planning for corporate acquisitions, divestitures, or reorganizations. Instead, the focus was on Federal income tax aspects of the transaction and the pretax economics. More recently, state and local tax issues have risen in significance because of increased state tax rates and increased state audit and enforcement activity.

A due diligence review is essentially a complete audit of the target to determine whether a client should acquire the target, how to acquire the target, and what the effects of acquiring the target will be. A due diligence is one of the most challenging projects that can be assigned because it encompasses virtually every state and local tax specialty including income, franchise and net worth, gross receipts taxes, property and real estate transfer taxes, and employment taxes. It is of significant importance, and must generally be completed in a very short period of time.

Before actually beginning any due diligence review, one must determine the type of transaction that is at issue. Following this, one must obtain an understanding of the target's business to provide the necessary follow-up expertise. After identifying the nature of the transaction, the scope and type of due diligence required can be determined.

There are two principal types of due diligence. "Full" due diligence generally covers transactions in which the target and its substructure survive the transaction. Full due diligence is required for transactions in which the target survives the transaction or the target's tax attributes survive the transaction. "Limited" due diligence generally covers transactions in which the target is not acquired. Limited due diligence procedures are appropriate when neither the target nor the target's tax attributes survive the transaction.

Even in these transactions, it is still important to obtain an understanding of the target's business operations and the multistate filing posture. First, the purchaser may confront business and tax issues that the target has historically experienced. Second, most states require that either the buyer or seller give the state notice of a bulk sale of business assets. Although the seller remains primarily liable for unpaid state taxes, failure to give timely notice to the state or to obtain a tax clearance certificate generally makes the buyer jointly liable for certain of the seller's unpaid state taxes.

In addition to identifying and quantifying tax exposures, a thorough due diligence also allows the parties to focus on the types of *representations and warranties* that are needed in the purchase agreement. Many times a mutually favorable split of tax costs and compliance can be achieved through the use of information obtained in the due diligence review.

Full Due Diligence for Stock Purchases or Tax-Free Reorganizations

In these types of transactions, the buyer generally requires broad representations and warranties covering all identified and potential tax liabilities of the target. These include representations that returns have been filed, representations that taxes have been paid, and a confirmation of the existence of tax reserves and the target's audit history. Part of this audit history should include a detailed listing of extensions of statutes of limitations. If a §338(h)(10) election is contemplated, the parties generally agree to make the election in the purchase contract. The purchase agreement usually assigns compliance responsibility for the year of sale, provides for cooperation in future audits, and provides for which taxpayer receives refunds of taxes from Federal and state group tax returns.

Limited Due Diligence for Taxable Asset Purchases

Generally, tax representations and warranties made in connection with these transactions are less encompassing than those found in stock purchase agreements. However, it is common to find representations relating to real/personal property taxes, transfer/sales taxes, apportionment of taxes for periods beginning prior to closing but ending after closing, concomitant filing responsibilities, and compliance with state bulk sale laws.

Potential Past Tax Exposure — Income and Franchise Taxes

As a part of any due diligence, the following activities need to be performed for each legal entity acquired: (1) make complete inquiries regarding nexus, (2) review target's returns to obtain relevant tax information, and (3) review concluded and pending audits.

Nexus Issues and Review of Tax Returns

Any due diligence review requires an understanding of where the target is filing and what potential exposure exists in the applicable jurisdictions. In addition to inquiries regarding nexus, the consultant can obtain valuable information by reviewing the target's returns and related tax return and tax accrual workpapers. Some of the key items to focus on in a return review include:

1. The filing status and whether it is warranted
2. The basis of the tax (e.g., net income, capital, or both)
3. Allocation and apportionment data by jurisdiction
4. Apportionment data from prior years to assure that the target has been filing in all states in which it has nexus

One straightforward technique is to reconcile the total apportionment factor numerators to the amount of property, payroll, and sales reported on the tax return. Also, the following should be examined: the use and availability of NOLs and tax credits, depreciation adjustments and other state modifications, aggressive filing positions (such as treatment of nonbusiness income, expenses attributable to subsidiary capital), and the use of special purpose entities. As for the latter, it must be determined if these entities have been properly structured and operated. Frequently they have not been properly structured, "resulting" in significant tax exposure.

Potential Past Tax Exposure — Gross Receipt and Special Entity Taxes

For the business of the target, it may be necessary to become familiar with gross receipts taxes or special entity taxes. Some of these special entity taxes are bank taxes, taxes on financial institutions, insurance company gross receipts taxes, and Indian casino gambling taxes. Again, a review of nexus issues, applicable returns (with related workpapers), and audit history is required if the target is subject to these taxes.

Potential Past Tax Exposure — Sales and Use Taxes

The purpose of the inquiries made in the sales/use tax portion of the due diligence is to obtain a detailed understanding of the target's purchasing and selling functions as well as the target's overall multistate business operations.

Nexus Issues

As in an income tax due diligence, one must make the following key inquiries. Where does the target have physical presence? *De minimus* contact may now trigger audit exposure in some states. What are the activities of the target's sales personnel or representatives? Where is the target registered to collect sales/use taxes and should the target be registered in other jurisdictions? Some courts have held that mere registration to collect sales and use taxes does not create income tax nexus.

Review of Returns

It is important that there be a review of the target's sales and use tax returns. It should be assured that sales tax has been paid or accrued on fixed asset and expense purchases, and a list made of all locations with direct pay permits. It should be ascertained whether the target is taking advantage of statutory exemptions. If the target is overlooking exemptions, a "reverse sales and use tax audit" should be performed on the target after the acquisition to pursue refund opportunities.

Exemption Certificate Procedures

It also is important to review the target's procedures for exemption certificate maintenance. One especially needs to be alert to drop shipment situations to ensure proper exemption certificates have been obtained.

Use Tax Self-Assessment

Review of the target's use tax self-assessment procedures is highly desirable in order to determine potential exposures.

Audits

Information for both past and present audits should be obtained and reviewed, so that any current exposure can be quantified.

Potential Past Tax Exposure — Property Taxes

Property taxes are also frequently overlooked during due diligence reviews. With real property the following areas should be considered: determine compliance and appeal history, review available exemptions, and consider whether the assessed property value is overstated and should be appealed going forward.

With personal property, one should consider whether the target is in full compliance with state and local personal property tax laws, whether the property tax function (manual versus automated) is efficient, and whether the system is being acquired as part of the transaction. There also should be a review of the returns and tax calendar and a determination of appeal activity history and applicable exemptions or abatements.

Potential Past Tax Exposure — Payroll and Unemployment Taxes

An important area for the consultant to examine in the due diligence review is payroll and unemployment taxes. Here, one should determine the location of employees, review withholding issues and procedures, evaluate the standard used to determine independent contractor status, and review past and current audits. Sometimes the direction of a merger hinges on which entity has the better unemployment compensation rating as well as the state rules concerning "successor employers."

Potential Past Tax Exposure —
Real Property Transfer and Gains Taxes

A final area of importance in the due diligence review is real property transfer and gains taxes. In examining this area, one should review past acquisitions and dispositions involving interests in real property, determine whether such transactions were properly reported, and identify and quantify exposure.

DISCUSSION QUESTIONS

1. What are the common state tax issues that arise in a taxable stock acquisition?
2. What are the common state tax issues that arise in a table asset acquisition?
3. What are the common state tax issues that arise in tax-free reorganizations?
4. What nonincome/franchise tax issues should the consultant be concerned with in M&A transactions?
5. What state tax issues should a consultant be concerned with for a purchasing company in an M&A transaction?

PROBLEMS

Problem 1

For your state, determine its conformity with Federal rules for:
1. A, B, and C reorganizations
2. Section 338(h)(10)

Problem 2

Smithco is considering acquiring the assets of Jonesco. It had considered buying Jonesco stock, but Smithco is concerned about unknown or contingent liabilities. Smithco is a New Jersey company, which because it does mail-order sales has no nexus in other states. Jonesco is a California mail-order company, also with no nexus in other states. Jonesco has substantially appreciated assets. Would you recommend a taxable or tax-free acquisition, from a state income tax perspective? Why? What other tax issues should be considered?

Problem 3

Assume the same facts as in Problem 2 above, except that a taxable versus tax-free stock acquisition is being considered.

Problem 4

Swenco is a Delaware investment holding company with annual net income of $100 million. Swenco does not pay dividends. Its only subsidiary, XYZ Refining, refines crude oil, generating $70 million per year in income. XYZ files income taxes only in New Jersey, because its out-of-state sales are all in states in which it does not have nexus. Most of these out-of-state sales are to Oklahoma. Note that New Jersey does not have a throwback rule or allow consolidated tax returns. Swenco is considering acquiring the assets of WV Refining, about the same size as XYZ, except located in Pennsylvania. WV does business in several states; its Pennsylvania income accounts for 75% of its overall apportionment (100% property and payroll, 50% sales, double-weighted). WV is expected to generate $20 million of income per year. What type of entity should be used to acquire WV, and who should own it? How would your answer change if WV was expected to generate NOLs?

Problem 5

Gupta Products (GP) is a C corporation that sells mail-order items nationally from its office in Nevada. It has no property or payroll in other states, uses a common carrier for shipping, and generates $100 million of net income annually. It wants to acquire SYSHAUL company, so it can have better control over shipping. SYSHAUL would generate annual net income of $10 million. Should the assets or stock of SYSHAUL be acquired? What type of business entity should be used, and why?

ENDNOTES

132. California permits a taxpayer to either (1) make a state §338(h)(10) election even if the taxpayer did not make a Federal §338(h)(10) election, or (2) not make the election even if a Federal election was made.
133. For example, Nebraska's Incentive Growth and Employment Credit follows the business assets even if acquired in a taxable asset transaction.
134. For example, Alabama, California, Wisconsin.
135. For example, Delaware, New York, and Illinois.
136. See *Richards Auto City vs. Director, Division of Taxation*, 140 N.J. 523.
137. For example, New Jersey and New York.
138. Consider former California Revenue and Taxation Code §§17041 and 17276.
139. Section 17053.49.
140. Some states, such as New York, have an exemption from sales tax for contributions of assets to a wholly owned subsidiary immediately upon formation. However, New York will impose a sales tax on such transfers of assets if liabilities are also assumed by the subsidiary, on the theory that the liabilities represent taxable consideration for the property transferred to the subsidiary. In these situations, avoid the assumption of liabilities, if possible, or look for other restructuring options.

Free value-added materials available from the
Download Resource Center at www.jrosspub.com.

8

SPECIAL TAX INCENTIVES

INTRODUCTION

In the on-going operations of the firm, capital acquisition and disposition decisions are common. Often, these involve location choice decisions as well. For such decisions, effective tax management is crucial, since state and local taxes can play a significant role. If planned properly, sales and use, property, and income taxes can be minimized. This chapter discusses capital budgeting and location choice decisions in the context of one of the most important aspects: tax incentives offered by state and local authorities. In particular, the following are considered: general tax incentives offered to all companies, negotiated (firm-specific) tax incentives, collateral effects on income tax apportionment, and other nontax incentives.

STATE-WIDE TAX INCENTIVES

States offer a number of tax benefits that include those for sales or use, income, property, and other taxes. They roughly can be categorized into the following general categories: area-specific incentives, employee-related incentives, industry-specific incentives, equipment incentives, building restoration incentives, and resource-related incentives.

Before discussing these categories, one of the largest tax-savings items related to location and relocation activites should be mentioned: depreciation. As shown in Tax Management in Action 3.1, all major states generally conform to Federal depreciation rules. Accordingly, depreciation is not generally a relevant incentive factor.

Area-Specific Incentives

Many states have tax incentives aimed at encouraging economic development in specific parts of the state. These are often either in areas of higher-than-normal unemployment and/or with a declining infrastructure (often called "enterprise zones"), or in areas designated for foreign trade (often called "foreign free trade zones").

One of the most difficult aspects of planning for such incentives is being able to identify what incentives apply to which specific sites. It may sound simple, but when there are many overlapping jurisdictions involved, it has proven time and time again to be very difficult to determine exactly which incentives apply to which street address. Those interested in this issue, and in particular how the authors have addressed it using an innovative array of software, should contact the authors via the e-mail address listed in the Acknowledgments.

Enterprise zones offer a variety of tax benefits, depending on the state. The possibilities are sales/use tax, income tax, and property tax breaks. To illustrate, consider one of the most successful programs, California's. California's enterprise zone program is an innovative partnership comprised of state government, local government, and private businesses. The enterprise zone program encourages business development in thirty-nine designated areas through special zone incentives. Companies situated within enterprise zones can take advantage of state and local incentives and programs not available to businesses outside the enterprise zones.

Tax credits and benefits available to companies locating in enterprise zones include:

- Tax credits for sales or use taxes paid up to $20 million of qualified machinery purchased per year
- A hiring credit of up to $27,000 (or more) for each qualified employee hired
- A 15-year carryover of up to 100% of net operating losses (NOLs) (albeit the deduction may be postponed in times of crisis in California public finance)
- Expensing up to $40,000 of certain depreciable property
- Lender income deductions for loans made to zone businesses
- Preference points on state contracts

Example 8.1. A retailer locates its store in California in a designated enterprise zone. It purchases furniture and fixtures for the new store, on which it pays $75,000 in sales taxes. It can then apply for a tax credit for the $75,000 in sales taxes.

In addition, local incentives may be available that include reduction or elimination of local permit and construction-related fees, expeditious processing of plans and permits, reduced utility rates, reduced land costs, assistance in employee hiring (including one-stop shopping for required certifications for Federal, along with state and local, hiring tax credits), low-cost financing, and low-interest revolving loans.

These nontax incentives often dominate the tax incentives. For example, the expediting of construction permits often cuts construction time for new building in half, resulting in tremendous savings. Similarly, the assistance in certifications often means the difference between a firm actually getting the jobs credits it is entitled to or not getting these credits.

A small but increasing number of states offer foreign trade zones. Foreign trade zones allow a variety of sales/use, property, and income tax breaks, depending on the state. The idea is that transactions occurring within these zones are treated as if they occurred outside U.S. borders, and so should not be subject to tax. It is an incentive to encourage international investment into the state.

To illustrate, consider one of the most successful: Arizona's foreign trade zone incentives. The area is treated as though legally outside of the U.S. Customs territory. Merchandise may be brought in duty-free for purposes such as storage, repackaging, display, assembly, or manufacturing. Imports may be landed and stored quickly without full customs formalities. In addition, Arizona is the only state that has enacted special legislation that makes businesses located in a zone, or subzone, eligible for an 80% reduction in state real and personal property taxes.

> **Example 8.2.** A Japanese firm locates a distribution center in a designated foreign trade zone in Arizona. The land and building normally would be subject to $100,000 of county real estate taxes. Assuming other conditions are met, the firm may be able to reduce the property taxes by $80,000, or 80%.

Employee-Related Incentives

Most jurisdictions are very concerned with the creation of jobs. Accordingly, tax incentives of a variety of sorts offer incentives for hiring and retaining workers. Most states have these; often, they are for areas with high unemployment and may be part of enterprise zone incentives. A typical example is Alaska's two programs. Its Work Opportunity Tax Credit (WOTC) applies if a company hires people from the seven kinds of groups: Alaska Temporary Assistance Program (ATAP) and Aid for Families with Dependent Children (AFDC) recipients, food stamp recipients, veterans, vocational rehabilitation recipients, ex-felons, and high-risk youth. The credit amount is 40% of each employee's qualified wage in the first year. But the total credit amount is no more than $2,400.

Its Welfare to Work (W2W) Credit applies if a company hires long-term ATAP and AFDC clients. The company will be qualified for a 2-year W2W tax credit. In the first year, the credit equals 35% of the first $10,000 in paid wages, but does not exceed $3,500; in the second year, 50% of the first $10,000 of wages with the maximum credit amount of $5,000.

> **Example 8.3.** An Alaskan manufacturing corporation hires an employee in 2000 who is an AFDC recipient. The worker is paid $15,000 by the corporation that year. The W2W credit is limited to $3,500 for 2000, which reduces the company's Alaska corporate income tax.

Industry-Specific Incentives

Jurisdictions sometimes provide incentives for specific industries. Most covet manufacturers because of their high "ripple-through" effect on the economy. The incentives for them are typically equipment related (see next subsection) or enterprise zone related. Other states encourage natural resource industries and an increasing number of "soft" industries like film production, biotechnology, and software development.

A good example of incentives for natural resources can be found with Colorado's Increased Purchase of Coal Credit. Only corporate taxpayers can be eligible for this credit. To stimulate the coal mining in the state, a company is encouraged to purchase more tons of coal than it did in the previous years after January 1, 1988. The credit equals $1 for each increment of a ton of coal when current year's purchase exceeds last year's purchase. A 3-year carryforward is permitted when there is unused portion. Furthermore, when the company does not wish to carry its credit forward to future years, the state government also allows that the company transfers its credit to its coal mining company so that the credit can reduce the purchase price.

An excellent example of film production incentives is Missouri's film production tax credit. The Missouri Department of Economic Development may issue a film production company state income tax credits equaling up to 25% of the company's expenditures in Missouri necessary for the making of a film. However, this credit will not exceed $250,000 in tax credits per project. To qualify for the incentive, the production company must spend $300,000 or more in Missouri (i.e., payments made to Missouri companies, organizations, or individuals) in the making of the film. Also, the entire film production tax credit program is capped at $1 million per year.

Example 8.4. A California movie producer makes a movie that it shoots on location in St. Louis, Missouri. While there, it spends $400,000 in qualifying expenditures. It is eligible for up to $100,000 in tax credits against its Missouri income tax.

Equipment Incentives

States typically offer tax benefits for two categories: manufacturing equipment purchases and researched development (R&D) investment. The equipment purchases incentive is sometimes tied to enterprise zone incentives and may come under a variety of names. The most common titles are investment credit, equipment credit, and manufacturer's incentive credit (also known as MIC). The R&D incentives typically include tax benefits for both R&D equipment and R&D "soft" costs (such as salaries of scientists and engineers).

A fine example of tax benefits for R&D can be found for Kansas. Starting in 2001, corporations have been allowed to take an R&D credit against income taxes for expenditures that are incurred for increasing research activities in Kansas. These expenses are defined in the same way as under §41 of the Internal Revenue Code (IRC) for the Federal R&D credit. The credit is 6.5% of the difference between the actual qualified R&D expenses for the year and the average of the actual expenditures made during the year and the two previous tax years. The credit allowed in any one tax year is limited to 25% of the credit plus any carryforward. Any remaining unused credit may be carried forward in 25% increments until the total amount of credit is used.

Example 8.5. A Kansas biotech corporation spends $100,000 in qualifying R&D in 2000. The average of its 1998, 1999, and 2000 R&D is $80,000. Therefore, $20,000 of its 2000 R&D is eligible for the 6.5% credit to reduce its Kansas corporate income tax.

The epitome of equipment tax benefits can be found for Texas. Enacted for 2000, a capital investment credit is available to businesses provided that some conditions are met: the business pays wages at least 110% of the county average, offers group health care benefits to all full-time employees and pays 80% of the premium, and makes a minimum $500,000 qualified capital investment. The credit is equal to 7.5% of expenditures.

Building Restoration Incentives

Many states offer such incentives to encourage business to restore old structures. An example of this incentive can be found in Maine's Historic Property

Rehabilitation Tax Credit. This nonrefundable credit became available beginning January 1, 2000. The amount of the credit is equal to the amount available in IRC §47. The recapture provisions are the same as in that code section, too. The credit is limited on the Maine tax return, however, to $100,000 per taxpayer.

Resource-Related Incentives

States also offer a variety of tax incentives for firms to improve the state's environment. For example, Delaware has tax credits available through the Blue Collar Jobs Act. These apply to companies that reduce their wastes or are involved in recycling.

Firm-Specific (Privately Negotiated) Incentives

If a firm plans a substantial new investment in a new location, it can often privately negotiate with state and local tax authorities for incentives. Officials are sometimes willing to give these incentives if the investment creates jobs in the state. Another reason is the "ripple-through" effect of the investment on the surrounding economy, with the concomitant increases in other types of tax collections. Usually, the firm or its outside advisors should work with a location specialist in negotiating these benefits. States, in turn, often have departments of economic development that either negotiate the incentives or put the firm in touch with state/local representatives who can make such negotiations. In some cases, the firm can increase tax incentives by getting more than one state to compete for the investment, partly through increasing offers of tax incentives.

> **Example 8.6.** An automobile manufacturer is trying to decide whether to open a new plant in one of two adjoining states in the Southeast. It projects that the "ripple-through" effects of the plant on the local economy (in either state) would provide 5,000 jobs. Although the corporation would only pay $60,000 per year in taxes, the ripple-through effect on the local economy would increase corporate income, personal income, property, and sales tax collections by $1 million per year, in total. It is able to negotiate for no property taxes and special income tax credits, which together reduce its tax bill by $200,000 per year.

In the past, firms have been able to receive individual benefits and, if the investment becomes unprofitable, leave the area (or downsize) without having to refund previous tax incentives. Recently, however, many local governments have begun to be less generous, as the excerpt in Tax Management in Action 8.1 indicates.

Tax Management in Action 8.1

Incentives and Location Choice

In an article appearing in the *Wall Street Journal*,* it was reported that many cities, states, and counties offer firm-specific incentives to entice business to locate in their area. The article reported the results of a KPMG Peat Marwick survey of Fortune 1000 companies. In the survey, 160 of the 203 respondents said they received the following incentives:

Property tax rebates	51%
Income/franchise tax incentives	48%
Job training	11%
Employment or payroll tax credits	9%
Utility rebates	8%
Other	14%

The article also reported that many local governments are beginning to demand refunds of previous incentives from companies that reneged on their promises (leaving the area, not hiring as many workers as planned, and the like). When the government puts such refunds in a contract, they are commonly referred to as "clawback" or "recapture" provisions. As an alternative, some localities award incentives over time, instead of up front.

*Localities Force Firms to Keep Their Promises, *Wall Street Journal*, 10/26/96, p. A2.

Collateral Effects on Income Tax Apportionment

If the firm is multistate, how will additional capital change its apportionment factors? The net affect will be to apportion more income to the state in which the acquisition is made. If the tax rate in the capital-expansion state is higher than in the other states in which it operates, overall taxes may increase despite the above incentives.

> **Example 8.7.** A manufacturing firm has its principal facilities in a state with a 6% tax rate. It locates a new plant in a state with an 8% tax rate, in which it receives property tax exemptions worth $5 million per year. Data for the two plants are as follows (in $ millions):

	Existing Plant	**New Plant**
Net income	60	40
Sales	300	200
Property	100	50
Payroll	50	20

Assuming the firm did not previously have nexus in the new state, the change in income tax would be as follows:

Tax before new plant 60 × 6%		=	$3.6

Tax after new plant (assume all sales are in-state and are double weighted in both states' apportionment formulas):

Old state:

Sales factor 300/600 = 0.6 × double weight	=	1.20	
Property factor 100/150	=	0.67	
Payroll factor 50/70	=	0.71	
		2.58	
	÷	4	
Apportionment factor	=	0.64	
Times income	×	$100	
Income apportioned to old state		$64	
Tax at 8%			$5.1

New state:

Apportionment factor		
(complement of old state factor)	0.36	
Income	× $100	
Income apportioned to new state	$36	
Taxes at 6%		$2.2

Total income taxes		$7.3
Effective tax rate: $7.3/$100	=	7.3%

As can be seen, the firm's effective income tax rate has moved from 6 to 7.3%, which is reflected in its annual report to shareholders.

NONTAX INCENTIVES

In addition to tax incentives, most states offer a number of nontax incentives that can exceed the tax benefits. These benefits can be characterized into state financing, other (state-wide), and local (city) incentives.

State Financing

Many states offer the following or their equivalents:

- Industrial Development Bonds
- Pollution Control Financing
- Small Business Loan Guarantees
- SBA 500 Loans
- State Capital Access Programs
- Sudden and Severe Dislocation Loan Programs
- Technology Investment Partnership Programs
- Export Finance Loan Guarantees
- Old Growth Diversification Loans
- Revolving Loan Programs
- Environmental Loans
- Hazardous Waste Reduction Loans
- Recycling Loans
- Public Infrastructure Financing
- Rural Economic Development Financing
- Infrastructure Programs
- Community Development Block Grants
- USDA Rural Developments

Other State Incentives

Many states offer the following or their equivalents:

- Electric Industry Restructuring
- Venture Capital Networks
- Manufacturing Technology Centers
- State Health Insurance Plans
- Recycling Zones
- Favorable Labor Laws (sometimes called "right to work" jurisdictions)
- Favorable Pollution Control Laws
- Low Regulation (that is, reduction of "red tape")

Local (City) Incentives

Many cities, counties, and other taxing districts offer the following (or their equivalents):

- Economic Revitalization Manufacturing Property Tax Rebates
- Capital Investment Incentive Payments
- Local Financing Redevelopment Agency
- Local Revolving Loan Funds
- Local Business Assistance Programs
- Low-Cost Utilities

DISCUSSION QUESTIONS

1. Do tax incentives run afoul of constitutional law restrictions? Explain.
2. Which is more important — tax incentives, nontax incentives, or other reasons — for locating in a new state? Explain.
3. Assume that tax incentives are a zero sum game. That is, whatever one state gains in new business, another state loses. Do incentives make sense in such a setting?
4. Is a state (or area of a state) with the best tax incentives the best place to do business?

PROBLEMS

Problem 1

What are the tax incentives offered in your state?

Problem 2

Rework Example 8.7, assuming your state is the new state.

Problem 3

Rework Example 8.7, assuming your state is the old state.

Problem 4

Assume you are advising a client on whether to operate in new states with multiple tax incentives. However, the client firm has never had any business connections to the states before. What are the tax tradeoffs of locating in the new states?

Free value-added materials available from the
Download Resource Center at www.jrosspub.com.

9

TAXATION OF ELECTRONIC COMMERCE[141]

INTRODUCTION

One of the most dramatic revolutions to take place in the business world recently is the emergence of electronic commerce (also known as e-commerce). E-commerce can be simply defined as the exchange of goods and services by electronic means. The growth of e-commerce as a viable means of conducting business has been made possible because of the development and growth of the Internet, particularly the Web. These business trends are referred to by various names such as the "Internet or Cyberspace Economy," the "Digital Economy," or simply the "New Economy."

What is remarkable about e-commerce is its size and its incredible growth rate. Although estimates abound, a study by the University of Texas's Center for Research in Electronic Commerce finds that the U.S. Internet economy alone accounted for 2.5 million jobs and generated over $520 billion in economic activity back in 1999, less than a decade after the Web was established and just 6 years after the Web became readily available for commercial use. More astonishingly, between 1995 and 1999, this sector of economy grew at a compounded annual rate of over 100%. This contrasts with the 2.8% growth rate in the U.S. gross domestic product (GDP) over the same period. The size of the Internet economy rivals some of the more mature industries in the U.S., such as energy ($223 billion) and automobiles ($350 billion). E-commerce likely topped the $1 trillion mark in 2003.

A major implication of the size of the Internet economy and its startling growth rate is that it has greatly expanded the scope for e-commerce. Apart from the growth of new businesses in the cyberspace sector, more and more existing businesses are also starting to use the Internet to enhance their business in some way. Thus, even though the Web is a relatively recent phenomenon, the prospects of its continued growth are boundless. As the Internet and e-commerce become larger contributors to the economy, it becomes important to understand the implications of these trends on the government, businesses, and society in general.

In particular and perhaps not surprisingly, one of the more hotly debated issues surrounding the Internet and e-commerce is the taxation of cyberspace transactions. The purpose of this chapter is to discuss some of the more important issues surrounding the taxation of the Internet and e-commerce. In particular, the discussion will focus on the state and local tax issues, although similarly important issues exist with respect to the Federal and international tax consequences of these transactions. The questions range from the very basic such as *should* the Internet be taxed to the fairly complicated such as *could* the Internet be taxed and if so, how.[142]

To appreciate the arguments for or against these questions, one must first understand what is unique about transactions in cyberspace. The primary attribute of these transactions that makes them fundamentally different from those conducted in any other market is that cyberspace transactions lack many of the physical attributes of traditional transactions. For example, in contrast with the sale or exchange of tangible goods and services that characterizes typical business transactions, e-commerce usually involves the sale or exchange of intangible goods and services, such as computer software and travel and financial services. Increasingly, however, e-commerce has also begun to involve the digital delivery of tangible goods, such as newspapers, magazines, books, and music, over the Internet. In addition, determining the location and sometimes even the identity of the parties involved becomes difficult or irrelevant in Internet transactions.

These characteristics of Internet transactions pose serious challenges to state and local tax systems that have evolved to handle transactions occurring in the "old" economy. Not that all of these characteristics are unique; many apply to any mediated transaction, be it over the telegraph, through the mails, or via telephone. However, state and local governments are concerned that the growth of e-commerce is causing substantial loss of tax revenues because these governments are not equipped to handle such transactions. If so, it is likely that such losses will become huge as the size of the Internet economy grows.

On the other hand, there is a concern that taxing Web-based transactions could choke off the growth of this sector. This concern has attracted widespread attention of policymakers and legislators. In view of its startling growth, its remarkable potential, and concerns that the state and local tax systems may require fundamental reform to deal with the new economy, Congress has placed a moratorium on any new state and local taxes on the Internet.

This moratorium is contained in the Internet Tax Freedom act of 1998 (IFTA), Public Law (P.L.) 105-277, 112 Statutes at Large 2681. (The act is reproduced in Tax Management in Action 9.1.) The moratorium was slated to end in 3 years on October 2001. However, when it was amended in 2002 by P.L. 107-75 (H.R. 1552), the sunset was postponed until November 1, 2003.

Tax Management in Action 9.1

The Internet Tax Freedom Act (ITFA)

ITFA (formerly known as S.442, now Title XI of P.L. 105-277, the Omnibus Appropriations Act of 1998), reproduced below, establishes the Advisory Commission on Electronic Commerce.

TITLE XI — MORATORIUM ON CERTAIN TAXES

SEC. 1100. SHORT TITLE.
This title may be cited as the "Internet Tax Freedom Act."

SEC. 1101. MORATORIUM.
(a) Moratorium. — No State or political subdivision thereof shall impose any of the following taxes during the period beginning on October 1, 1998, and ending 3 years after the date of the enactment of this Act —
   (1) taxes on Internet access, unless such tax was generally imposed and actually enforced prior to October 1, 1998; and
   (2) multiple or discriminatory taxes on electronic commerce.
(b) Preservation of State and Local Taxing Authority. — Except as provided in this section, nothing in this title shall be construed to modify, impair, or supersede, or authorize the modification, impairment, or superseding of, any State or local law pertaining to taxation that is otherwise permissible by or under the Constitution of the United States or other Federal law and in effect on the date of enactment of this Act.
(c) Liabilities and Pending Cases. — Nothing in this title affects liability for taxes accrued and enforced before the date of enactment of this Act, nor does this title affect ongoing litigation relating to such taxes.
(d) Definition of Generally Imposed and Actually Enforced. — For purposes of this section, a tax has been generally imposed and actually enforced prior to October 1, 1998, if, before that date, the tax was authorized by statute and either —
   (1) a provider of Internet access services had a reasonable opportunity to know by virtue of a rule or other public proclamation made by the appropriate administrative agency of the State or political subdivision thereof, that such agency has interpreted and applied such tax to Internet access services; or
   (2) a State or political subdivision thereof generally collected such tax on charges for Internet access.
(e) Exception to Moratorium. —
   (1) In general. — Subsection (a) shall also not apply in the case of any person or entity who knowingly and with knowledge of the character of the material, in interstate or foreign commerce by means of the World Wide Web, makes any communication

Tax Management in Action 9.1 (continued)

The Internet Tax Freedom Act (ITFA)

for commercial purposes that is available to any minor and that includes any material that is harmful to minors unless such person or entity has restricted access by minors to material that is harmful to minors —

(A) by requiring use of a credit card, debit account, adult access code, or adult personal identification number;

(B) by accepting a digital certificate that verifies age; or

(C) by any other reasonable measures that are feasible under available technology.

(2) Scope of exception. — For purposes of paragraph (1), a person shall not be considered to be making a communication for commercial purposes of material to the extent that the person is —

(A) a telecommunications carrier engaged in the provision of a telecommunications service;

(B) a person engaged in the business of providing an Internet access service;

(C) a person engaged in the business of providing an Internet information location tool; or

(D) similarly engaged in the transmission, storage, retrieval, hosting, formatting, or translation (or any combination thereof) of a communication made by another person, without selection or alteration of the communication.

(3) Definitions. — In this subsection:

(A) By means of the World Wide Web. — The term "by means of the World Wide Web" means by placement of material in a computer server-based file archive so that it is publicly accessible, over the Internet, using hypertext transfer protocol, file transfer protocol, or other similar protocols.

(B) Commercial purposes; engaged in the business. —

(i) Commercial purposes. — A person shall be considered to make a communication for commercial purposes only if such person is engaged in the business of making such communications.

(ii) Engaged in the business. — The term "engaged in the business" means that the person who makes a communication, or offers to make a communication, by means of the World Wide Web, that includes any material that is harmful to minors, devotes time, attention, or labor to such activities, as a regular course of such person's trade or business, with the objective of earning a profit as a result of such activities (although it is not necessary that the person make a profit or that the making or offering to make such communications be the person's sole or principal business or source of income). A person may be considered to be engaged in the business of making, by means of the World Wide Web, communications for commercial purposes that include material that is harmful to minors, only if the person knowingly causes the material that is harmful to minors to be posted on the World Wide Web or knowingly solicits such material to be posted on the World Wide Web.

(C) Internet. — The term "Internet" means collectively the myriad of computer and telecommunications facilities, including equipment and operating software, which comprise the interconnected world-wide network of networks that employ the Transmission Control Protocol/Internet Protocol, or any predecessor or successor protocols to such protocol, to communicate information of all kinds by wire or radio.

Tax Management in Action 9.1 (continued)

The Internet Tax Freedom Act (ITFA)

(D) Internet access service. — The term "Internet access service" means a service that enables users to access content, information, electronic mail, or other services offered over the Internet and may also include access to proprietary content, information, and other services as part of a package of services offered to consumers. Such term does not include telecommunications services.

(E) Internet information location tool. — The term "Internet information location tool" means a service that refers or links users to an online location on the World Wide Web. Such term includes directories, indices, references, pointers, and hypertext links.

(F) Material that is harmful to minors. — The term "material that is harmful to minors" means any communication, picture, image, graphic image file, article, recording, writing, or other matter of any kind that is obscene or that —

(i) the average person, applying contemporary community standards, would find, taking the material as a whole and with respect to minors, is designed to appeal to, or is designed to pander to, the prurient interest;

(ii) depicts, describes, or represents, in a manner patently offensive with respect to minors, an actual or simulated sexual act or sexual contact, an actual or simulated normal or perverted sexual act, or a lewd exhibition of the genitals or post-pubescent female breast; and

(iii) taken as a whole, lacks serious literary, artistic, political, or scientific value for minors.

(G) Minor. — The term "minor" means any person under 17 years of age.

(H) Telecommunications carrier; telecommunications service. — The terms "telecommunications carrier" and "telecommunications service" have the meanings given such terms in section 3 of the Communications Act of 1934 (47 U.S.C. 153).

(f) Additional Exception to Moratorium. —

(1) In general. — Subsection (a) shall also not apply with respect to an Internet access provider, unless, at the time of entering into an agreement with a customer for the provision of Internet access services, such provider offers such customer (either for a fee or at no charge) screening software that is designed to permit the customer to limit access to material on the Internet that is harmful to minors.

(2) Definitions. — In this subsection:

(A) Internet access provider. — The term "Internet access provider" means a person engaged in the business of providing a computer and communications facility through which a customer may obtain access to the Internet, but does not include a common carrier to the extent that it provides only telecommunications services.

(B) Internet access services. — The term "Internet access services" means the provision of computer and communications services through which a customer using a computer and a modem or other communications device may obtain access to the Internet, but does not include telecommunications services provided by a common carrier.

(C) Screening software. — The term "screening software" means software that is designed to permit a person to limit access to material on the Internet that is harmful to minors.

The Internet Tax Freedom Act (ITFA)

(3) Applicability. — Paragraph (1) shall apply to agreements for the provision of Internet access services entered into on or after the date that is 6 months after the date of enactment of this Act.

SEC. 1102. ADVISORY COMMISSION ON ELECTRONIC COMMERCE.

(a) Establishment of Commission. —There is established a commission to be known as the Advisory Commission on Electronic Commerce (in this title referred to as the "Commission"). The Commission shall — (1) be composed of 19 members appointed in accordance with subsection (b), including the chairperson who shall be selected by the members of the Commission from among themselves; and (2) conduct its business in accordance with the provisions of this title.

(b) Membership. —

    (1) In general. — The Commissioners shall serve for the life of the Commission. The membership of the Commission shall be as follows:

        (A) 3 representatives from the Federal Government, comprised of the Secretary of Commerce, the Secretary of the Treasury, and the United States Trade Representative (or their respective delegates).

        (B) 8 representatives from State and local governments (one such representative shall be from a State or local government that does not impose a sales tax and one representative shall be from a State that does not impose an income tax).

        (C) 8 representatives of the electronic commerce industry (including small business), telecommunications carriers, local retail businesses, and consumer groups, comprised of —

            (i) 5 individuals appointed by the Majority Leader of the Senate;

            (ii) 3 individuals appointed by the Minority Leader of the Senate;

            (iii) 5 individuals appointed by the Speaker of the House of Representatives; and

            (iv) 3 individuals appointed by the Minority Leader of the House of Representatives.

    (2) Appointments. — Appointments to the Commission shall be made not later than 45 days after the date of the enactment of this Act. The chairperson shall be selected not later than 60 days after the date of the enactment of this Act.

    (3) Vacancies. — Any vacancy in the Commission shall not affect its powers, but shall be filled in the same manner as the original appointment.

(c) Acceptance of Gifts and Grants. — The Commission may accept, use, and dispose of gifts or grants of services or property, both real and personal, for purposes of aiding or facilitating the work of the Commission. Gifts or grants not used at the expiration of the Commission shall be returned to the donor or grantor.

(d) Other Resources. — The Commission shall have reasonable access to materials, resources, data, and other information from the Department of Justice, the Department of Commerce, the Department of State, the Department of the Treasury, and the Office of the United States Trade Representative. The Commission shall also have reasonable access to use the facilities of any such Department or Office for purposes of conducting meetings.

Tax Management in Action 9.1 (continued)

The Internet Tax Freedom Act (ITFA)

(e) Sunset. — The Commission shall terminate 18 months after the date of the enactment of this Act.

(f) Rules of the Commission. —

(1) Quorum. — Nine members of the Commission shall constitute a quorum for conducting the business of the Commission.

(2) Meetings. — Any meetings held by the Commission shall be duly noticed at least 14 days in advance and shall be open to the public.

(3) Opportunities to testify. — The Commission shall provide opportunities for representatives of the general public, taxpayer groups, consumer groups, and State and local government officials to testify.

(4) Additional rules. — The Commission may adopt other rules as needed.

(g) Duties of the Commission. —

(1) In general. — The Commission shall conduct a thorough study of Federal, State and local, and international taxation and tariff treatment of transactions using the Internet and Internet access and other comparable intrastate, interstate or international sales activities.

(2) Issues to be studied. — The Commission may include in the study under subsection (a) —

(A) an examination of —

(i) barriers imposed in foreign markets on United States providers of property, goods, services, or information engaged in electronic commerce and on United States providers of telecommunications services; and

(ii) how the imposition of such barriers will affect United States consumers, the competitiveness of United States citizens providing property, goods, services, or information in foreign markets, and the growth and maturing of the Internet;

(B) an examination of the collection and administration of consumption taxes on electronic commerce in other countries and the United States, and the impact of such collection on the global economy, including an examination of the relationship between the collection and administration of such taxes when the transaction uses the Internet and when it does not;

(C) an examination of the impact of the Internet and Internet access (particularly voice transmission) on the revenue base for taxes imposed under section 4251 of the Internal Revenue Code of 1986;

(D) an examination of model State legislation that —

(i) would provide uniform definitions of categories of property, goods, service, or information subject to or exempt from sales and use taxes; and

(ii) would ensure that Internet access services, online services, and communications and transactions using the Internet, Internet access service, or online services would be treated in a tax and technologically neutral manner relative to other forms of remote sales;

(E) an examination of the effects of taxation, including the absence of taxation, on all interstate sales transactions, including transactions using the Internet, on retail businesses and on State and local governments, which examination may include a review of the efforts of State and local governments to collect sales and use taxes owed on in-State purchases from out-of-State sellers; and

The Internet Tax Freedom Act (ITFA)

    (F) the examination of ways to simplify Federal and State and local taxes imposed on the provision of telecommunications services.

  (3) Effect on the Communications Act of 1934. — Nothing in this section shall include an examination of any fees or charges imposed by the Federal Communications Commission or States related to —

    (A) obligations under the Communications Act of 1934 (47 U.S.C. 151 et seq.); or

    (B) the implementation of the Telecommunications Act of 1996 (or of amendments made by that Act).

(h) National Tax Association Communications and Electronic Commerce Tax Project. — The Commission shall, to the extent possible, ensure that its work does not undermine the efforts of the National Tax Association Communications and Electronic Commerce Tax Project.

SEC. 1103. REPORT.

Not later than 18 months after the date of the enactment of this Act, the Commission shall transmit to Congress for its consideration a report reflecting the results, including such legislative recommendations as required to address the findings of the Commission's study under this title. Any recommendation agreed to by the Commission shall be tax and technologically neutral and apply to all forms of remote commerce. No finding or recommendation shall be included in the report unless agreed to by at least two-thirds of the members of the Commission serving at the time the finding or recommendation is made.

SEC. 1104. DEFINITIONS.

For the purposes of this title:

(1) Bit tax. — The term "bit tax" means any tax on electronic commerce expressly imposed on or measured by the volume of digital information transmitted electronically, or the volume of digital information per unit of time transmitted electronically, but does not include taxes imposed on the provision of telecommunications services.

(2) Discriminatory tax. — The term "discriminatory tax" means —

    (A) any tax imposed by a State or political subdivision thereof on electronic commerce that —

      (i) is not generally imposed and legally collectible by such State or such political subdivision on transactions involving similar property, goods, services, or information accomplished through other means;

      (ii) is not generally imposed and legally collectible at the same rate by such State or such political subdivision on transactions involving similar property, goods, services, or information accomplished through other means, unless the rate is lower as part of a phase-out of the tax over not more than a 5-year period;

      (iii) imposes an obligation to collect or pay the tax on a different person or entity than in the case of transactions involving similar property, goods, services, or information accomplished through other means;

      (iv) establishes a classification of Internet access service providers or online service providers for purposes of establishing a higher tax rate to be imposed on such providers than the tax rate generally applied to providers of similar information services delivered through other means; or

Tax Management in Action 9.1 (continued)

The Internet Tax Freedom Act (ITFA)

(B) any tax imposed by a State or political subdivision thereof, if —
  (i) except with respect to a tax (on Internet access) that was generally imposed and actually enforced prior to October 1, 1998, the sole ability to access a site on a remote seller's out-of-State computer server is considered a factor in determining a remote seller's tax collection obligation; or
  (ii) a provider of Internet access service or online services is deemed to be the agent of a remote seller for determining tax collection obligations solely as a result of —
    (I) the display of a remote seller's information or content on the out-of-State computer server of a provider of Internet access service or online services; or
    (II) the processing of orders through the out-of-State computer server of a provider of Internet access service or online services.

(3) Electronic commerce. — The term "electronic commerce" means any transaction conducted over the Internet or through Internet access, comprising the sale, lease, license, offer, or delivery of property, goods, services, or information, whether or not for consideration, and includes the provision of Internet access.

(4) Internet. — The term "Internet" means collectively the myriad of computer and telecommunications facilities, including equipment and operating software, which comprise the interconnected world-wide network of networks that employ the Transmission Control Protocol/Internet Protocol, or any predecessor or successor protocols to such protocol, to communicate information of all kinds by wire or radio.

(5) Internet access. — The term "Internet access" means a service that enables users to access content, information, electronic mail, or other services offered over the Internet, and may also include access to proprietary content, information, and other services as part of a package of services offered to users. Such term does not include telecommunications services.

(6) Multiple tax. —
  (A) In general. — The term "multiple tax" means any tax that is imposed by one State or political subdivision thereof on the same or essentially the same electronic commerce that is also subject to another tax imposed by another State or political subdivision thereof (whether or not at the same rate or on the same basis), without a credit (for example, a resale exemption certificate) for taxes paid in other jurisdictions.
  (B) Exception. — Such term shall not include a sales or use tax imposed by a State and 1 or more political subdivisions thereof on the same electronic commerce or a tax on persons engaged in electronic commerce which also may have been subject to a sales or use tax thereon.
  (C) Sales or use tax. — For purposes of subparagraph (B), the term "sales or use tax" means a tax that is imposed on or incident to the sale, purchase, storage, consumption, distribution, or other use of tangible personal property or services as may be defined by laws imposing such tax and which is measured by the amount of the sales price or other charge for such property or service.

(7) State. — The term "State" means any of the several States, the District of Columbia, or any commonwealth, territory, or possession of the United States.

Tax Management in Action 9.1 (continued)

The Internet Tax Freedom Act (ITFA)

(8) Tax. —

(A) In general. — The term "tax" means —

(i) any charge imposed by any governmental entity for the purpose of generating revenues for governmental purposes, and is not a fee imposed for a specific privilege, service, or benefit conferred; or

(ii) the imposition on a seller of an obligation to collect and to remit to a governmental entity any sales or use tax imposed on a buyer by a governmental entity.

(B) Exception. — Such term does not include any franchise fee or similar fee imposed by a State or local franchising authority, pursuant to section 622 or 653 of the Communications Act of 1934 (47 U.S.C. 542, 573), or any other fee related to obligations or telecommunications carriers under the Communications Act of 1934 (47 U.S.C. 151 et seq.).

(9) Telecommunications service. — The term "telecommunications service" has the meaning given such term in section 3(46) of the Communications Act of 1934 (47 U.S.C. 153(46)) and includes communications services (as defined in section 4251 of the Internal Revenue Code of 1986).

(10) Tax on Internet access. — The term "tax on Internet access" means a tax on Internet access, including the enforcement or application of any new or preexisting tax on the sale or use of Internet services unless such tax was generally imposed and actually enforced prior to October 1, 1998.

TITLE XII — OTHER PROVISIONS

SEC. 1201. DECLARATION THAT INTERNET SHOULD BE FREE OF NEW FEDERAL TAXES.

It is the sense of Congress that no new Federal taxes similar to the taxes described in section 1101(a) should be enacted with respect to the Internet and Internet access during the moratorium provided in such section.

SEC. 1202. NATIONAL TRADE ESTIMATE.

Section 181 of the Trade Act of 1974 (19 U.S.C. 2241) is amended —

(1) in subsection (a)(1) —

(A) in subparagraph (A) —

(i) by striking "and" at the end of clause (i);

(ii) by inserting "and" at the end of clause (ii); and

(iii) by inserting after clause (ii) the following new clause: "(iii) United States electronic commerce,"; and

(B) in subparagraph (C) —

(i) by striking "and" at the end of clause (i);

(ii) by inserting "and" at the end of clause (ii);

(iii) by inserting after clause (ii) the following new clause: "(iii) the value of additional United States electronic commerce,"; and

(iv) by inserting "or transacted with," after "or invested in";

(2) in subsection (a)(2)(E) —

The Internet Tax Freedom Act (ITFA)

    (A) by striking "and" at the end of clause (i);

    (B) by inserting "and" at the end of clause (ii); and

    (C) by inserting after clause (ii) the following new clause: "(iii) the value of electronic commerce transacted with,"; and

(3) by adding at the end the following new subsection: "(d) Electronic Commerce. — For purposes of this section, the term 'electronic commerce' has the meaning given that term in section 1104(3) of the Internet Tax Freedom Act."

SEC. 1203. DECLARATION THAT THE INTERNET SHOULD BE FREE OF FOREIGN TARIFFS, TRADE BARRIERS, AND OTHER RESTRICTIONS.

(a) In General. — It is the sense of Congress that the President should seek bilateral, regional, and multilateral agreements to remove barriers to global electronic commerce through the World Trade Organization, the Organization for Economic Cooperation and Development, the Trans-Atlantic Economic Partnership, the Asia Pacific Economic Cooperation forum, the Free Trade Area of the America, the North American Free Trade Agreement, and other appropriate venues.

(b) Negotiating Objectives. — The negotiating objectives of the United States shall be —

    (1) to assure that electronic commerce is free from —

        (A) tariff and nontariff barriers;

        (B) burdensome and discriminatory regulation and standards; and

        (C) discriminatory taxation; and

    (2) to accelerate the growth of electronic commerce by expanding market access opportunities for —

        (A) the development of telecommunications infrastructure;

        (B) the procurement of telecommunications equipment;

        (C) the provision of Internet access and telecommunications services; and

        (D) the exchange of goods, services, and digitalized information.

(c) Electronic Commerce. — For purposes of this section, the term "electronic commerce" has the meaning given that term in section 1104(3).

SEC. 1204. NO EXPANSION OF TAX AUTHORITY.
Nothing in this title shall be construed to expand the duty of any person to collect or pay taxes beyond that which existed immediately before the date of the enactment of this Act.

SEC. 1205. PRESERVATION OF AUTHORITY.
Nothing in this title shall limit or otherwise affect the implementation of the Telecommunications Act of 1996 (Public Law 104-104) or the amendments made by such Act.

SEC. 1206. SEVERABILITY.
If any provision of this title, or any amendment made by this title, or the application of that provision to any person or circumstance, is held by a court of competent jurisdiction to violate any provision of the Constitution of the United States, then the other provisions of that title, and the application of that provision to other persons and circumstances, shall not be affected.

In particular, IFTA enjoins state and local governments from imposing multiple or discriminatory taxation on e-commerce, as well as any new taxes on Internet access. However, before commencing a discussion of the interesting, exciting, and challenging state and local issues Internet-based transactions pose for all aspects of tax policy, it is useful to simply get a perspective of what the Internet is.

THE INTERNET AND INTERNET COMMERCE

The origins of the Internet can be traced to the 1960s and efforts of researchers working for the U.S. Department of Defense (DOD).[143] The DOD was also heavily involved in funding computing research at academic and research centers around the world. However, competition among computer manufacturers led to the development of different proprietary operating systems. Because computer resources were costly at that time and the existence of different systems required much duplication of effort, demand grew for a means of sharing resources and research. That led to the development of the first networks, which connected computers at different universities.

To facilitate communication between computers in different networks required developing standard protocols for communication, which produced what is now referred to as the Internet Protocol (commonly referred to as an IP). This development was a major step because it provided the rules for computer communication and support to solve problems in transmission, thereby ensuring that data reach their destination.

Initial questions about network connections such as who provides the connections and who pays for them were resolved by government funding. In 1985, the National Science Foundation (NSF) funded a network linking five academic supercomputing centers. The NSF offered other regional and university computers to physically connect to this network so as to form a "backbone" for internetworking. As traffic increased, agreements were reached with private companies to provide a faster backbone, which became increasingly popular, and connectivity to the network came to be known as the Internet.

Note that e-commerce was in existence at this time, albeit only among pre-existing business partners, using expensive private networks (both land based and space based), running cumbersome software on expensive hardware. During the early 1980s, for example, many U.S.-based garment manufacturers and distributors were linked with department chains, so that when a store's predetermined economic order quantity was reached for a certain item, these items were ordered by the purchaser's mainframe directly from the vendor's mainframe.

By 1995, the NSF stepped out of the picture. That led to the private development of backbone services by some of the national telecommunications operators. These national operators lease access to the networks already established (e.g., those of universities) at the regional level, thereby providing their users access to the Web. They also lease access to Internet Service Providers (ISPs), which in turn provide retail access to consumers and businesses. Most consumers and businesses today access the Internet via modems that dial into the ISPs through twisted pair telephone lines. Others access via faster modems through their cable television providers. Still others, desiring access at university-like speed, access through DSL connections integrated into existing telephone systems. DSL access is more expensive but has the great advantage of being "always on," running at the highest speeds, and not requiring an extra telephone line.

In effect, what started out as closed and isolated networks comprised primarily of academics and researchers has mushroomed into an open, interconnected network that is accessible to all consumers and businesses. Further, rather than being government sponsored and government run, the Internet is now user funded and run by commercial providers. This transformation of the Internet, while unleashing a huge potential for taxable commerce, has also opened up a whole host of issues that traditional tax systems, particularly the sales and use tax systems, were not designed to deal with. These challenges can be considered as falling into two main sets of transactions that may be collectively considered as "Internet commerce:" (1) the sales of access to the Internet and (2) the sales of good and services provided directly or indirectly through the Internet.

CONSTITUTIONAL LIMITATIONS ON THE STATES' POWER TO IMPOSE TAXES

General Principles

The Web has spawned a new form of business: the micro-multinational. Now even the smallest companies can access customers worldwide, at very low marginal cost, with off-the-shelf Web pages. Moreover, more and more business is being conducted by even the largest of firms. With the tremendous growth in business activities conducted by out-of-state companies in any given state, tensions have escalated between state taxing authorities and multistate enterprises with respect to the states' authority to impose taxes.

As discussed extensively in earlier chapters, states' rights to impose taxes on out-of-state businesses are limited by Federal constitutional provisions. The basic question pertains to how far a state's jurisdiction extends in terms of its ability to tax out-of-state businesses. Because e-commerce typically involves sale of goods or services by remote sellers, the central issue in determining sales or use tax collection responsibilities and income tax filing obligations concerns the business's nexus with the taxing jurisdiction. Unfortunately, the nexus landscape is far from stable, and theories about the states' taxing jurisdiction with respect to remote sellers continue to evolve, including slight physical presence, attributional nexus, affiliate nexus, and economic presence nexus.

In general, a state can impose a tax on an interstate business if such business has sufficient nexus with the state under both the Due Process Clause and the Commerce Clause of the U.S. Constitution. For several years, the Court's decisions discussed the nexus standard interchangeably under both clauses. However, it clarified its position in the landmark 1992 *Quill* decision.

The Slight Physical Presence Test and the Quill Case

The case of *Quill Corporation v. North Dakota*, 504 U.S. 298 (1992), involved North Dakota's attempt to require an out-of-state mail-order company that had neither outlets nor employees and either insignificant or nonexistent intangible property in the state to collect and pay a use tax on goods purchased for use within the state and that were delivered to the customers by mail or common carrier from out-of-state locations. The U.S. Supreme Court ruled against North Dakota, stating that the bright-line test of physical presence it established in *National Bellas Hess, Inc.*, 386 U.S. 753 (1967), is still required by the Commerce Clause to bring out-of-state vendors within the ambit of a state's sales and use tax laws and that mere economic presence is not sufficient for this purpose. Specifically, the Court ruled that such physical presence is not required to satisfy the Due Process Clause and while, in past cases involving the application of state taxing statutes to out-of-state sellers, it relied on both clauses without precisely distinguishing between the two clauses, they are "analytically different."

The Court stated that under the Due Process Clause:

> the relevant inquiry [is] whether a defendant had minimum contacts with the jurisdiction....In that spirit, we have abandoned more formalistic tests that focused on a defendant's "presence" within a State in favor of a more flexible inquiry into whether a defendant's contacts with the forum made it reasonable, in the context of our federal system of government, to require it to defend a suit in that State....Applying these principles, we have held that if a foreign corporation purposefully avails itself of the benefits of an economic market in the forum State, it may subject itself to the State's *in personam* jurisdiction even if it has no physical presence in the State.

Despite the similarity in phrasing, the nexus requirements of the Due Process Clause and the Commerce Clause are not identical. The two standards are animated by different constitutional concerns and policies. Due process centrally concerns the fundamental fairness of governmental activity. Thus, at the most general level, the due process nexus analysis requires that we ask whether an individual's connections with a State are substantial enough to legitimate the State's exercise of power over him. We have, therefore, often identified "notice" or "fair warning" as the analytic touchstone of due process nexus analysis. In contrast, the Commerce Clause, and its nexus requirements, are informed not so much by concerns about fairness for the individual defendant as by structural concerns about the effects of state regulation on the national economy....Accordingly, we have ruled that that Clause prohibits discrimination against interstate commerce...[requiring] a substantial nexus and a relationship between the tax and the State-provided services [and] limit the reach of State taxing authority so as to ensure that State taxation does not unduly burden interstate commerce. Thus, the "substantial-nexus" requirement is not, like due process' "minimum-contacts" requirement, a proxy for notice, but rather a means for limiting state burdens on interstate commerce. Accordingly,...a corporation may have the "minimum contacts" with a taxing State as required by the Due Process Clause, and yet lack the "substantial nexus" with that State as required by the Commerce Clause.

The Theory of Agency or Attributional Nexus

Under this theory, a taxing jurisdiction may assert nexus by attributing to the taxpayer the presence or activity of another person or entity. Thus, even though the taxpayer may not have sufficient presence within the taxing state, it may become subject to its tax. The leading case for this proposition is that of *National Geographic Society v. California Board of Equalization*, 430 U.S. 551, 97 S. Ct. 1386 (1977).

In this case, the U.S. Supreme Court held that an out-of-state mail-order seller with two offices in California conducting business unrelated to its mail-order line could be held responsible for collection of use tax on its mail-order sales delivered into the state by a common carrier. Significantly, the Court did suggest that the type of tax (use tax in this case versus a gross receipts tax) reduced the amount of nexus the taxing jurisdiction was required to show because the out-of-state seller becomes liable only by failing or refusing to collect the tax from the in-state customer. Further, the sole burden imposed on the out-of-state seller is that of an administrative responsibility of collecting and remitting the tax (cf. *Tyler Pipe*).

The Affiliate Nexus Theory

Related to the agency or attributional nexus theory discussed above is the theory of affiliate nexus. Under this theory, the nexus of one corporation is attributed to another (parent, subsidiary, or affiliate) under certain circumstances. Thus, under the affiliate nexus theory some states try to bring entire consolidated groups under their jurisdiction. However, the states have not been very successful with their claim of affiliate nexus. For example, in *SFA Folio Collections v. Tracy*, the Ohio Supreme Court rejected the Ohio Department of Taxation's claim that the in-state presence and activities of a corporation (a retail store) created nexus for its sister corporation (an out-of-state mail-order vendor). Similarly, in *Bloomindales By Mail Ltd. v. Department of Revenue*, a Pennsylvania court refused to impute the nexus of a parent corporation (that had a chain of retail stores, some in the state) to its subsidiary (an out-of-state mail-order company). The court found that the retail stores did not solicit orders of the mail-order company or in any way act as its agent.

Nexus Through Economic Presence

Geoffrey Inc. v. South Carolina Tax Commission is a case that has received widespread attention for the proposition that economic presence may be sufficient for establishing nexus. In this case, the South Carolina Supreme Court held that a Delaware passive investment company, whose sole connection with South Carolina was the licensing of a trademark used in the state, was subject to the state's income tax. The court reasoned that the company had purposefully directed its activities at the state's economic forum and that it had sufficient connection with the state through its intangibles and accounts receivables in the state. The court refused to accept that the physical presence requirement under *Quill* was necessary for its state income tax to attach to the taxpayer.

Since 1993, a number of states have adopted South Carolina's approach in *Geoffrey* and are requiring entities with an economic presence within the state through intangibles to pay the state income tax. For example, Arkansas now requires that holding companies receiving royalty income from an Arkansas business should file an Arkansas corporate income tax return. Some of the other states that have adopted the *Geoffrey* approach are Florida, Hawaii, Iowa, New Mexico, Tennessee, Texas, and Wisconsin. There are other states that are considering adopting this approach. Some states have actually incorporated economic nexus standards in their statutes, especially with regard to the income taxation of financial institutions (e.g., Massachusetts).

STATE SALES AND USE TAXES

Sales and use taxes have long been a cornerstone of state tax revenue bases. State and local governments have typically viewed the sales and use tax as a reliable source of revenue, less susceptible to the fluctuations of the business cycle than income taxes, and one that entails little administrative costs because the tax collection responsibilities are shifted onto the retailers. From a tax administrator's point of view, this arrangement makes this tax efficient and hence very attractive.

Further, the tax yields large amounts of revenues even at fairly low rates with broad exemptions for the sale of services, intangibles, and realty. Thus, although initially adopted during the Depression as an emergency measure necessitated by the unique economic circumstances of the times, it is not surprising that currently 45 states and over 7,500 local jurisdictions have adopted transaction taxes, and nationwide these taxes provide the largest single source of state tax revenues.

Despite the inherent advantages of low rate, high yields, and limited collection costs, sales and use taxes are far from being trouble free. Taxpayers frequently complain that there is very little consistency or coordination among the states with regard to the tax base or systems of tax administration. Perhaps more alarmingly, sales tax rates continue to rise, with the average combined state, county, and municipal level sales tax rate increasing every year since 1981. The averaged reached 8.25% in 1998,[144] and has continued to rise.

The dissatisfaction with the implementation and concerns with the structure of sales and use taxes have become the subject of a much sharper debate in the e-commerce environment. As discussed more fully in Chapter 4, sales and use taxes were originally designed to deal with an environment where commerce involved the purchase and sale of tangible personal property between a buyer and seller both of whose identity and location were known with certainty. However, all of these basic environmental assumptions are challenged in an e-commerce economy, resulting in problems with the assessment and collection of sales and use taxes.

Problems of Applying Sales and Use Tax Laws to E-Commerce Transactions

The emergence of the digital economy creates a number of problems from a sales and use tax viewpoint. First, perhaps the biggest problem in the context of e-commerce transactions is the heavy dependence of sales and use taxes on geographical and political borders. In the classical brick-and-mortar environment, the buyer and seller typically are present at the same physical location at the same time. In contrast, municipal, county, state, or even national borders are meaningless in an e-commerce world, even for traditional businesses that are expanding to the Web (also known as "clicks-and-mortar" enterprises). Thus, determining the location (more precisely, the situs) of a sales transaction becomes difficult, which in turn makes it unclear as to which taxing body has jurisdiction over the transaction.

Second, the identity of the purchaser must be known with certainty for sales and use taxes to attach. However, knowing the identity or location of the purchaser in an e-commerce transaction is neither necessary nor always feasible. Mostly, just a valid credit card number is sufficient to consummate the transaction, which may arguably identify the purchaser but not necessarily the location. Even this clue to the purchaser's identity may disappear with the advent of certain new forms of payment such as "cyber cash" or "electronic wallets." Under these arrangements, money can be stored on computer chips or other memory devices and electronically transferred to the vendor without any personally identifiable information about the purchaser being made known to the vendor. Thus, absent the conventional audit trails of credit card or check payments, the purchaser's identity remains anonymous.

Third, it should be noted that the issues of location and identity of the purchaser continue to be a vexing problem even in the case of use taxes, which are sourced to the destination of the receipt and use of the purchased goods. Because digital products are sent to Uniform Resource Locators (URLs) and e-mail addresses rather than a physical street address, it remains unclear where the goods might have been purchased and used. For instance, a purchaser could download a book while waiting in an airport terminal of a city she may have gone to for a business trip and read the book during the flight from that city to her home city. Put simply, the vendor in this case would have a virtually impossible task of determining the amount of sales or use tax that should be collected from the purchaser.

Finally, the problem of multiple jurisdictions and nonuniformity of the sales and use tax laws among the various jurisdictions pose a potentially daunting compliance cost burden on retailers. This is likely a nontrivial problem and it exists even if the issues of location and identity were resolved. Moreover, the compliance cost problem is relevant even for the sale of nondigital products (i.e., tangible personal property), especially for smaller vendors.

The fundamental attraction of the Web is that the market of even a small business potentially is international rather than local or even regional. The requirements of vendor registration and then collection and remission of use taxes to multiple jurisdictions can overwhelm small businesses, and perhaps even drive them away. Although compliance with sales and use taxes is costly for all multistate sellers, it has been suggested that such costs for firms with collection responsibilities in all forty-five states with sales and use taxes range from 14% of the sales tax collected for large retailers to 87% of such taxes for small retailers.[145]

Sales Tax Issues in Internet-Delivered Services: Taxing Services in the Cyberspace Economy

An issue that is likely to become increasingly important with the greater use of the Internet is the imposition of sales taxes on services delivered via the Internet. The U.S. Supreme Court's decision in *Oklahoma Tax Commission v. Jefferson Lines*, 514 U.S. 175, provides interesting insights into the sales tax issues that arise with Internet-delivered services.[146]

First, the facts. In *Jefferson Lines* the taxpayer provided bus service in Oklahoma and other states. Oklahoma imposed a sales tax on transportation services. The taxpayer collected and remitted the sales tax on all intrastate ticket sales, that is, for travel that originated and terminated within the state, but not for tickets sold in Oklahoma for travel to other states. Oklahoma asserted jurisdiction over all tickets sold in the state, regardless of where the travel terminated. The taxpayer asserted that because a portion of the services in the case of interstate travel was rendered outside the state, Oklahoma's sales tax levy on those sales violated the Commerce Clause's restraint on taxing interstate commerce.

Recall that under the four-pronged test laid down in the *Complete Auto* case,[147] a state tax will survive a Commerce Clause challenge only if it (1) is applied to an activity that has substantial nexus with the taxing state, (2) is fairly apportioned, (3) does not discriminate, and (4) is fairly related to the services provided by the taxing state. In applying these tests to *Jefferson Lines*, the Court found that the only test in real question was whether the Oklahoma sales tax was fairly apportioned with respect to the interstate travel, as the other tests were easily met by the facts of the case.

Further, recall that under the Court's decision in *Container Corp.*,[148] a tax is considered fairly apportioned only if it is both internally and externally consistent. A tax is internally consistent if every state was to adopt the same tax and yet multiple taxation would not occur. External consistency is concerned with the economic justification of the state's claim on the value taxed and whether the tax reaches beyond the portion of value fairly attributable to the economic activity occurring within the taxing state. In deciding that the external consistency test was met, the Court laid down two general rules regarding the sales taxation of interstate services: (1) a sales tax should be an unapportioned tax and (2) a sale of services is a local event.

A Sales Tax Should be Unapportioned

Distinguishing sales taxes from income or gross receipts taxes, the Court stated that "a sale of goods is most readily viewed as a discrete event facilitated by the laws and amenities of the place of sale, and the transaction itself does not readily reveal the extent to which completed or anticipated interstate activity affects the value on which a buyer is taxed." Thus, the sales can be taxed measured by the gross charge for the purchase without dividing the tax base among the different states in which activities might occur either before or after the sale. On the issue of interstate transportation services, the Court specifically rejected an apportionment formula based on mileage even if administratively feasible because the taxpayer did not prove that Oklahoma's tax grossly distorted the result out of all proportion to the business transacted in the state. Further, the Court was reluctant to abandon its precedent and in the end "lose the simplicity of our general rule sustaining sales taxes measured by full value."

Sale of Services: A Local Event

The Court also stated that just as in the case of the sale of goods, a sale of services could be easily treated as a local state event. While acknowledging that far fewer of its decisions have concerned the sale of services relative to the sale of goods, the Court stated that its past decisions on the taxation of gross sales receipts in the hands of a seller of services adequately support the view that the taxable event is local. As an example, the Court cited its decision in *Western Live Stock v. Bureau of Tax Revenue*, 303 U.S. 250 (1938), in which it upheld New Mexico's gross receipts tax imposed on advertising revenues for a magazine wholly prepared, edited, and published within the state but distributed both within and outside the state. Similarly, the Court identified the local sales event in *Jefferson Lines* as the agreement, payment, and delivery in the state of some of the services, which was sufficient to justify an unapportioned tax. Further, the Court rejected the taxpayer's argument that the provision of services consisted of a series of separate sales, stating that "nothing in our case law supports the view that when delivery is made by services provided over time and through space a separate sale occurs at each moment of delivery."

Applicability of Jefferson Lines to Cyberspace

The critical factor that led the Court to uphold Oklahoma's sales tax on the interstate transportation services in *Jefferson Lines* was that there was some local state event, specifically the agreement, payment, and delivery of some of the services, in the taxing state. Extending this analysis to cyberspace transactions challenges this basic premise because, as discussed before, that is a world without geographical boundaries.

STATE CORPORATE INCOME TAXES

Although most of the debate surrounding the taxation of e-commerce has centered on sales and use taxes, e-commerce also raises important corporate income tax questions regarding the apportionment of income to the various states. State corporate income taxes are imposed on income derived from business activities, including e-commerce. However, states vary in their approach to where such income is sourced. For multistate corporations, states typically use an apportionment formula composed of a payroll factor, property factor, and a sales factor to determine the portion of the income taxable within each state. Most of the complications for the income taxation of e-commerce relate to the sales factor and arise from the classification of the product being sold.

Sourcing Rules for Tangible Personal Property, Intangible Property, and Services

There does not as yet exist widespread agreement as to whether software and other electronic content on-line comprise tangible personal property, intangible property, or services. To the extent such sales are considered to be of tangible personal property, the usual destination-based rules would apply and income would be sourced to the state where the customer is located. The case is not as cut and dried if such sales are considered to be the sale of services or intangibles, which is what the majority of states will likely consider them. Although most states source the sale of intangibles/services to the state where the vendor is located (i.e., an origin-based rule), some states are likely to source these sales to where the customer is located (i.e., a destination-based rule). The theory for the origin-based rule is that that is where the income-producing activity was performed, whereas the theory for the destination-based rule is that that is where the benefit of the service/intangible was received.

The variation among the states does not stop at the origin-based and destination-based sourcing rules; they are merely the start of other issues that can potentially lead to more complications as discussed below.

- *The income-producing-activity rule.* Jurisdictions that tax sales of services or intangibles based on where the income-producing activity is performed typically use an all-or-nothing rule or a pro-rata allocation rule when the costs of performance occur in multiple jurisdictions. For example, California considers sale of services or intangibles to occur within the state if the income-producing activity is performed in the state. If the income-producing activity were performed both within and in another state, California would tax the activity if a greater proportion of the income-producing activity were performed within the state. Some states, such as Connecticut and Texas, prorate the revenues based on the percentage of costs of performance or the fair value of the services rendered, respectively.

■ *The destination-based rule.* Some states include revenues from the services or intangibles based on where the services are consumed. For example, Minnesota follows this rule for receipts from performance of services together with a proration if the intangible property is used in more than one state.

■ *The throwback rule.* In states that follow this rule, corporations making sales of tangible personal property into states in which they are not subject to tax are required to throw back or source the sale to the state from which the goods were shipped. However, the sale of services or intangibles is not subject to the sales throwback rules; hence, the classification of the product being sold in e-commerce will determine whether the throwback rule applies or not.

■ *Potential for double taxation.* Given that some states tax services based on where the services are performed (e.g., Massachusetts) whereas some tax them based on where the services are received (e.g., Minnesota), it is possible that taxpayers might be subjected to double taxation on the same receipts.

A PROTOTYPICAL EXAMPLE OF E-COMMERCE TAX ISSUES

The following example illustrates some of the central tax issues surrounding the Internet and e-commerce transactions.[149] Consider first that a computer software manufacturer (Taxpayer) is based in Massachusetts. This taxpayer has a network of sales representatives soliciting sales around the country who report to the sales office in Connecticut. All sales are shipped via U.S. mail to retail outlets around the country. Based on these simple facts, the likely income and sales tax consequences for Taxpayer are as follows:

1. Income tax consequences:
   ■ Taxpayer would have to file tax returns only in Massachusetts and Connecticut.
   ■ Sales to states other than Massachusetts and Connecticut would be sourced outside Massachusetts and not subject to throwback to Massachusetts.

2. Sales tax consequences:
   - Taxpayer will have collection responsibility in most states.
3. Some benefits of the above scenario are likely to be as follows:
   - *Income tax:* A single sales factor apportionment would apply and Taxpayer is likely to be eligible for the investment tax credit.
   - *Sales tax:* Exemption for machinery and materials would be available to Taxpayer.
   - *Property tax:* Exemption for machinery used in manufacturing would be available to Taxpayer.
     a. Rationale: "Canned software" typically considered tangible personal property.

Now consider the same example with a simple change in the facts. Assume that Taxpayer now delivers 100% of sales of its software to its customers electronically.

1. Income tax consequences:
   - Taxpayer would have filing responsibilities in most states because software is now considered "intangible property" (that is, no P.L. 86-272 protection).
   - All sales are now sourced back to Massachusetts.
   - Intangible property sales sourced to where income-producing activity takes place.
   - Significant increase in Massachusetts income tax liability.
2. Sales tax consequences:
   - Collection responsibilities are likely reduced.
   - Electronically transferred software considered intangible property in many jurisdictions.
   - Sale of intangible property exempt from sales tax in about one-half the jurisdictions.
3. Tax benefits:
   - May become ineligible for certain income, sales, and property tax benefits.
   - Rationale: Many of these benefits apply to the manufacture and sale of tangible personal property.

THE INTERNET TAX FREEDOM ACT (ITFA) OF 1998

This statute represents one of the few instances in which the U.S. Congress has intervened between the private sector and the state and local governments in the matter of taxation. Indeed, the only other instance in memory of such intervention is the enactment of P.L. 86-272 discussed earlier. The text of the act is reproduced in Tax Management in Action 9.1.

In particular, ITFA enjoins state and local governments from imposing multiple or discriminatory taxation on e-commerce, as well as any *new* taxes on Internet access. This prohibits taxes on Web-based transactions that are not generally collectible on similar transactions not performed over the Internet, as well as taxes at higher rates on Web-based versus other transactions. For example, "mail-order" sales conducted via the Web by a seller that has no property, payroll, or agents in the state could not be taxed by a state simply because of contacts in the state due to using the Web (e.g., the leasing of Web access in the state). Similarly, there can be no use tax collection requirement for a firm that has no contacts with the state except in-state Web-based access to its out-of-state server, or the use of an ISP with nexus in the state.

The key ingredients of the act are:

■ Placing a moratorium on certain taxes on the Internet
■ Establishment of an Advisory Commission on Electronic Commerce
■ Report of the Commission

The Moratorium — What It Is and What It Is Not

It is important to note what the moratorium does not do. Specifically, §101 of the act provides that no state or political subdivision shall impose any of the following taxes:

■ Taxes on Internet access, unless such tax was already in force prior to October 1, 1998 (when the act first became effective)
■ Multiple or discriminatory taxes on electronic commerce

Moreover, under the ITFA moratorium, current state and local taxing authority is preserved. That is, the act does not modify or supersede any state or local law concerning taxation that is permissible under the U.S. Constitution or other Federal law in effect. Further, existing liabilities and pending cases also are not affected by the act. Finally, the moratorium does not apply to any person or entity that in interstate or foreign commerce knowingly sells or transfers by means of the World Wide Web material that is harmful to minors. This exception does not apply if the person or entity requires the use of a verified credit card, debit account, adult access code, or adult personal identification.

The Advisory Commission on Electronic Commerce

Section 102 of the act requires the establishment of an Advisory Commission on Electronic Commerce. The act provides for the following:

- Composition of the Commission, including appointments, vacancies, etc.
- Rules of the Commission
- Duties of the Commission

Composition of the Advisory Commission

ITFA also provides that the Commission shall be composed of nineteen members with:

- Three representatives from the Federal government, comprised of the Secretaries of Commerce and the Treasury and the U.S. Trade Representative (or their delegates)
- Eight representatives from state and local governments (including one representative from a state that does not impose a sales tax and one from a state that does not impose an income tax)
- Eight representatives of the electronic commerce industry, telecommunications carriers, local retail businesses, and consumer groups

The act also provides that the Commission shall have a chairperson, selected by the Commission members from among themselves, and that the commissioners serve for the life of the Commission.

Duties of the Advisory Commission

Under the act, the Commission is required to conduct a thorough study of Federal, state and local, and international taxation and tariff treatment of transactions using the Internet and Internet access and other comparable intrastate, interstate, and international sales activities. The study is to include an examination of:

- Barriers imposed in foreign markets on U.S. providers of property, goods, services, or information engaged in electronic commerce
- How imposition of such barriers will affect U.S. consumers and competitiveness of U.S. citizens in property, goods, services, and information in foreign markets, and the growth and maturing of the Internet
- Collection and administration of consumption taxes on electronic commerce in other countries

Report of the Advisory Commission

Section 103 of the act required that the Commission transmit its report to Congress within 18 months after enactment. The report was to include the findings of the Commission's study. These were subject to the conditions that any recommendations agreed to by the Commission shall be tax and technologically neutral and apply to all forms of remote commerce. No finding or recommendations were to be included unless agreed to by at least two-thirds of the members of the Commission. The Commission issued its report to Congress in April 2000. The report contains some formal "findings and recommendations" based on votes by two-thirds or more of the commissioners and also contains several "policy proposals" based on votes by a simple (but not two-thirds) majority of the commissioners. The report is reproduced in Tax Management in Action 9.2.

Tax Management in Action 9.2

Advisory Commission on Electronic Commerce's Report to Congress (April 2000)

Executive Summary

The Advisory Commission on Electronic Commerce (AECC) met in four in-person meetings: Williamsburg, Virginia; New York City, New York; San Francisco, California; and Dallas, Texas. At its final meeting in Dallas on March 20 and 21, 2000, the Commission voted on a number of proposals bearing on the subject of the Commission's charter. Certain of those proposals received a 2/3rds vote and, pursuant to the statute, represent findings and recommendations of the Commission. Other proposals, including those pertaining to state sales and use taxes, received a majority vote of the Commissioners and are identified as such throughout the report. Under the terms of the statute, those proposals do not constitute formal findings or recommendations of the Commission.

The domestic tax proposals, if implemented by Congress, would establish an environment that continues to foster innovation and technological advancement in the development of the Internet and electronic commerce ("e-commerce") while, at the same time, recognizing the role of state and local governments to continue providing needed services to their citizens. The proposals, adopted by a majority of the Commissioners, are consistent with the belief that governments should keep the tax and administrative burden on consumers and businesses as low as possible. They are also consistent with the view that federal policies in this area should respect the sovereignty of sub-federal jurisdictions and interstate commerce. The best way to strike a balance between the national and state interests will be through earnest and open debate among all affected parties.

In addressing whether and how the Internet should be subject to taxation, a major priority should be reducing or removing barriers to access to perhaps the most advanced and useful medium of communications and commerce yet devised. That imperative has infused the various access and telecommunications tax discussions in this proposal, which will, cumulatively, drive down the cost of connecting to the Internet and consequently increase the numbers of those who can afford to connect.

Tax Management in Action 9.2 (continued)

Advisory Commission on Electronic Commerce's Report to Congress
(April 2000)

The advent of e-commerce raises new challenges for traditional state and local tax systems. It should not be presumed that the collection of sales and use taxes on Internet transactions is an inevitability. There is, however, a need to begin a dialogue that will lead to the substantial simplification and reform of the current tax systems if they are to continue to remain viable in the 21st century. Now is not the time to ignore the challenge of reform, and it is not the time for incremental adjustment. Rather, now is the time to take a hard look at state and local transaction taxes, to determine whether they can be restructured in light of technological change, and then to take action. These proposals are intended to enable all consumers, whether or not they make purchases on the Internet, to enjoy the benefits of a new, restructured sales and use tax system. The hallmark of the system should be simplicity, efficiency and fairness.

Our system of federalism mandates that the burden of producing such a system falls on the states. The proposals adopted by a majority of the Commissioners suggest giving the states five years to simplify their state and local transaction tax systems in a manner which would equalize the burdens of tax collection for local and remote sellers. The system should not be more burdensome on a business that collects and remits taxes to several taxing jurisdictions than it is to a business that collects and remits taxes in a single taxing jurisdiction. By eliminating any disparate burden on interstate commerce, states will have a pathway toward a system that extends their collection of existing state taxes to remote sellers. In the interim, there should be several clarifications to remote sales tax collection duties that would benefit both state and local governments and vendors by drawing some "bright lines" for guidance. These guidelines would provide clarity, thereby reducing costly litigation and uncertainty and enabling equitable treatment of retailers and "e-tailers," as well as consumers who do not have Internet access. In addition, the sale of certain products available in both digital and tangible forms should be exempt from sales tax during the moratorium period.

No party in the debate has sought to increase tax revenues through more taxes. Therefore, it is appropriate for states whose overall sales and use tax revenue collections increase as a result of use tax collections on remote sales to make a substantial and proportional reduction in their overall sales tax rates, thus maintaining revenue neutrality in overall sales and use tax collections.

The proposal will achieve these goals through the following five-part approach:

1. Substantially reducing the overall burden on consumers due to state and local sales taxes by radically simplifying state and local tax systems, and reducing the aggregate collection costs of all transactions, which will allow all sellers to pass on those cost savings to taxpayers;
2. Creating a simple and equitable system for state and local sales taxes that would impose equal obligations and costs on all sellers, local or remote, regardless of sales channel or technology utilized;
3. Addressing concerns regarding the digital divide and the regressive character of state and local transaction taxes by eliminating the disparate tax treatment of main street and Internet sales, banning taxes on Internet access and reducing overall transaction tax rates;

Advisory Commission on Electronic Commerce's Report to Congress
(April 2000)

4. Eliminating the federal excise tax on communications services, simplifying state and local telecommunications taxes and eliminating multiple and discriminatory taxation of telecommunications services and property; and

5. Protecting the privacy of consumers by minimizing the disclosure of personal information for tax collection purposes.

E-commerce raises new tax compliance and administrative issues for national income tax and consumption tax systems. An international perspective is necessary to address this subject since e-commerce potentially crosses national borders to a greater extent than other, traditional forms of doing business. Therefore, it is important for every nation to give serious consideration to the impact on its trading partners of any new or amended rules for taxation of e-commerce. In order to minimize the potential for double taxation, an international consensus for the taxation of e-commerce should be developed. The Organization for Economic Cooperation and Development ("OECD") is the appropriate forum to sponsor the required international dialogue, which will require input from the business community and non-OECD countries.

The Advisory Commission on Electronic Commerce believes the Congress of the United States can facilitate the international dialogue by adopting the proposal described herein. The proposal receiving a majority vote of the Commissioners is based on the conclusion that existing, internationally accepted tax rules should be applied to e-commerce. No new taxes are required. In addition, the goals of simplification, neutrality, greater certainty, and avoidance of double taxation are equally significant.

The Advisory Commission on Electronic Commerce was established pursuant to P.L. 105-277, Div C, Title XI Stat. 2681-719, and codified as 47 U.S.C.S. § 151 Sec. 1102 (H.R. 4328) (referred to herein as the "Internet Tax Freedom Act" or the "Act"). As set forth in the Act, the Commission's statutory mandate is to study "federal, state and local, and international taxation and tariff treatment of transactions using the Internet and Internet access and other comparable intrastate, interstate or international sales activities."[150]

The Act requires the Commission to complete its study within 18 months and transmit its findings, including any legislative recommendations, to Congress. The Act directed Senate and House leadership to appoint 19 commissioners including: the Secretary of Commerce, the Secretary of the Treasury and the United States Trade Representative (or their respective delegates), eight representatives from state and local governments (including one from a state or local government that does not impose a sales tax, and one representative from a state that does not impose an income tax), and eight representatives from the e-commerce industry (including small businesses), telecommunications carriers, local retail business and consumer groups.[151]

Formal Findings and Recommendations of the Commission

1. Digital Divide
The following items received more than 2/3rds (15) of the Commissioners' support and are considered recommendations:

Tax Management in Action 9.2 (continued)

Advisory Commission on Electronic Commerce's Report to Congress (April 2000)

- Clarify federal welfare guidelines expressly to permit the states to spend Temporary Assistance to Needy Families Program (TANF) surpluses (unobligated balances) to provide needy families access to computers and the Internet, and to provide training in computers and Internet use.
- Encourage states and localities to partner with private technology companies to make computers and the Internet widely accessible for needy families, libraries, schools, and community centers and to train needy families how to use computers and the Internet. Incentives for these partnerships may include:
  - federal and state tax credits and incentives for private technology companies that partner with state and local governments; and
  - federal matching funds for state and local expenditures.
- Encourage the Administration and Congress to continue gathering data for empirical research that will inform federal, state and local policymakers on measures that will lead to the reduction, and eventual elimination, of the Digital Divide by empowering families in rural America and inner cities to participate in the Internet economy.

2. **Privacy Implications of Internet Taxation**
   The following items received more than 2/3rds (16) of the Commissioners' support and are considered recommendations:
   - Explore the privacy issues involved in the collection and administration of taxes on e-commerce, with special attention given to the costs that any new system of revenue collection may have upon other values that U.S. citizens hold dear, and the steps taken in systems developed to administer taxes on e-commerce to safeguard and secure personal information.
   - Take great care in the crafting of any laws pertaining to online privacy (if any such laws are necessary), because policy missteps could endanger U.S. leadership in worldwide e-commerce.

3. **International Taxes and Tariffs**
   The following item received more than 2/3rds (18) of the Commissioners' support and is considered a recommendation:
   - Support implementing and making permanent a standstill on tariffs at the earliest possible date.

Majority Policy Proposals of the Commission

1. **Sales and Use Taxes**
   The following items received a majority (11) of the Commissioners' support:
   - For a period of five years, extend the current moratorium barring multiple and discriminatory taxation of e-commerce and prohibit taxation of sales of digitized goods and products and their non-digitized counterparts.
   - Clarify which factors would not, in and of themselves, establish a seller's physical presence in a state for purposes of determining whether a seller has sufficient nexus with that state to impose collection obligations.

Tax Management in Action 9.2 (continued)

Advisory Commission on Electronic Commerce's Report to Congress
(April 2000)

- Encourage state and local governments to work with and through the National Conference of Commissioners on Uniform State Laws ("NCCUSL") in drafting a uniform sales and use tax act that would simplify state and local sales and use taxation policies so as to create and maintain parity of collection costs (net of vendor discounts) between remote sellers and comparable single-jurisdiction vendors that do not offer remote sales.
- Establish a new advisory commission responsible for oversight of the progress of NCCUSL's efforts to create a uniform sales and use tax act.

2. **Business Activity Taxes**
   The following item received a majority (11) of the Commissioners' support:
   - Clarify the circumstances that determine whether a seller has sufficient nexus with a state to be required to meet business activity and income tax reporting and payment obligations of that state.

3. **Internet Access**
   The following item received a majority (11) of the Commissioners' support:
   - Make permanent the current moratorium on any transaction taxes on the sale of Internet access, including taxes that were grandfathered under the Internet Tax Freedom Act.

4. **Taxation of Telecommunications Services and Providers**
   The following items received a majority (11) of the Commissioners' support:
   - Eliminate the 3% federal excise tax on communications services.[152]
   - Eliminate excess tax burdens on telecommunications real, tangible and intangible property.
   - Afford similar treatment of telecommunications infrastructure in states that exempt purchases of certain types of business equipment from sales and use taxes.
   - Encourage state and local governments to work with and through NCCUSL in drafting a uniform telecommunications state and local excise tax act, within three years, that would require states to follow one of two simplified tax structure models.

5. **International Taxes and Tariffs**
   A. Tariffs
      The following item received a majority (11) of the Commissioners' support:
      - Support the formal, permanent extension of the World Trade Organization's current moratorium on tariffs and duties for electronic transmissions or transaction tax rates.
   B. International Taxes on Goods and Services
      The following items received a majority (11) of the Commissioners' support:
      - Recognize the OECD's leadership role in coordinating international dialogue concerning the taxation of e-commerce; affirm support for the principles of the OECD's framework conditions for taxation of e-commerce; and support the OECD's continued role as the appropriate forum for (1) fostering effective international dialogues concerning these issues; and (2) building international consensus.

Tax Management in Action 9.2 (continued)

Advisory Commission on Electronic Commerce's Report to Congress
(April 2000)

- Encourage and support (including adequately funding) the U.S. Government's efforts to further international dialogue concerning the taxation of e-commerce, which are consistent with the principles outlined above.
- Refrain from adopting legislative proposals affecting international transactions or activities that are inconsistent with the principles enumerated above.

6. **The Need for Improved Knowledge of International Ramifications**
   The following item received a majority (11) of the Commissioners' support:
   - Congress should increase its oversight of the international ramifications of domestic Internet commerce decisions.

Formal Findings and Recommendations

1. Digital divide — to provide access to needy families to both computers and the Internet
2. Privacy implications of Internet taxation — to explore the privacy issues involved in the collection and administration of taxes on e-commerce and to take care in the crafting of any laws pertaining to online privacy (if any such laws are necessary)
3. International taxes and tariffs — to support implementing and making permanent a standstill on tariffs at the earliest possible date

E-COMMERCE TAXATION — MUCH ADO ABOUT NOTHING?

Although the arguments about whether to impose taxes on the Internet and e-commerce have been passionate on both sides, there is little by way of empirical evidence on what are the likely effects of either course of action. There has been some preliminary work done on the issue by Robert Cline and Thomas Neubig of Ernst & Young and Donald Bruce and William Fox of the University of Tennessee.[153] Their findings in these studies are discussed here.

Cline and Neubig estimate that the sales and use tax not collected in 1998 because of the increase in remote sales due to the Internet is less than $170 million, or one-tenth of 1% of total state and local government sales and use tax collections. They argue that the small amount of lost tax revenue is due, in large part, to the fact that 80% of current e-commerce is business-to-business (B2B) sales, which are not subject to sales tax, and most e-commerce sales are of intangible services, such as travel and financial services, which generally are not subject to sales tax.

In contrast, Bruce and Fox estimated that by 2003 the total revenue loss for all states due to e-commerce will be over $10 billion. They estimate the revenue loss for Arizona alone to be over $183 million in 2003. What is the rationale for their very different point of view than that of Cline and Neubig? Bruce and Fox contend that the devil is in the details.

Specifically, they state that:

- Not all B2B transactions are exempt from sales tax.
- About 52% of B2B transactions are taxable.
- Businesses have about 40–50% compliance with the use tax.
- About 70% of business-to-consumer (also called B2C) sales are taxable.

ENDNOTES

141. For more detail on this topic, browse the Web site for Professor Karayan's courses on taxation of e-enterprises at http://www.csupomona.edu/~jekarayan/acc439.
142. There is a growing body of literature on the subject of e-commerce taxation. One of the most astute, yet readable, of these remains the paper written by R. Bruce Josten, Executive Vice President of the U.S. Chamber of Commerce, entitled "E-Commerce Taxation: Issues in Search for Answers" (September 1999) that was submitted to the Advisory Commission on Electronic Commerce. This chapter is organized in much the same way as his paper.
143. Much of this discussion is based on Edward A. Morse, "State taxation of Internet commerce: something new under the sun?" *Creighton Law Review*, 30, 1113 (1997).
144. George S. Isaacson, "A Tax Whose Time has Passed? Problems with State Sales and Use Taxes in an Electronic Commerce Environment" (paper presented at the University of Southern California Federal Tax Institute, 2000), based on information obtained from Vertex, Inc., a developer of state and local tax compliance software.
145. Robert J. Cline and Thomas S. Neubig, "Masters of Complexity and Bearers of Great Burden: The Sales Tax System and Compliance Costs for Multistate Retailers," Ernst & Young Economics and Consulting and Quantitative Analysis Group, September 1999.
146. See "*Jefferson Lines* as ticket to cyberspace? Taxing electronic services," by Arthur Angstreich, James R. Fisher, and Eric J. Miethke in *Tax Notes* (July 27, 1998), for an extended analysis of this case and a policy proposal for an origin-based tax policy for the sales taxation of Internet-delivered services.
147. *Complete Auto Transit v. Brady*, 430 U.S. 274 (1977).
148. *Container Corp. of America v. Franchise Tax Board*, 463 U.S. 159 (1983).
149. This example is adapted from "The taxation of the cyberspace: state tax issues related to the Internet and electronic commerce," by Karl A. Frieden and Michael E. Porter, *State Tax Notes* 11, 1363 (1996).

150. ITFA, 47 U.S.C. §151, §1102(g)(1998).
151. ITFA, 47 U.S.C. §151, §1102(a)(1998).
152. The authors just have to tell readers that this tax was enacted in 1898 as a temporary measure to finance the Spanish-American War. At that time, this tax essentially was a "luxury tax," which has been a common war tax.
153. "The Sky is Not Falling: Why State and Local Revenues Were Not Significantly Impacted by the Internet in 1998," by Robert Cline and Thomas Neubig, Ernst & Young Economic Consulting Group, June 1999. Source: "E-Commerce in the Context of Declining State Sales Tax Bases," by Donald Bruce and William Fox, University of Tennessee, February 2000.

Free value-added materials available from the
Download Resource Center at www.jrosspub.com.

PART IV:
OTHER AREAS

10

INCOME TAXATION OF EMPLOYEES AND SOLE PROPRIETORSHIPS

INTRODUCTION

Income taxation of employees and sole proprietorships has been saved until last in this book because the key issues were discussed when dealing with corporate income taxes. However, there are some corporate-individual differences, and these are presented in this chapter.

FEDERAL-STATE CONFORMITY

As with corporate income taxes, many states do not match Federal law, but increasingly have conformed. A key figure is Federal adjusted gross income, from which state differences are taken as adjustments in reaching state adjusted gross income. The biggest difference is grounded in differences in geographic jurisdiction. Analogous to the Federal, in some states income tax applies to the worldwide income of state residents but only the state-source income of nonresidents.

When it comes to personal income taxes, there are two basic sets of rules: the first for residents and the second for nonresidents and part-year residents. A "nonresident" is an individual who is not a resident; a person usually is a resident if physically present in the taxing jurisdiction for other than a "temporary or transitory purpose." As a rule of thumb, a person who moves into a state to take a job, start a business, or retire — or who is physically present in the state for more than 9 months — becomes a resident when he or she enters the state.

The distinction is made because in many states residents are taxed on their worldwide income but nonresidents are only taxed on their state-source income. Income is state-source if earned in the state, such as rents or royalties from property physically located or used in the state and from business operations in the state.

Similar to the situation for corporate income taxes, the latter can be problematical for multistate businesses. For them, an averaging mechanism, normally a three-factor Massachusetts formula, is used. It averages the ratios of property, payroll, and sales within and without the state, and is used to apportion business income into the state. The same issues regarding unitary taxation versus separate accounting apply to employees and sole proprietors as were discussed for corporate taxpayers.

The big issue for employees and sole proprietors that was not covered in the corporate income tax discussions in this book is residency. Nonresidents are taxed sourced to a state. For example, income generated by the rendering of personal services in a state is sourced to the state. There are special rules for certain occupations. For example, nonresident salespersons apportion commission income by the ratio of state sales to total sales volume. Athletes and entertainers identify revenue from performances in each state. For example, a football player whose team plays three of its fifteen games in California would have to apportion 20% of his salary for the year to California. Professionals — such as CPAs — must do so on a job-by-job or hourly basis. Employees who have continuously been employed sometimes must prorate their pay for the year on a relative workday basis. In practice, this rule may be honored more in the breach. Technically, California taxes business people who fly into a California airport for a business meeting and then fly home.

Nonresidents are not taxed on passive income from investments not located in a state. Under the ancient Roman doctrine that intangibles have situs where their owners' reside, portfolio income such as interest or dividends is not taxed by the state where an employee or sole proprietor does not reside. Trading in securities can amount to a business, so a nonresident who buys and sells with such regularity in a state to amount to transacting a business there may be taxed on the resulting income.

Returns on investment in intangibles, such as patents or franchises, are taxed only if the property is being used in the state. This applies to current returns, such as royalties, and to profits on disposition. Thus it behooves persons moving in and out of a high-tax state to time gains and losses optimally. Realty or tangible personal property generates state-source income if it is physically located in a state.

Income or loss from pass-through entities, such as trusts, partnerships, and S corporations, retains its character. That is, owners are taxed under the conduit theory. Thus portfolio dividends and interest — as opposed to those that are part of a business — are not taxed to nonresident owners unless the property acquired a business situs in the state while in the hands of the pass-through entity.

So what contacts make someone a resident of a state? A "resident" generally is defined as a person who is physically present in a jurisdiction for other than a temporary or transitory purpose. (As explained below, it is not controlling that such an individual's domicile, or legal residence, is in the state or elsewhere.) Also deemed a resident are persons domiciled in the state but who are physically absent for any period during the tax year for a temporary or transitory purpose. Anyone who is not a "resident" is automatically a "nonresident."

Thus it often is important to determine just what is a temporary or transitory purpose. The underlying theory is that the state with which a person has the closest connection during the taxable year is the state of his or her residence.

Residence and domicile are not the same thing. Residence determines taxability of income, not domicile. The definition of residence is based on domicile but is not synonymous with it. For example, the laws of the state of domicile govern the allocation of income between spouses. That is, if the taxpayers are domiciled in a community property state, property earned during marriage is considered earned one-half by each spouse, unless there is a community property agreement to the contrary (such as a valid prenuptial agreement).

Thus, the definition of domicile is important. It basically is the fixed home and permanent establishment of the taxpayer, that is, the place to which he or she intends to return when absent. Domicile is where the heart is. Dorothy may have been a resident of Oz, but her domicile was Kansas.

Interestingly, a taxpayer may have only one domicile at one time. But domicile can change in the wink of an eye, and do so repeatedly. Change of domicile requires three elements. The first is the abandonment of the taxpayer's prior domicile.

Facts evidencing this largely are in the control of the taxpayer. Good planners consider this. Keeping one's room at Mom's house, and storing valuable items such as collections and cars there, can keep it a domicile even when the taxpayer works elsewhere.

Physically moving to and living in a state usually is necessary to change from an out-of-state domicile to an in-state one. But it is not sufficient. There also must be an intent to remain in the new locality permanently and indefinitely. Again, the facts can be preserved by perceptive tax planning which help show that this has not occurred.

Spouses who live together have the same domicile, barring unusual circumstances. However, some states (e.g., California) allow a person to retain his or her domicile regardless of the domicile of the spouse.

Now that we have looked at the definition of domicile, let us turn our attention to Dorothy's Oz, that is, the definition of residence. A resident must be physically present in the state for a purpose that is not temporary or transitory. This is determined regardless of domicile. In the alternative, one can become a resident if one is domiciled in the state, provided any absence from the state is for a purpose that is temporary or transitory.

A resident remains a resident even though temporarily absent from the state, even if he or she establishes domicile elsewhere. Thus even though there is only one domicile, a taxpayer may be considered a resident for tax purposes by more than one state at the same time. The double taxation that can result is softened somewhat by many a state's equivalent of the Federal foreign tax credit. (It also is softened by incorrect return positions, the vast majority of which are unintentional.) This does not do away with double taxation entirely, however.

Not every state grants such a credit, and some credit only income taxes paid to another state on income from a source within the other state, but only if the tax does not result purely from dual residency. Furthermore, in some cases no credit applies to states which themselves provide another state income tax credit, such as Arizona.

There are some regulations and cases that help determine the law in the various states. The most extensive are in California. For example, Regulations §17014 provides a facts and circumstances test to the key phrases "temporary or transitory purpose," and examples of "other than temporary or transitory purpose" are given in Regulations §17014(b). These include an individual who is in this state to improve his or her health and whose illness is of such a character as to require a relatively long or indefinite period to recuperate.

Also not temporary is a taxpayer who is physically present in the state for business purposes that will require a long or indefinite period to accomplish or is employed in a position that may last permanently or indefinitely. Finally, one who has retired from business and moved to the state, with no definite intention of leaving shortly thereafter, is a resident under these regulations.

Examples of "temporary or transitory purpose" are given in Regulations §17014(b). An individual who is simply passing through the state on his or her way to another state or country is not a resident. Nor does one become a resident merely by coming to a state for a rest or vacation, provided that it is not extensive or regular. Practitioners sometimes call this the Disney World rule.

Doing a deal in a state does not make one a resident. Coming to New York to complete a particular transaction, or perform a particular contract, or fulfill a particular engagement, which will require presence in the state for but a short period, is a temporary or transitory purpose. Athletes and entertainers often fall under this rule. They do not get off tax free, however. Most states source that performance of personal services to where they are rendered.

An underlying theory applies in close calls: the state with which a person has the closest connection during the taxable year is his or her state of residence. As discussed more fully below, this point often is never reached because of the operation of two presumptions. The first is the seasonal visitor rule. (It is codified into the 6 months or less presumption found in California Regulations §17014[b].) It states that taxpayers who spend 6 months or less of the taxable year in a state and who maintain a permanent abode elsewhere are deemed nonresidents. There is a catch, however. In the words of the regulation, this results "providing he does not engage in any activity or conduct within this state other than that of a seasonal visitor, tourist or guest."

The cases discussed below indicate that people can be seasonal visitors or guests even though they own homes, property, investments, or businesses in California or are socially involved in the California scene.

The opposite result occurs for long visits, as embodied by the 9-months presumption of Revenue and Taxation Code §17016. This statute provides that people physically present in California no less than 9 months in any one tax year are presumed to be there for a purpose that is not temporary or transitory. This statutory presumption is rebuttable based on facts and circumstances.

A variety of factual issues have been involved repeatedly when resident status is in question. One common one is the effect of maintaining homes in two or more states. The definition of residence for tax purposes is not the same as that used in normal conversation.

The tax residence of the multiple home taxpayer often turns on where the "closest connections" are. Facts that have been cited in cases include:

1. The amount of time taxpayer spent in the state relative to each other potential state or country of residence.
2. The number of months taxpayer's immediate family as a whole was maintained in each place. One key question here is where the children, if any, live particularly if they attend school.
3. The relative substantiality of each house or apartment, i.e., a mansion in one place versus a summer cottage in another.
4. Who occupies the residence when not occupied by taxpayer; the issue turns on whether family members (or servants) do so, or whether it is rented out, and if so, for how long.

If the taxpayer files resident returns in another state, this evidences, but not conclusively, that the purpose in state is temporary or transitory. Other factors that have come up are the location of the most substantial and active bank accounts maintained and voter registration. As to the latter, sometimes the question of where the taxpayer actually voted is at issue, and if so, whether in person or by absentee ballot. As these facts are entirely within the control of the taxpayer, a little planning can go a long way.

Other factors include the state where cars, boats, planes, and other toys are maintained and licensed, along with other social activities, like memberships in clubs, lodges, or churches, and the relative intensity of activity outside of the state.

Two other factors are of recent vintage. Did the taxpayer claim residence in order to reap the deep discount on his or her childrens' in-state college tuition? If so, the taxpayer virtually admitted residence, and it is extremely unlikely to win a nonresidency claim.

The final factor of interest here is simple: where did the taxpayer claim homeowner's property tax exemptions? The homeowner's exemption is not determinative of residence for income tax purposes, but is taken as strong indication of residence if it was used to reduce property taxes. Some states have a veteran's homeowners' exemption, too, and allow veterans to apply for subsidized home loans. Both of these typically require a declaration of residence in state. This admission against interest should be determinative. Note that because the veteran's exemption is less than homeowner's and one cannot get both, as a practical matter the veteran's exemption is obsolete and is never applied for.

Those taxpayers who do not have multiple living quarters often have determinations based on the relative significance of business activities in versus out of the state. Note that it is not necessary to have one state of residence for income tax purposes. An individual may be held to be a resident by more than one state for the same time period; among other reasons, different states have different rules. On the other hand, in order to establish nonresidence, it is not always necessary to prove that one is a resident somewhere else.

Moving to or from a state raises the issue of when does a taxpayer become a resident or cease to be one. "When" residence attaches usually is not a problem: a taxpayer is a resident when he or she arrives in the state to reside permanently or indefinitely. Thus residency relates back to crossing the border. However, sometimes there is a considerable transition period due to business obligations in the former state. Taxpayers, particularly these days, also may be unable to sell their prior residence or leave part of their family in the old home to finish the school year. There also may be other entanglements.

It is possible for spouses to become, or cease to be, residents at different times. A change of residence usually involves change of domicile as well, so if husband and wife move at different times, they may have a period of time when their domiciles are different. This can create interesting results when one spouse is domiciled in a separate property state.

Taxpayers who take a job in another state or country transform into nonresidents when they leave the state, unless the job is temporary or transitory. Business assignments outside the state, particularly in foreign countries, have created much controversy in recent years. Generally speaking, someone domiciled in a state remains a resident if he or she is outside the state on a contract with a definite termination date, as is the case with most foreign employment. However, a contract for more than 2 years typically is sufficient to break the connection; many practitioners feel that 18 months gives sufficient comfort for a return position.

A single taxpayer who severs most of his or her connections with the state when leaving, even though he or she continues to own real property located there that is leased or rented to someone else, will usually be considered a non-resident. This would exclude income from employment, but not from the rentals. A married taxpayer who takes family along and severs most ties also transmutes into a nonresident, but those who do not almost always remain a resident for the entire assignment. Again, remember that even if the taxpayer were to become a nonresident, a resident spouse — that is, one who stays behind — in a community property state will be taxed on his or her community half of the out-of-state income.

As noted above, there are special rules for soldiers and sailors. These generally deem them to be nonresidents when outside of a state on permanent duty. They are a good example of the rare Federal legislation in the area of state and local taxation. The rules are embodied in Title 50 of the U.S. Code, and were enacted as part of the *Soldiers and Sailors Civil Relief Act of 1940*. Generally, a service person is not considered to have changed residence solely because of permanent military orders. Compensation for military services performed in a state where the member is a nonresident cannot be sourced to that state.

The domicile of a service person is the state of domicile at the time he or she entered service. A service person can change domicile by changing the home of record. However, a service person who is married can retain his or her own domicile regardless of the domicile or residence of the spouse. A civilian spouse's domicile is normally that of the soldier or sailor. But if both spouses are service members, each will retain his or her own domicile unless specific action is taken to change it.

Although the determination of residency thus is fact bound, there are some good rules of thumb. For example, as explained above, persons physically present in a state for 6 months or less in a tax year, and who throughout the year maintain a permanent home elsewhere which is their permanent domicile, are rarely considered residents. Instead, they will be considered as being in this state for temporary or transitory purposes providing they do not engage in any activity other than that of a seasonal visitor, tourist, or guest. The reverse, however, is not deemed true. But it usually is: coming to see Niagara Falls does not make one a resident.

The effect of domicile can be overriding. Then again, an individual may be domiciled in a state but not be a resident. For example, a person who goes on a 5-year assignment abroad, but who intends to come back to the state when it is finished, can be considered domiciled in the state, but he or she is not a resident because he or she is outside the state for more than a temporary or transitory purpose.

Taxpayers need not show that they are a resident of any particular state or country to avoid residence status; they merely need to show that they are not residents in that state. Thus, the person referred to in the last paragraph need not become a resident of another country to avoid residence in the state that was left: physical absence plus the required state of mind is sufficient. The person could, for example, be on a space mission to Mars or be circumnavigating the globe in a rowboat.

On the other hand, an individual may be a resident of a state though domiciled elsewhere. If the Sultan of Brunei, who owns the Beverly Hills Hotel but maintains lavish palaces and estates throughout the world, were to spend most of the year in California every year because he liked the weather, he would be a California resident although most likely domiciled in Brunei. An actual case was decided in 1955 on the issue, the *Appeal of Amado*. There the taxpayers were domiciled in New York for most of the period involved, but they spent most of their time in California. They were held to be California residents.

As similar decision came in the *Appeal of Ralph and Marvelle Currier*, a 1969 decision. There the taxpayer was a Southern Pacific Railroad Company employee who was required to move frequently due to the nature of his job. As a result, he had lived in California for over 2 years before moving his family fairly permanently to Arizona. He then was transferred back to work in California.

The Franchise Tax Board — the body that conducted the tax audit — invoked the 9-months presumption of California residence. The State Board of Equalization — the elected body that hears appeals from the Franchise Tax Board, among other things — agreed with the taxpayer that the facts proved that he was domiciled in Arizona. Nevertheless, they held that his work assignment in California was for an indefinite period. Thus he was in the state for other than a transitory purpose, and taxable as a California resident.

As a result of California's unsatisfying efforts to tax President Nixon as a resident during his extensive absence from the state after being elected President, special rules classify nonmilitary Federal brass, like congresspersons, Cabinet members, and high-level bureaucrats, as California residents if they remain domiciled in California.

Notwithstanding these rules, the area has been a hive of litigation for years. A rebuttable presumption alluded to above was added to the law to establish a bright line for long-term visitors to California. "Every individual who spends in the aggregate more than nine months of the taxable year within this state shall be presumed to be a resident."

The 9-month residence rule is not hard and fast: it is truly a rebuttable presumption, and thus can be overcome by good facts. This was done in the case of *Appeal of Edgar Montillion Woolley* decided in 1951. The taxpayer was an actor who was permanently domiciled in New York. He came to California in 1944 and stayed for about a year. This included over 9 months in 1945. While in California he acted in pictures and radio broadcasts.

He lived in a hotel the entire time, renting on a weekly basis. He did not intend to stay so long, but illness and a studio strike caused him to change his plans serendipitously. The State Board of Equalization held that, even though he lived in California for over 9 months in 1945 and for over a year all toll, he was in California for only for a temporary or transitory purpose and therefore was not a resident.

Another similar result occurred in the 1962 *Appeal of Joseph and Rebecca Peskin*. They were in California most of the year for several years, up to 10 months in one year, and owned businesses and property in California. Nevertheless, the taxpayers were able to rebut the presumption of residence due to their close connections with their home state, Illinois.

This 9-months presumption hurts taxpayers, but in theory never helps them. Being in the state for less than 9 months does not, in and of itself, establish non-residency. Indeed, in theory — and as one taxpayer found out the hard way — one can be a California resident even though not present in California at all during the year.

As much of the law in the area is case law, most of the examples you will hear will be actual matters determined by the State Board of Equalization or the courts. There is a case on point here. *Appeal of Morgan and Ann Jones* was a 1972 case where the taxpayers were in California for 8 months in 1961 and held to be residents. In this case the taxpayers maintained little formal contact with California. For example, they voted in Texas and had Texas driver's licenses. Nevertheless, the State Board of Equalization held that no "under 9 months" presumption existed. The Board also ruled for residency in 1962, when the taxpayers were present in California for less than 6 months.

Appeal of Raymond and Ann Stefani was a 1984 case involving a California professor. He taught at a school in Switzerland while on sabbatical leave from his California position. Nevertheless, he was held to have remained a California resident, based on a regulation that stated that "a person may be a resident even though not in the state during any portion of the year."

Members of the U.S. Armed Forces on active duty fare better. The Franchise Tax Board's 1965 *Legal Ruling No. 300* held that they become nonresidents when leaving California for duty out of state, unless the duty is temporary. This rule does not, however, prevent the soldier's spouse from being taxed on one-half of the couple's community income if the spouse is a California resident.

The effect of a temporary assignment can be surprising. In *Appeal of Cecil and Bonai Sanders*, the State Board of Equalization held in 1971 that unless military orders required a "permanent change of station," duty is "temporary rather than permanent or indefinite" and thus California residence is not automatically shucked off.

These rules do not apply to civilian employees, as illustrated by a 1983 case, *Appeal of Ronald and Joyce Surette*. There the taxpayers spent 3 years in West Germany while the husband worked for the U.S. Army, but not as a member of the armed forces. They were held to continue to be California residents throughout the 3 years because they owned a California home and never changed their California driver's licenses and voter registrations.

Similarly, in *Appeal of Dennis and Emiko Leggett*, a 1984 case, the taxpayer worked almost the entire year aboard U.S. naval vessels but still was ruled a California resident.

Taxpayers who leave the state for business have had varying luck with appeals. The State Board of Equalization has repeatedly stated that the state with which a person has the closest connections is where that person is a resident. Those who win tend to have cast off as many ties to California in the course of what appears at the outset to be a long or indefinite project outside the state, or to have kept as many contacts with another state or country while traveling to California for a short, specific, or limited activity.

One good case in this regard is *Appeal of Richard and Kathleen Hardman*, which was decided in 1975. There a writer who worked in the U.K. for almost all of the year — 1969 — was determined to be a nonresident. This was the finding even though during 1969 and 1970 he was physically present in California for about 11 months.

Two factors weighed most in the decision. First, the taxpayers intended an extended stay in the U.K.; the period was shortened after the fact. Second, the taxpayers abandoned social, legal, and financial contact with California when they originally left.

It was followed in 1986 by *Appeal of Berry Gordy, Jr.* There the taxpayer owned extensive holdings of real estate and business investment interests in Michigan. He also continued to license his cars, vote, and consult professionals such as doctors, dentists, attorneys, certified public accountants, and insurance agents in Michigan. He was determined not to have become a California resident merely because of his presence in the state.

Taxpayers can be considered residents for odd reasons, such as leaving one's family behind in California while going on a foreign assignment. Note that California community property laws can act to deem as earned by the spouse who stays one-half of the income earned by the spouse abroad. Thus, only half of the expatriating spouse's income is removed from California's reach if the expatriate is declared a nonresident. All of the resident spouse's earnings and, of course, earnings from rental realty located in California (and perhaps even bank accounts) are California source income and thus taxed even if the expatriate is declared a nonresident.

For example, in *Appeal of John and Beverly Simpson*, an engineer who worked in Australia from October 1970 through May 1972 was denied his claim that he was a nonresident in 1971. In this 1975 case, the damning facts were that his family did not leave California to go with him, and the job he went on was intended to last for just 1 year.

The importance of expatriating one's family was emphasized in the 1976 *Appeal of Anthony and Beverly Zupanovich*. There a taxpayer who was in Vietnam on an assignment that spanned 4 calendar years was held to remain a resident for the first 3. The State Board of Equalization language clearly indicated the importance of his family remaining behind when it stated that "although appellant's absence turned out to be rather lengthy, his family life, his social life, and much of his financial life remained centered in California throughout the years in question."

The tribunal also stated that such "connections...are important both as a measure of the benefits and protection that the taxpayer has received from the laws and government of California, and also as an objective indication of whether the taxpayer entered or left this state for temporary or transitory purposes."

This approach was reflected in a 1976 case, *Appeal of William and Mary Louise Oberholtzer*. There the taxpayer on-site in France for his entire year-and-a-half assignment retained his house, a car, and child in school in California. Furthermore, French law caused him to be treated as a French resident. Nevertheless, he was not allowed to claim that he became a nonresident when he left California for France.

In the 1980 *Appeal of Pierre and Nicole Salinger*, the taxpayer — who at one time had campaigned for senator in California and served as President Kennedy's press advisor — spent a year working in Europe, but had not abandoned his social and political ties with California. He was held to remain a California resident, even though he subsequently has remained based in Europe.

One can be a resident though one's time in California is limited, according to *Appeal of E. L. and Virginia Cord*. This is a 1958 State Board of Equalization decision. It held that the taxpayers were California residents during the 3 tax years at issue. However, in 1 year they were in California for only 4 months, and in the other 2 about 7 months. The determining factor was that the largest portion of their investments was in California, and they never stayed in any other state longer than they were in California.

The outer limits of the doctrine have been tested in cases dealing with sailors. A seaman was held to be a California resident in *Appeal of Olav Valderhaug* in

1954. This was decided even though he was never in California for more than 3 months a year. The reason for California residence was that his family lived here.

In *Appeal of Charles F. Varn*, the taxpayer was a merchant seaman who never worked in California. But he was deemed to have become a California resident the day he married one, because he had no closer connection with any other state or country.

Finally, let us turn to chewing gum. Wrigley's widow lost her claim of non-residency despite having extensive business, social, banking, political, and other interests in Chicago. Three aspects turned the Board's mind against her. In their words, a "...long continued preference for (spending her time in) California, when coupled with her extensive and long continued financial interests within the state, the burial of her husband in California, the retention of two large homes within the state and the exchange of her large apartment in Chicago for smaller quarters there, convinces us that...California had become her principal place of abode."

A "nonresident alien" can be taxed as a California resident, even if in this country illegally. Thus in *Appeal of Riad Ghali*, an Egyptian residing in the U.S. due to political disfavor at home was clearly a nonresident alien for Federal tax purposes. Technically, he was here illegally because he had not properly sought asylum; the Federal authorities were aware of his presence, however. The 1971 case ruled that he was a California resident, and thus taxable on non-California source income.

The determination of residence, like the determination of domicile, often presents a very difficult problem. It is so fact based that no clear answers can be given. The Franchise Tax Board has a questionnaire that it demands be filled out whenever the issue comes up on audit. Here are some of the facts it is interested in.

1. Previous or other current addresses within and without California
2. The days within and without California and other states or countries over the past few years
3. Where the taxpayer's family was during those years, and where the taxpayer owned or rented a home
4. Where registration and licensing to vote, drive, own cars, pay taxes, and the like occurred
5. The location of bank accounts, religious, and social clubs

The questionnaire, which is available from the Franchise Tax Board, is a road map for tax planners. When someone is leaving California, get and keep as much written evidence that the assignment is long term — preferably over 2 years — or indefinite. Even the most self-serving memos or letters can prove useful. Get and keep evidence that will support answers to the questionnaire.

Sell off as many assets in California as possible, or give them away, even if it is to friends and family. Move bank accounts; this easily can be done with out-of-state credit cards, large brokerage house cash management accounts, and money market mutual funds. It may be as simple as updating an address.

Reregister to vote as an expatriate American, or in the new state when the taxpayer is living. Go inactive on any clubs; join the equivalent — such as a church — in the new location.

If the taxpayer does own a house in California, have it leased out long term. If it cannot be done that way, list it for sale while it is leased month for month.

Store assets outside the state, if possible: Nevada is not that far away. Be sure to change the address on the taxpayer's passport, driver's license, and vehicle registration.

The reverse is true for those coming to California.

Tax Management in Action 10.1

Resident/Nonresident Issues: An Outline of Examples from California

I. Significance of residence
  A. A resident is taxable on all income regardless of source.
  B. A nonresident is taxable only on income from in-state (e.g., California) sources.

II. Residence and domicile
  A. Personal income tax law makes a sharp distinction between these terms, which elsewhere are often used interchangeably.
    1. Residence determines taxability of income.
    2. The definition of residence is based on domicile but is not synonymous with it.
    3. Laws of the state of domicile govern the allocation of income between spouses.
  B. Definition of domicile
    1. Place of true, fixed home and permanent establishment; place to which one intends to return when absent; place where a person has voluntary fixed habitation of self and family with the intention of making a permanent home [18 California Code of Regulations Section ("Reg.") 17014(c)].
    2. A person may have only one domicile at one time.
    3. Change of domicile requires three elements:
      (a) Abandonment of prior domicile.
      (b) Physically moving to and residing in the new locality.
      (c) Intent to remain in the new locality permanently and indefinitely.
    4. As a general rule spouses who live together have the same domicile. However, since 1972 California law specifically allows a person to retain his or her California domicile regardless of the domicile of the spouse. The law previously provided that the domicile of the husband was the domicile of the wife unless the spouses were separated [Government Code Sec. 244(e)].
  C. Definition of residence
    1. A resident is a person who is either:
      (a) Present in the state for a purpose which is not temporary or transitory (regardless of domicile); or

Resident/Nonresident Issues: An Outline of Examples from California

    (b) Domiciled in the state and absent from the state for a purpose which is temporary or transitory.

    (c) A resident (regardless of domicile) remains a resident even though temporarily absent from the state [R & T Code Sec. 17014].

  2. A person may only have one domicile but may be considered a resident for tax purposes by more than one state at the same time. The tax effect may be mitigated by a credit granted by one state for tax paid to another on income from a source within the other state.

  3. This law defines residence for personal income tax purposes only. It does not govern the determination of residence for any other purpose, although the fact that a person does or does not file resident personal income tax returns may be taken into account in determining residence for other purposes.

III. **Regulations governing resident status**

  A. Meaning of "temporary or transitory purpose": a facts and circumstances test

    1. Examples of "other than temporary or transitory purpose" [Reg. 17014(b)]:

      (a) An individual who is in this state to improve his health and whose illness is of such a character as to require a relatively long or indefinite period to recuperate…

      (b) Or who is here for business purposes which will require a long or indefinite period to accomplish…

      (c) Or is employed in a position that may last permanently or indefinitely…

      (d) Or has retired from business and moved to the state with no definite intention of leaving shortly thereafter.

    2. Examples of "temporary or transitory purpose" [Reg. 17014(b)]:

      (a) An individual who is simply passing through this state on his way to another state or country…

      (b) Or is here for a brief rest or vacation…

      (c) Or to complete a particular transaction, or perform a particular contract, or fulfill a particular engagement, which will require his presence in this state for but a short period.

  B. Underlying theory: The state with which a person has the closest connection during the taxable year is his state of residence.

    1. Six months or less presumption [Reg. 17014(b)]: An individual who spends six months or less of the taxable year in the state and who maintains a permanent abode at the place of his domicile is considered a nonresident "providing [s]he does not engage in any activity or conduct within this state other than that of a seasonal visitor, tourist or guest." An individual may be a seasonal visitor or guest even though he owns a home in California, has a bank account there, or joins local clubs.

    2. Nine months or more presumption (R & T Sec. 17016): An individual who spends nine months or more of the taxable year in the state is presumed to be there for a purpose that is not temporary or transitory. This statutory presumption is rebuttable based on facts and circumstances.

Tax Management in Action 10.1 (continued)

Resident/Nonresident Issues: An Outline of Examples from California

(a) Presence for less than nine months does not create a presumption of nonresidence. A person may be a resident even though not present in the state at all during the taxable year [Reg. 17016].

IV. Issues in determining resident status
   A. Maintaining homes in California and another state: Where is the tax residence?
   B. Moving to California: Are you a resident when you cross the border?
   C. Moving out of California: Are you a nonresident when you cross the border?
   D. Special rules for military personnel.

V. The multiple residence taxpayer
   A. Determination must be made in terms of "closest connection." Questions that will be asked include:
      1. Number of months taxpayer and spouse spent in California, other states, and elsewhere (e.g., traveling)
      2. Number of months family as a whole was maintained in each place
      3. Relative substantiality of residence, e.g., mansion in California vs. condo in Dallas
      4. Who occupies California and other residence when not occupied by taxpayer?
      5. Where do children live, attend school?
      6. Does taxpayer file returns as a resident of another state?
         (a) As a practical matter — A taxpayer who files resident returns in Hawaii and nonresident in California is not saving any taxes and will probably not be hassled much. One who claims residency in Nevada or Texas is more likely to be questioned.
      7. Where are most substantial and active bank accounts maintained?
      8. Where is voter registration? Actually voted? Absentee ballot?
      9. Where are autos maintained and registered?
      10. Memberships in clubs, social organizations, churches; relative activity
      11. Where professional services are obtained — medical, legal, accounting
      12. Did taxpayer claim California or other state residence for college tuition purposes?
      13. Driver's license
      14. Did taxpayer claim the homeowner's exemption on property tax?
         (a) The homeowner's exemption is not determinative of residence for income tax purposes, but is one item to be taken into account.
         (b) The veteran's exemption or a Cal-Vet loan application require a declaration of California residence and would be determinative. Since the veteran's exemption is less than homeowner's and you cannot get both, as a practical matter the veteran's exemption is obsolete.
      15. Relative significance of business activities and connections in California vs. other state(s).
   B. It is not necessary to have one state of residence for income tax purposes.
      1. An individual may be held to be a resident by more than one state for the same time period. Different states have different rules. Credits for taxes paid to other states may mitigate the tax effect.

Tax Management in Action 10.1 (continued)

Resident/Nonresident Issues: An Outline of Examples from California

2. This happens most often to the civilian spouse of nonresident military individual.
3. On the other hand, in order to establish nonresidence in California, it is not always necessary to prove that one is a resident somewhere else. See *Appeal of Richard W. Vohs* (1973), SBE, CCH, Para. 204-980 and 205-270.

VI. Moving to California: When does taxpayer become a resident?
A. Usually not a problem — California considers a taxpayer a resident when he or she arrives in California to reside permanently or indefinitely. However, sometimes there is a considerable transition period due to business obligations in former state, inability to sell prior residence, leaving part of family in old home to finish school year, etc.
  1. Questions asked are similar to those for dual-home taxpayers above. Date of change is the date when the scale of "closest connection" tipped to California.
  2. Husband and wife may not become residents at the same time.
   (a) Change of residence usually involves change of domicile as well. When spouses move at different times, they may have a period of time when their domiciles are different. This can create interesting results when one spouse is domiciled in a separate property state.
   (b) Old Reg. § 17016(d) held that a married woman's residence was her husband's (even if she had never set foot in the place herself). This regulation has been repealed recently. It was on the books but ineffective for a number of years after 1975, when California law changed with respect to the domicile of married women.

VII. Moving out of California: When (if ever) does taxpayer become a nonresident?
A. General rule — A taxpayer who leaves California to accept employment in another state on a permanent or indefinite basis becomes a nonresident when he or she leaves the state.
B. Business assignments outside California, particularly in foreign countries, have created much controversy in recent years. Generally speaking FTB considers a California domiciliary to remain a resident if he is outside the state on a contract with a definite termination date, as is the case with most foreign employment.
  1. A single taxpayer who severs most of his connections with California when he leaves, even though he owns real property here which is leased or rented to someone else, will usually be considered a nonresident.
  2. A married taxpayer who takes a spouse and family along and severs most California ties will also be considered a nonresident.
  3. A married taxpayer who leaves spouse and family in California will almost always be held to be a resident for the entire period of absence.
   (a) Even if the taxpayer in this instance is a nonresident, the resident spouse will be taxed on his or her community one-half of the foreign-earned income.
  4. For tax years beginning after 12/31/93, an individual domiciled in California who is out of state for at least 18 consecutive months under an employment-related contract is a nonresident, as would be an accompanying spouse. (A return to California for up to 45 days is ignored in determining the 18-month period.) The rule does not apply, however, to taxpayers with income from

intangibles in excess of $200,000 in any tax year during which the contract is in effect.

VIII. Special rules for military personnel

A. Limitations imposed on the application of residency rules to active duty military personnel by Soldiers and Sailors Civil Relief Act of 1940 (SSCRA) [Title 50, USC Appendix Sec. 574].

   1. A person may not be considered to have changed residence or domicile for tax purposes solely by reason of being stationed elsewhere on permanent military orders.

   2. Compensation for military services performed in a state where the member is a nonresident is not considered to have its source in that state.

   3. These provisions also apply to commissioned officers of the U.S. Public Health Service (P. L. 94-178 applicable to years beginning on or after 1/1/76).

   4. These provisions do not apply to:

     (a) Military retired or reserve personnel.

     (b) Active duty personnel in the state of their domicile.

B. California application of State and Federal laws to military personnel

   1. Domicile of service member

     (a) The domicile of a service member is the state of domicile at the time the member entered the service.

     (b) A service member may elect to change domicile. A change of home of record is generally considered a change of domicile. However, the three conditions for change of domicile must also be met.

       (i) Change of home of record to California will be considered presumptive evidence of California residence while the member is stationed here.

     (c) A married service member may retain his or her own domicile regardless of the domicile or residence of the spouse.

       (i) A civilian spouse's domicile is normally that of the service member.

         (A) The spouse may be considered a California resident for income tax purposes.

       (ii) If both spouses are service members, each will retain his or her own domicile unless specific action is taken to change it.

   2. Member domiciled in California

     (a) While stationed in California — Resident, taxable on all income including military compensation.

     (b) While outside California on PCS orders — Nonresident, taxable only on income from California sources.

       (i) Home port of ship governs determination of residence.

       (ii) From 1944 to 1963 the Franchise Tax Board regulations provided that a California domiciled member remained a resident taxable on all income, including military compensation, regardless of duty station, until official change of domicile or separation from service. The SBE held in *Appeal of Naylor* (1963), XII SBE 82, CCH Para. 202-310, that the Franchise Tax Board could not administratively impose on military personnel a standard of residence different from that provided

---

Tax Management in Action 10.1 (continued)

Resident/Nonresident Issues: An Outline of Examples from California

by statute. As a result, PCS orders outside the state are generally considered to create absence for a purpose which is not temporary or transitory, and, hence, nonresidence (FTB Legal Memo 503, 2/24/64). (For an exception to this rule, see *Appeal of Sanders*, XVIII SBE 84, 6/2/71.)

 (c) The civilian spouse of a member domiciled in California who remains in California while the member is absent remains a California resident.

  (i) Pursuant to California community property law, the resident spouse is taxed on one-half of the military compensation (FTB Legal Memo 503, 2/24/64). (Note that SCCRA tax provisions do not apply in the state of the member's domicile.)

 3. Member domiciled outside California

  (a) While stationed in California — Nonresident, taxable only on California source income. (Note that military compensation for services performed in California is not California source income to a nonresident member.)

  (b) The civilian spouse of a nonresident member stationed in California on PCS orders becomes a resident when he or she enters the state to reside with the member.

   (i) All income of the resident spouse is taxable in California.

   (ii) Division of income between spouses is governed by the laws of their domicile.

   (iii) Protection extends to 100% of military compensation.

Tax Management in Action 10.2

Printed Sources for State and Local Tax Rules: An Outline for California

I. **General**

 A. THE LAW: California Revenue and Taxation Code

  1. "How California Taxes are Enacted" from California Chamber of Commerce, *The Legislative Process in California*

  2. *The Statutes of California* (California State Printing Office)

  3. *West's Annotated California Codes: Revenue and Taxation*

  4. *Deering's Revenue and Taxation Code* (annotated with forms)

 B. THE REGULATIONS: *18 California Code of Regulations* (California Administrative Register)

 C. THE CASES:

  1. Bancroft Whitney ("BW"), *California Official Reports, 3rd Series* (California Supreme Court cases)

  2. BW, *California Appellate Reports, 3rd Series* (California Appellate cases)

  3. West's, *California Reporter* (all California cases)

  4. West's, *Pacific Reporter* (selected California cases)

  5. California State Board of Equalization ("SBE"), *Opinions of the State Board of Equalization* (1930 to date)

  6. West's, *Opinions of the Attorney General of California*

Tax Management in Action 10.2 (continued)

Printed Sources for State and Local Tax Rules: An Outline for California

7. SBE, *SBE Sales Tax Counsel Rulings*
8. Franchise Tax Board ("FTB") *FTB Legal Rulings*
9. FTB, *California Tax Cases* (1930-62)
10. Commerce Clearing House ("CCH"), *California Tax Cases* (1938 to date)
11. CCH, *California Tax Reporter New Matters* (1948 to date)
12. Recorder Publishing Company, *LARMAC Consolidated Index to the Constitution and Laws of California*
13. APS Publishing, *Report of Cases Determined Before the SBE* (through 1962)
14. SBE, "Hearing Procedure Before the SBE" (unbound)
15. [California Legislature's] Commission on California State Government Organization and Economics, *The Tax Appeals System in California*

D. SECONDARY MATERIALS:
   1. "Master" tax guides
      a) California only
         (1) Bock, *Guidebook to California Taxes* (CCH; annual paperback)
         (2) Frentz, *California Tax Handbook* (RIA [Prentice-Hall]; annual paperback)
      b) All states
         (1) CCH and PH each have both an all-state guidebook and newsletter
   2. Looseleaf services
      a) California only
         (1) CCH, *State Tax Reporter — California* (all taxes; CCH has a similar service for each state)
         (2) RIA, *State and Local Tax Service — California* (separate reporter for property taxes; similar service for each state)
         (3) SBE, "SBE Quick Index"
      b) All states in one place
         (1) *State Tax Guide* (both CCH and RIA)
         (2) RIA, *State Tax Action Coordinator, Western Region*
         (3) The large CPA firms publish guides to states taxes, e.g., Ernst & Young "Guide to State Taxes in the U.S.A."
   3. Treatises
      a) Petersen, *California Taxation*, MB [stopped when MB was bought out]
      b) California Continuing Education of the Bar ("CEB"), *California Taxes* (discontinued)
      c) Witkin, *Summary of California Law, 8th Edition* (BW)
      d) Rice, *California Tax Planning* (MB, 2nd Edition)
      e) West's, *California Digest 2nd*
      f) *California Digest of Official Reports, 3rd Series* (BW)
      g) *Cal. Jur., 3rd Edition* (BW)
      h) Hon. Arthur K. Marshall, *California Practice Vols 11 & 12: State Local Taxation* (BW)
      i) Hale & Kramer, *State Tax Liability and Compliance Manual* (MB)
      j) AICPA, *Minimizing the Corporate Interstate Tax Burden*
      k) National Tax Association, *Annual Proceedings*

Tax Management in Action 10.2 (continued)

Printed Sources for State and Local Tax Rules: An Outline for California

     l) Winkler & Kirlin, *California Policy Choices* (L.A. Taxpayers Association)

     m) California CPA Foundation Annual *California Tax Conference*

4. Journals
   a) Panel Publishers, *Journal of State Taxation*
   b) Interstate Tax Press, *Interstate Tax Report*
   c) Tax Executives Institute ("TEI"), *The Tax Executive*

5. Newsletters (not referred to above)
   a) CCH *State Tax Review* (weekly; RIA has similar newsletter)
   b) Spidell's, *California Tax Letter* (proactively seeks answers from FTB and SBE to practice questions
   c) Petersen, *California Taxation Reporter* (MB) [continuing status in question due to MB's merger]
   d) California Taxpayers Association, *California Tax News* (bi-monthly)
   e) L.A. Taxpayers Association, *L.A. Tax Report*
   f) Federation of Tax Accountants, *Tax Administrators News*
   g) SBE and FTB mailing lists, e.g., California FTB *Tax News*
   h) Various large CPA firms, e.g., Deloitte & Touche *Interstate Tax Alert*

6. Forms
   a) FTB, *California Tax Forms* (California's equivalent to the Federal "Package X"); order via FTB Form 3598 to:
      Franchise Tax Board
      Tax Forms Request Unit
      P. O. Box 307
      Rancho Cordova, CA 95741-0307
      Telephone (800) 338-0505-3700 [the F.A.S.T. Phone Service]
   b) FTB, other tax forms order via Form FTB 4012 or F.A.S.T. Phone Service
   c) Correspondence:
      Franchise Tax Board
      P. O. Box 942840
      Sacramento, CA 94240-0040

7. Texts
   a) Ajalat and Soto, *State and Local Taxes* (unpublished)
   b) Hellerstein and Hellerstein, *State and Local Taxation* (West's)
   c) Hellerstein, *State Taxation* (Warren, Gorham & Lamont)
   d) Hartman, *Federal Limitations on State and Local Taxation* (BW)
   e) Oldman and Schoettle, *State and Local Taxes and Finances*

8. "Legal" forms
   a) Marshall, *California Code Forms — Revenue and Taxation Code* (West's)
   b) *California Legal Forms* (MB)
   c) Robinson, *Legal Forms System* (Clark Boardman)
   d) Rabkin and Johnson, *Current Legal Forms with Tax Analysis* (MB)

9. Associations
   a) California Chamber of Commerce State Tax Committee
   b) California Taxpayers Association
   c) L.A. Taxpayers Association

Tax Management in Action 10.2 (continued)

Printed Sources for State and Local Tax Rules: An Outline for California

        d) Tax Executive Institute
        e) National Tax Association
        f) Various industry associations, e.g., American Electronics Association
   10. Research
        a) Henke, *California Law Guide*
   11. Citation
        a) *A Uniform System of Citation* (Harvard Law Review, 15th Edition)
        b) *Auto-Cite* (Lawyers Co-op Publishing Co. [runs on Lexis; similar service available on Westlaw, CCH Access, and RIA/PHInet])
   12. Citators
        a) Sheppards, *California Citations* (statutes, cases, ordinances, and law review articles; runs on Lexis)
        b) *Auto-Cite* (Lawyers Co-op Publishing Co. [runs on Lexis; similar service available on Westlaw, CCH Access, and RIA/PHInet])
   13. Computerized Research
        a) *Lexis* (California Court Cases, SBE rulings, SBE cases, FTB rulings, and Attorney General's opinions)
        b) *Westlaw* (West's) (California Court Cases and Attorney General's opinions)
        c) *CCH Access*
        d) *RIA/PHInet*

II. Specific areas

  A. Income tax
    1. FTB, *Personal Income Tax Law* (FTB: annotated California statutes)
    2. FTB, *Annual Report*
    3. FTB, *Mailing list* (newsletter, notices of proposed regulations, and other items of current interest including sales tax counsel rulings)
    4. Major FTB publications
        a) *Uniform Apportionment Manual*
        b) *Guide for Corporations Commencing Business in California*
        c) *Guide for Corporations Which May Be Subject to the Provisions of the California Bank and Corporations Bank Law*
        d) *Instructions for Filing a Combined Report*
        e) *Uniform Division of Income For Tax Purposes Act ("UDITPA") Techniques Manual*
        f) *UDITPA Apportionment Manual*
        g) *Corporations Audit Manual*
        h) *Exempt Organization Manual*
        i) *Field Audit Manual*
        j) *Guide to Multi-State Audit*
        k) *Personal Income Tax Audit Manual*
        l) *Guide for Corporations Filing a Combined Report*
  B. Sales tax
    1. SBE Department of Business Taxes, *Business Tax Law Guide*
    2. SBE, *California Excise Tax Laws* (annotated laws)
    3. SBE, *Annual Report*

Tax Management in Action 10.2 (continued)

Printed Sources for State and Local Tax Rules: An Outline for California

    4. SBE, *Mailing list*
    5. SBE publications, regulations, and pamphlets
    6. CCH, *All State Sales Tax Reporter*
    7. SBE, "Letters to Interested Parties"
C. Property Tax
    1. SBE, *California Property Tax Laws* (annotated California statutes)
    2. Ehrman & Flavin, *Taxing California Property, Assessment, Equalization* (BW)
    3. Ehrman & Flavin, *Taxing California Property* (Boll publishing Company, 2nd Edition)
    4. SBE Division of Assessment Standards, *Assessors Handbook* (extremely useful when on point; many topics are covered)
    5. International Association of Assessing Officers, *Assessment and Valuation Legal Reporter*
    6. International Association of Assessing Officers, *Assessors Journal*
    7. International Association of Assessing Officers, *Property Assessment Valuation*
    8. Los Angeles County ("L.A. Cty.") Assessor Standards Division letters
    9. Los Angeles County Assessment Appeals Board, *Rules*
   10. SBE, "Letters to Assessors"
D. Miscellaneous
    1. Los Angeles City Clerk, *City of Los Angeles Business Tax Ordinance*
    2. San Francisco Tax Collector, *City of San Francisco Payroll Expense Tax and Business Tax Ordinances*
    3. L.A. Cty. Assessor Standards Division, *Los Angeles County Taxpayers Guide*
    4. Los Angeles Tax Foundation, *Municipal Business Tax Reference Guide* (covers L.A. County)
    5. CCH, *Inheritance and Gift Tax Reporter* (for prior law)
    6. California State Controller, *California Inheritance and Gift Tax Laws* (for prior law)
    7. CCH, *All State Unemployment Insurance Reporter*
    8. CCH, *Payroll Management Guide*
    9. SBE, *California Excise Tax Laws* (annotated)
   10. Legislative Bill Room (916) 445-2323

Free value-added materials available from the
Download Resource Center at www.jrosspub.com.

APPENDICES

APPENDIX A: STATE AND LOCAL TAX RESEARCH

State and local tax research is similar to the Federal, except that fewer and less organized materials are available. Much of the law is "administrative": it is not written, but carried in the hearts of the tax authorities. All too much is a matter of first impression which can only be determined by analogy and Federal precedent.

THE FONTS OF STATE AND LOCAL TAX RULES

Tax rules can be determined from two basic sources: primary and secondary sources. Primary sources are official governmental pronouncements. For state and local taxation, these include statutes enacted by legislative bodies, regulations and rulings issued by the tax administrators, and judicial opinions in court cases dealing with tax matters. Official sources increasingly are being published on the Web. Legislative, judicial, and administrative primary sources of tax law for most jurisdictions, such as states like New York, can be found on the Web.

These can readily be found through tax gateway Web sites such as *www.taxsites.com* or *www.taxworld.org*. A gateway Web site is made up only of links to other Web sites. These are useful because of the constant changes in Web sites. Most states have all of their forms and publications available from their Web sites.

Albeit more authoritative, primary sources often are extremely difficult to fathom, even for the most experienced tax planners. This is the main reason why there are secondary sources. They are unofficial, edited views of what the tax rules are published by nongovernmental sources, much easier to understand, and particularly useful when learning about something for the first time. Among the most topical, and most accessible, are those found in newspapers, such as the Wednesday front page tax column of the *Wall Street Journal*. There also are professional tax journals, state and local tax treatises, and publications sponsored by tax professionals, such as the American Bar Association for lawyers and AICPA for accountants.

These, too, can be located through gateway Web sites, such as *www.taxsites.com*. For example, each of the Final 4 accounting firms, and the large international law firms, publish state and local tax commentaries and advisories on their Web sites. More importantly, there are several outstanding commercial publications, which are Web accessible (as well as still being printed). One that was mentioned above is Commerce Clearing House. These, too, can be located by browsing a gateway tax Web site.

Commercial tax publications are organized in one of two formats. Tax services are arranged by topics, like an encyclopedia. They read like textbooks, and are keyed into primary sources through footnotes. In contrast, annotated reporters read like a dictionary. They are one-stop shops for all official tax rules, and are organized around tax codes, ruling, and cases.

COMMERCE CLEARING HOUSE (CCH)

CCH is a leading publisher of state and local tax reference materials and commentaries. Among these materials are

- **State Tax Reporter** — Fifty-state and D.C. service, updated monthly, and covers personal and corporate income, franchise, sales/use, property, employment, and limited city taxes.
- **Multistate Corporate Income Tax Guide** — Two-volume reporter, updated monthly, limited to corporate income tax, and contains numerous charts, general discussion of various aspects of state tax such as apportionment, unitary, business/nonbusiness, and general discussions of each state.
- **Multistate Sales and Use Tax Guide** — Nine volumes covering all fifty states, updated monthly, limited to sales and use tax, and contains numerous charts, state explanations, law and regulations.
- **All States Guide** — Two volumes, updated monthly, covers income, franchise, sales and use and other miscellaneous taxes, and contains numerous charts and state explanations.
- **Payroll Management Guide** — Four volumes (two volumes covering state and local tax), updated monthly.

- **Multistate Part-Year/Nonresident Return Guide** — Two-volume service, updated monthly, and contains charts and state-by-state commentary of individuals filing multiple state returns.
- **Electronic Research Services** — All of these services are available on-line, in a Web-based system called the CCH Tax Research Network.

WESTLAW

Westlaw also provides basic tax research materials on-line. All state statutes are available as well as many full-text state courses. Limited coverage of regulations and proposed state legislation is also available.

RESEARCH INSTITUTE OF AMERICA (RIA)

- **State and Local Taxes — All States Guide** — This is available in print, on CD-rom that is updated monthly, and on-line via a Web-based interface. It contains charts and state-by-state commentary, and covers income, sales, and property taxes.

BUREAU OF NATIONAL AFFAIRS (BNA)

Tax Management Inc. is part of the of the Bureau of National Affairs group. Its publications are available both in print and via a Web-based interface.

- **State Management Multistate Tax Portfolios** — A series of twenty-five portfolios covering various aspects of state income, sales, franchise and property taxation, updated monthly. Other portfolios have been commissioned.
- **Payroll Administration Guide** — This has five print volumes (two volumes cover state and local tax), and contains charts and state-by-state commentary.

OTHER PUBLICATIONS

- **RIA All States Handbook** — Published annually, and contains charts and calendars covering income, sales/use, property, and other state taxes.
- **RIA Guide to Sales and Use Taxes** — Published annually, state-by-state commentaries on sales/use tax.

- **CCH State Tax Handbook** — Published annually, with charts covering income, sales/use, property, and other state taxes.
- **CCH Guidebook to Michigan [California, New York, and Nine Other] Taxes** — Published annually, chart covering income, sales/use, property, and other taxes.
- **Multistate Corporate Tax Guide (Panel Guide)** — Published annually by Panel Publication, contains charts and commentary on income and sales/ use taxes, and is two volumes.
- **State and Local Tax Compendium for REITs** — Published annually by National Association of Real Estate Investment Trusts, Inc. (NAREIT), and state-by-state coverage of income and franchise taxes relating to REITs.
- **Partnership Federal and State Income Tax Reporting** — By Michael N. Jennings and Daniel R. Bolar, and published annually by JB Publications.
- **S Corporations — State Law and Taxation** — Complete discussion of state tax issues affecting S corporations, published by Callahan and Callahan, and is updated infrequently at best.

JOURNALS

- **Tax Management Multistate Tax Report** — Published monthly by Tax Management, Inc., a subsidiary of BNA (800) 372-1033, requires an annual subscription, provides update of income, franchise, sales/use, and property tax developments.
- **Journal of State Taxation** — Published monthly by Panel Publishers, Inc. (516) 484-0006, it contains articles written by state tax practitioners.
- **The Journal of Multistate Taxation** — Published bimonthly by Warren Gorham Lamont, a division of RIA (800) 950-11252, requires an annual subscription, and has articles written by state tax practitioners.
- **Tax Administrators News** — Published monthly by the FTA (202) 624-5890, requires an annual subscription.
- **Multistate Tax Compact Publications** — Guides and handbooks on various topics.
- **Various State Department of Revenue Newsletters** — Write to state and ask to be placed on mailing list.
- **State Tax Notes** — Published weekly by Tax Analysts (703) 533-4484, requires an annual subscription, provides update of income, franchise, sales/use, and property tax developments.
- **State Tax Review** — Published weekly by CCH, 4025 W. Peterson Ave., Chicago, IL 60646-6085, requires an annual subscription, and

provides update of income, franchise, sales/use, and property tax developments.

ORGANIZATIONS

Tax Administrator Organizations

Federation of Tax Administrators (FTA) is comprised of four regional tax administrator groups:

1. SEATA (Southeastern Association of Tax Administrators)
2. NSTOA (Northeastern State Tax Officials Association)
3. MSATA (Midwest States Association of Tax Administrators)
4. WSATA (Western States Association of Tax Administrators)

The FTA is headquartered at 444 North Capitol Street, N.W., Washington D.C. 20001, and it holds an annual meeting that is open to the public, as do the regional groups, and holds various sections and committee meetings to discuss such tax areas as tobacco tax, motor fuel tax, electronic filing, revenue estimating, etc. It maintains current mailing and phone lists of state tax administrators and their staffs, updated every February, and files amicus briefs, conducts research into state tax issues, and engages in other activities.

The FTA developed a uniform exchange of information agreement, including most of the states, that became effective January 1993.

OTHER ASSOCIATIONS

- **Tax Executives Institute (TEI)** is headquartered at 1001 Pennsylvania Ave., N.W., Suite 320, Washington, D.C. 20004-2505, and is a national organization of tax executives from large corporations. It is comprised of numerous local chapters, with membership limited to taxpayers, not limited to state and local taxes, and sponsors meetings, seminars, and schools.
- **Committee on State Taxation (COST)** is sponsored by the Council of State Chambers of Commerce, and is active in all areas of taxation, sponsors meetings and seminars, with membership limited to taxpayers.

APPENDIX B: PRESENT VALUE

The concept of present value is based on the idea of interest. Interest is rent on the use of someone else's money. Simple interest is calculated by multiplying the amount borrowed (called the present value) by the applicable interest rate. This rate often is nominally expressed as an annual rate, so loans for periods other than a year often have an applicable rate of a multiple of the annual rate (e.g., for a 1 1/2 year loan, multiply the annual rate by 1.5). Using this formula indicates the future amount (principle plus interest) that has to be repaid.

The existence of interest suggests that getting a dollar now is not the same as getting it a year from now. This is because a dollar now can be invested and grow to more than a dollar over the year. That is, the present value is not the same as the future value. This can be expressed mathematically as $FV = PV \times (1+R)^n$, where R is the annual interest rate and n is the number of years involved. Similarly, $PV = FV/(1+R)^n$

For ease of use, present values have been worked out and presented in tables such as the following, which shows the present values of $1 due at the end of n periods at various interest rates:

Period (n)	1%	2%	3%	4%	5%	6%	7%	8%	9%	10%
1	.9901	.9804	.9709	.9615	.9524	.9434	.9346	.9259	.9174	.9091
2	.9803	.9612	.9426	.9246	.9070	.8900	.8734	.8573	.8417	.8264
3	.9706	.9423	.9151	.8890	.8638	.8396	.8163	.7938	.7722	.7513
4	.9610	.9238	.8885	.8548	.8227	.7921	.7629	.7350	.7084	.6830
5	.9515	.9057	.8626	.8219	.7835	.7473	.7130	.6806	.6499	.6209
6	.9420	.8880	.8375	.7903	.7462	.7050	.6663	.6302	.5963	.5645
7	.9327	.8706	.8131	.7599	.7107	.6651	.6227	.5835	.5470	.5132
8	.9235	.8535	.7894	.7307	.6768	.6274	.5820	.5403	.5019	.4665
9	.9143	.8368	.7664	.7026	.6446	.5919	.5439	.5002	.4604	.4241
10	.9053	.8203	.7441	.6756	.6139	.5584	.5083	.4632	.4224	.3855

Sometimes it is not one lump sum in the future that is of concern, but a series of periodic payments. A good example is the payoff of a state lottery prize of $20,000 per year for 20 years. Although the present value of each of the twenty payments can be calculated using the formula above, another formula can be used. In particular, the present value of an annuity of $1 per period for n periods is

$$\sum_{t=1}^{n} \frac{1}{(1+r)^t} = \frac{1 - \dfrac{1}{(1+r)^n}}{r}$$

This, too, has been calculated and placed in ready-to-use tables, such as the following:

n	1%	2%	3%	4%	5%	6%	7%	8%	9%	10%
1	0.9901	0.9804	0.9709	0.9615	0.9524	0.9434	0.9346	0.9259	0.9174	0.9091
2	1.9704	1.9416	1.9135	1.8861	1.8594	1.8334	1.8080	1.7833	1.7591	1.7355
3	2.9410	2.8839	2.8286	2.7751	2.7232	2.6730	2.6243	2.5771	2.5313	2.4869
4	3.9020	3.8077	3.7171	3.6299	3.5460	3.4651	3.3872	3.3121	3.2397	3.1699
5	4.8534	4.7135	4.5797	4.4518	4.3295	4.2124	4.1002	3.9927	3.8897	3.7908
6	5.7955	5.6014	5.4172	5.2421	5.0757	4.9173	4.7665	4.6229	4.4859	4.3553
7	6.7282	6.4720	6.2303	6.0021	5.7864	5.5824	5.3893	5.2064	5.0330	4.8684
8	7.6517	7.3255	7.0197	6.7327	6.4632	6.2098	5.9713	5.7466	5.5348	5.3349
9	8.5660	8.1622	7.7861	7.4353	7.1078	6.8017	6.5152	6.2469	5.9952	5.7590
10	9.4713	8.9826	8.5302	8.1109	7.7217	7.3601	7.0236	6.7101	6.4177	6.1446

Calculations of future amounts and present values of lump sum, as well as for annuities, can be done on most business calculators, as well as in spreadsheet programs. Tables and calculators also are available on the Web.

Free value-added materials available from the
Download Resource Center at www.jrosspub.com.

INDEX